Revealing The Truth

Through my personal experiences at the place of H.H. Dorje Chang Buddha III during my twelve years there as a bhiksuni, which include disappointment, sadness, pain, and awakening.

Shi Zheng Hui

Translated by Suonan Ciren Rinpoche

Great River Books
Salt Lake City, Utah

Homage to Sakyamuni Buddha

Translated from the Chinese book 揭開真相

Originally published by 禾年實業有限公司　October 2013

Author: Shi Zheng Hui

Translator: Suonan Ciren Rinpoche.

Editorial assistance: Cairang Baizhen Rinpoche

For Information, contact:　　　Great River Books
　　　　　　　　　　　　　　161 M Street
　　　　　　　　　　　　　　Salt Lake City, UT 84103
　　　　　　　　　　　　　　www.greatriverbooks.com
　　　　　　　　　　　　　　801-532-4833
　　　　　　　　　　　　　　info@greatriverbooks.com

Library of Congress Cataloging-in-Publication Data

Names: Zhenghui, Shi, 1970- author.
Title: Revealing the truth : through my personal experiences at the place of
  H.H. Dorje Chang Buddha III during my twelve years there as a bhiksuni,
  which include disappointment, sadness, pain, and awakening / by Shi Zheng
  Hui ; translation by Suonan Ciren Rinpoche.
Other titles: Jie kai zhen xiang. English | Through my personal experiences
  at the place of H.H. Dorje Chang Buddha III during my twelve years there
  as a bhiksuni, which include disappointment, sadness, pain, and awakening
Description: Salt Lake City, Utah : Great River Books, 2016.
Identifiers: LCCN 2015030181 | ISBN 9780915556496 (trade pbk.)
Subjects: LCSH: Zhenghui, Shi, 1970- | Buddhist nuns--California--Biography.
  | Spiritual life--Buddhism.
Classification: LCC BQ999.Z44 A3 2016 | DDC 294.3/92092--dc23
LC record available at http://lccn.loc.gov/2015030181

Table of Contents

Preface by the Author

I am a monastic bhiksuni. I graduated from the Department of Law of the Taiwan National Political Science University. On the day of my graduation ceremony, the first thing I did was to go into a temple. Twenty years have passed since I entered the order of monastics. I clearly know the law of cause and effect. All things are due to the induction and retribution of causality. The Buddha-dharma is to enable us to untie this net of causality and let us become free and completely liberated. The law of cause and effect follows us all the time like a shadow. Therefore, to attain accomplishment and liberation, I must be responsible with regard to the law of cause and effect. That is why the narrations in this book of *Revealing the Truth* are all real facts. The true stories in the book are what I saw, heard, experienced, and participated in at a temple and a home base where H.H. Dorje Chang Buddha III lived during the twelve years from 2001 to 2013.

During these twelve years, I was disappointed at times and also had feelings of sadness and grief. Sometimes, I was in agony and despair. Then, through discovering and analyzing the terrible hidden constraint in my inner mind, I became awakened.

Now, I would like to clearly inform people in the world. You should never readily believe and rely on a name representing a so-and-so lineage to trust a person claiming or being claimed to be a Buddha, a Bodhisattva, or a patriarch master, a so-and-so great dharma king, a so-and-so great rinpoche, or a so-and-so great dharma master with a superficially sound lineage of Buddha-dharma. Otherwise, you will generally be fooled and deceived. I saw so many dharma kings, venerable ones, great rinpoches, and great dharma teachers during these twelve years. I saw their mindsets and images in daily life and at dharma ceremonies, and I was able to detect their hidden and secret personal natures. Once their conduct of the mind was unveiled, all that could be seen were mixtures of true and false. It is hard to describe in a few words who were really great holy ones. I have realized that only the genuine Buddhism is the most authentic and most supreme method of liberation. Also, there is only one place that has Buddha-dharma, which is the true and utmost precious method of liberation. That is the answer that I have searched for and found in my deep inner mind. With that answer, I have been awakened, stood up, and have ultimately acquired a great dharma of Tathagata. I have become the humble one that I am today.

Shi Zheng Hui, a humble bhiksuni, after finishing this book based on true stories of these twelve years

1

The Condition that Planted the Seed for Revealing the Truth

I am a very common and ordinary person. However, I am a monastic bhiksuni after all. I deeply understand that I must abide by the complete set of Grand Precepts that were awarded to me in three dharma assemblies. The purpose of cultivating myself and learning Buddhism is to attain accomplishment and to become liberated. I must not lie and harm myself for millions of eons to come. If I tell lies to deceive people even one time for any purpose, I will definitely meet with ferocious retributions in this lifetime and even fall into the hell realm. Therefore, I must tell facts and truth in this book of mine.

In 1993, I graduated from the Department of Law of National Taiwan Political Science University. During the first semester of my senior year, I had already taken and passed the exam for court registrar. A person who works with law greatly emphasizes logic and reasoning, pays great attention to science and evidence, and always relies on facts. Even with these traits, I was still unable to find the answers for the ultimate truth about human life and the universe in the field of law. However, I clearly knew that human life is the accumulation of birth, aging, illness, and death. Weren't there ways to eliminate these sufferings? If not, even being alive would be meaningless. I was determined to find the answer. After researching, I heard that Buddhism has the most to do with truth and can solve this problem. That was why I chose the path of entering the order of monastics to become a bhiksuni. My intention was to search for the answer to human life in the field of religion and solve the problem of birth and death.

After I became a monastic and received the precepts, I attended the colloquium of chanting sutras in the morning and in the evening every day at the temple. The schedule was very regular and life was very smooth. As to the dharma gates of cultivation, all I knew was chanting the Buddha's name, prostrating to the Buddha, and practicing the contemplation of the Pure Land. The goal was to ascend to the World of Ultimate Bliss with the help of Amitabha Buddha's power of vow. However, was doing so really effective? It did not have the proof of science! I could only force myself into believing, since I never saw Buddhas. Do They really exist? This was the reason I thought that I, with the impediment of suspicion still lingering in my faith, was a common and ordinary person. Occasionally, I also read commentaries and works authored by some great virtuous ones of Buddhist circles. My understanding of the dharma from these writings was quite fuzzy, seemingly knowing but not knowing. My overall impression was that the study of Buddhism was just about talks on emptiness and discussions on subtleties; it was too high and profound to comprehend.

In August 2000, I had the karmic condition of respectfully listening to the recorded dharma lessons expounded by the Great Dharma King Vajradhara Yangwo Yeshe Norbu. The superb discourses of the dharma in plain language, incisive reasoning, and strong logic made me feel like I was drinking nectar. It was like having a bucket of cool and refreshing fluid poured down the top of my head and waking up from a long dream. I felt like I had gotten hold of an utmost precious treasure. I listened to the dharma lessons repeatedly and did not feel tired even after listening for ten hours in a day.

Although I knew almost nothing about the concept of "Great Dharma King Vajradhara," at least I knew in my mind that this great dharma king was recognized by a dharma king who was a reincarnation of a great patriarch of Tibetan Buddhism. An elder virtuous one, who was also a very good cultivator, told me that he saw the document of recognition in person and therefore the title was not self-conferred. The document of recognition stated that the Great Dharma King once took the position of Dusongqianba (Dusum Khyenpa) or, simply speaking, was Dusongqianba. This elder virtuous one also told me that the Great Dharma King had extremely high realization. He mentioned an example of the Great Dharma King's realization involving a great virtuous one named Hui Hui who was over ninety years old and was a famous master of Buddhism from Jiangxi Province of China. It was a holy event that they both were present at a Buddhist altar.

At that time, Hui Hui asked the Great Dharma King to invoke Amitabha Buddha to come. He said that he did not ask to see Amitabha Buddha in a dream or a state of meditation. He did not want to see Amitabha Buddha as an illusion. He wanted to see the true Amitabha Buddha face to face right on the spot. This Great Dharma King Dusongqianba accepted his request right away and immediately sat on the dharma throne and was about to practice the dharma of invoking Amitabha Buddha. Suddenly, Hui Hui changed his mind and said that he no longer wanted to see Amitabha Buddha. The reason was that he was confident that he would ascend to the World of Ultimate Bliss in this lifetime. At that time, he would see the Buddha every day. Therefore, he asked the Great Dharma King to invoke the great dharma protector Mahakala to come. The Great Dharma King said, "Whom do you really want to see after all? You asked for too much! Considering that you are at such a senior age and are so pious, I will give it a try!" Then the Great Dharma King immediately changed the dharma being practiced to the dharma of the yidam and called out, "Mahakala arrive!" Right after the call, a roar of thunder was heard. Mahakala came from the sky to arrive right in front of Hui Hui and asked him loudly, "Why do you call me here?" Hui Hui was greatly scared and could not speak to reply. He retreated back and pressed himself against the wall. On that day, Hui Hui described his experience of seeing the great dharma protector Mahakala to people. He said that Mahakala was several tens of feet tall and was very formidable and mighty powerful, and His voice was swirling loudly like a sudden thunder. This elder virtuous one said that he was also present at the scene. The Great Dharma King was so serenely powerful that He was able to easily call the great dharma protector Mahakala to arrive. Just think about this fact. Who else could have done this?

To me, whether the Great Dharma King was Great Dharma King Vajradhara, Great Dharma King Dusongqianba, Great Dharma King Yangwo Yeshe Norbu, or an ordinary cultivator was not important at all. This is because His power of realization had already proven that He was a very great Buddha or Bodhisattva. Of course, this was just something I heard. Whether it was true or false was still questionable. However, I eventually chose to believe this story as true. Since then, respect, admiration, and adoration toward the Great Dharma King arose naturally in my mind. Without being concerned about whether He was Great Dharma King Vajradhara or Great Dharma King Dusongqianba, I imagined that He at least would be an accomplished highly realized person, a great holy one, or a great Bodhisattva without a doubt. How nice would it be if I could have the karmic condition of paying respect to the Great Dharma King in person! It was such a wish that later made me decide to go to the Great Dharma King's home base in the United States, and it caused disappointment, sadness, and suffering in me. In the end, I realized that I was a most stupid and ignorant person. Finally, I was able to wake up and stand up. I want to become liberated and accomplished. I absolutely cannot make even a tiny violation against the law of cause and effect. I must act in absolute accordance with the law of cause and effect. I will write only true facts without any fabrication. Therefore, I am going to tell cultivators the facts from my own experience in order to benefit all people.

In September 2000, one month after I started to respectfully listen to the recorded dharma lessons, I suddenly encountered an opportunity. A group of monastics was going to the United States to pay homage to a holy one. They asked me whether I would like to join. This was what I had been craving for even in dreams. How could I not join?

Some people told me that the holy one whom we were going to pay homage to was Great Dharma King Vajradhara. Some other people mentioned that the Great Dharma King was Dusongqianba instead. I did not care much about that. The name and title were not important to me! The most important thing was whether we were going to pay homage to a great Bodhisattva. If so, His name could be anything or He could be a beggar. I would follow Him regardless. I did not want to follow fame or title. I wanted to follow a holy one. The dharma in sutras tells us very clearly that we should follow holiness, not person. We should not follow name and appearance. We shall follow the ultimate reality.

Upon arriving in the United States, people were all talking with all kinds of descriptions. They said that an extremely magnificent dharma assembly was going to be held here. To tell the truth, I could hardly believe it. In a word, they said such an opportunity would be hard to encounter even in millions of eons. I attended this dharma assembly. However, I will postpone unveiling the facts of many incidents during this dharma assembly until later in this book.

After returning to Taiwan, the scenes of the Great Dharma King practicing the dharma constantly emerged in my mind. Because I was not able to go to the United States again, anxiety arose in me. That anguish caused trouble for me. Sometimes, I locked myself in a room, fretting; I had no desire to talk to or meet people. Day by day, I began to suffer from insomnia.

One morning after getting up, my mind went blank. I could only remember that I went to the United States to attend a dharma assembly but any memory about what the dharma assembly was and what happened during the dharma assembly was totally wiped out in my brain. However, an elderly dharma king's solemn and elegant demeanor of holiness and his voice like the loud and clear sound from a large bell remained in my mind and would flash up from time to time. Other than this, I totally forgot what had happened at the dharma assembly. On the other hand, other worldly matters were remembered clearly without loss. That was too mysterious. I visited a doctor for diagnosis. The doctor said that this might be caused by depression. The strange thing was that I remembered other things clearly. So the doctor was not certain. Other possibilities included the return of an old symptom from a severe concussion I had from an earlier car accident with a brief loss of memory and amnesia due to the irregularity of my thyroid functions. Anyway, I had no way of knowing or understanding. I tried all means to think but still could not recall what the dharma assembly was for and what had happened. This condition lasted until three days after I attended the Holy Buddha-Bathing Dharma Assembly held in May 2004. On the third evening after the Holy Buddha-Bathing Dharma Assembly, the complete process of the dharma assembly held in the year of 2000 suddenly reemerged. Due to the fact that my mind went blank for several years about this dharma assembly, I am not going to present it in the actual chronological order and will tell you this story later in the book.

2

A Hard-to-Make Choice between Conflicting Factors

After returning to Taiwan, I continued to listen to the recorded dharma lessons. However, I wondered when I would have the karmic condition to pay homage to the Great Dharma King again? Would my affinity with the dharma be disconnected? Time elapsed day by day. I heard nothing.

In May 2001, I saw the Great Dharma King in my dream. He told me, "Come to see me in America!" After waking up, I thought that my dream at night might have been caused by what I was thinking during the day. Moreover, how could I go there by myself, without any channel of communication? Although anxious, I did not have a way. Therefore, my mind wasn't overly occupied by the state that appeared in the dream. One month passed after having that dream. Surprisingly, one day a dharma master called me from the United States. I was told that the temple and the home base of the Great Dharma King was going to gather monastic practitioners for a meeting. Those who achieved a certain level could stay there as religious teachers (of Buddhism) to learn Buddhism, cultivate, and serve the people.

I began to evaluate myself. Although I wished to go very much, the fact was that I was not ready to leave my temple in Taiwan and was bound by feelings toward my parents. Still, I wanted to go to the Great Dharma King to beseech the dharma and did not want to miss this opportunity. My mind was struggling yet resigned to take a chance, since I might not even be selected. It would be a good experience just to go there with other people. Therefore, I started the trip to America with only a simple piece of luggage and without even saying farewell to my parents. What I did not know was that my path of cultivation after the age of thirty would change from then on.

While we were in the US, the results of who could stay were decided based on everyone's vote. The emotions of people became polarized. Those who did not get elected were very upset. Some even cried. The ones who were elected were wearing big smiles on their happy faces. The situation was quite different among people with opposite outcomes.

Though I got elected, I felt a great pressure because I was not mentally prepared for that. I decided to pass this great opportunity to other people. I thought that I could come again next time. As a result, I privately gave my slot to another monastic person.

However, seeing other elected people happily opening their luggage to prepare for moving in, my conflicting mind became undecided again, "Did I make a wrong decision? Am I really going to give up this opportunity?" A fellow sister came to inform me that this current karmic condition was the only one. There would be no such opportunity next time. She advised me to treasure this opportunity and not to give it up. The struggle in my mind started again, "Do I really want to give it up?" It was really hard for me to choose between these conflicting options!

Then I asked myself why I took the path of becoming a monastic. Wasn't that for ending the cycle of birth and death, for becoming accomplished and liberated, and for devoting myself to Buddhism? The life of a human being is bitter and short and does not have much meaning. Then why couldn't I give up all worldly matters? No! No! I couldn't give up like this. There would be no next time. I wanted to cultivate for accomplishment. I wanted to learn Buddha-dharma.

At that time, I had an extremely high mind of devotion and mind of renunciation. I decided to stay and work hard. I could not continue to wait. I wanted to hold onto this one and only opportunity. I made up my mind to stay in this temple in the United States and at the home base where the Great Dharma King was.

Earlier, I had decided to give up the opportunity and made a private agreement with another monastic person to pass my slot to her. Now I wanted to nullify the agreement, which caused her to cry and shout. She even declared that she was going to commit suicide and then let the Great Dharma King raise her spirit to a higher realm. That incident got the Great Dharma King's attention. In the end, the Great Dharma King offered to teach that monastic person a dharma, so this unexpected disturbance I caused was put off. I did not foresee that I committed a sin before establishing any merit. This whole thing was my fault!

Master Long Hui led us into the Great Dharma King's meditation site and residence. The living room we walked into was plain and simple. A set of old sofas was placed on the left side. On the right, there was an oval-shaped wooden table and two small sofa chairs plus a small tea table. Having this simple setting on the wooden floor conveyed a quiet and tranquil atmosphere.

The Great Dharma King definitely knew what I had thought. He asked Master Long Hui about my situation. Master Long Hui reported that I had made up my mind. Then the Great Dharma King specifically called me in and said, "Many places have monasteries and temples. It is okay if you want to go elsewhere. Or, you can come here next time."

After hearing what the Great Dharma King said, my mind took a pause. The Great Dharma King seemed to tell me to come next time. I thought that perhaps the Great Dharma King had seen the impediment in my mind and that was why He told me to come next time. I believed that the Great Dharma King would not see things wrong. Maybe my karmic condition for the dharma was not mature yet. I thought that I should listen to the Great Dharma King's instruction. So I agreed and then left the living room.

Now it was Master Long Hui's turn to be called in. The Great Dharma King immediately told her, "What is 'having made up the mind?' What kind of people did you select? The level is so low, failing at the first simple test."

Master Long Hui tried to explain for us, "They are really very pious." At that time, I panicked and hurriedly beseeched the Great Dharma King again to let me stay. I said, "Great Dharma King, I want to stay to learn Buddha-dharma. I am not going back. If I go back, the only thing waiting for me would be karmic constraints."

The Great Dharma King said, "Whether you stay or not is up to you. You are going to be religious teachers if you stay. You should also know that I do not have Buddha-dharma to teach you!"

I beseeched repeatedly. Seeing that I had made up my mind, the Great Dharma King kindly told us, "Okay! Okay! It will be you all. Since your abbot wants you to stay, you can stay. However, everything has to be governed by law. We still need to see whether the government agrees to let you stay or not. Only if the country permits you to stay, can you stay here to become religious teachers. Then, when the conditions arise in the future, you may still go back!"

Having gone through these twists and turns, I stayed. However, I knew that in my deep inner mind there still existed the un-severable love toward my parents that might emerge from time to time. I recalled that Master Milarepa also had to bid farewell to his mother to start his journey of learning Buddha-dharma at that time. All I could do was to turn this loving feeling into a longing hidden in the deepest corner of my heart. Then I would strive for attaining accomplishment and liberation in my current lifetime, to benefit my parents and repay their kindness and love to me.

3

How Could This Be Cultivation?

We moved into the home base and started our life there.

Master Long Hui, the current chairperson of the International Buddhism Sangha Association, was our leading sister. She took us around to let us familiarize ourselves with the environment. This place was rather big. Not only was the house big, there was also a large and beautiful backyard. In addition to a pond and a big lawn, there were fruit trees that bore fruit all year round, including oranges, lemons, avocados, olives, loquats, persimmons, dates, and others. Also, there was an American Indian-styled large kennel. There were several temples nearby. One of the temples was the Sanger Temple, on an even larger piece of land of nine acres. Many horses and cattle were raised on the pasture. There was also a natural lake, with many fish and water birds.

Speaking of dogs, this was a very troubling matter, especially at the beginning, when we were not yet acquainted with them. When we walked by, the dogs noticed. When they saw people coming, they ran happily out of the kennel. Although they were still within the fence, several of us who were new got very scared. Were these dogs? Really? Weren't we mistaken? How could they be dogs? They were as big as ponies.

They were very excited inside the wooden fence, jumping and barking. Sounds came from their hitting the wooden fence. Although they appeared very friendly, we were very afraid because we had never seen such Great Danes before. They were two feet seven inches tall at the back. When standing up, each dog's height was higher than ours. Of course they were more powerful than we were. That was very scary. Since we had never seen such big dogs before, we would feel very nervous whenever we thought about the fact that we were going to take care of them. (The two Great Danes were named "Weis" and "Jin Zhong Xue" respectively. Later, another one called "Ka Jun" also came.)

Actually, our regular duties were not complicated. Other than spending one hour in the morning to listen to the recorded dharma lessons, the duties were taking care of our residential environment, cleaning and sweeping, and serving as religious teachers at the temple. We also took turns to do grocery shopping, cooking, taking care of the Great Danes, and other chores. Because of the lack of experience in doing these tasks, we had to learn everything from the beginning. In particular, taking care of the Great Danes was quite hard. We needed to feed them and clean the dog house including removing their stools. At the beginning, we were not used to doing this. As soon as we entered the fence, they would jump toward us and eagerly wanted to play with us. However, they were really too strong for us. If not careful, one would be knocked to the ground and get the dog's hair and saliva and a strong dog odor all over one's body. Even that was not the worst part yet. We also had to pour water to flush away their urine and stools. That was really hard to bear. The strong foul smell made people dizzy. During that period, whenever I closed my eyes in my sitting meditation, the scene of their urine and stools would emerge in my mind. For quite a while, such an image could not be expelled from my mind. I have no words to describe how bad that experience was.

However, it was very strange that these dogs all prostrated to the Great Dharma King to show respect. We did not know why they would prostrate to the Great Dharma King without ever being taught by a person to do so. Master Long Hui said that they were Buddhists who had taken refuge. Later I also witnessed the refuge ceremony that the Great Dharma King performed for a dog named "Jie Ben."

At this place, I did not have as much time for meditation as in Taiwan. Although I kept my habit of getting up at a little after five o'clock in the morning and sitting in the yard to meditate, I still found that my practice of meditation deteriorated. My patience also grew worse. This was particularly due to the fact that all Buddhist brothers and sisters had to be with one another every day. However, some had very strong temperaments and were not easy to get along with. Often, there was a lack of good communication, resulting in continuous conflicts. That made me very surprised. How could this be cultivation? Such situations caused great torment in my inner heart. After a long time, I still could not adapt myself to get used to that. Compared to how I had been while in Taiwan, it was like being dropped off from heaven. The people and affairs here were much more complicated and harder than before. I could only repeatedly console myself, "I shall have patience. I just need to adapt to the situation. I will get used to that. Everything will be fine."

Of course, there was always something in return for giving up something! All hardship would be worthwhile if we could see the Great Dharma King. However, sometimes we did not see the Great Dharma King for a long period of time. Why? This was due to the fact that the Great Dharma King did not live here. It was not easy for the Great Dharma King to visit here. The Great Dharma King was also a professor at a university and had to work for the university. Even when He came occasionally, He could only stay for a short while. The Great Dharma King got along with us rather casually, showing that He was no different from common people. The Great Dharma King would typically ask about our living conditions and always compassionately care about us all. We generally felt that He was just a kind elder virtuous one, without showing something special. Neither did we see the superior power of realization that an eminent monk could have.

We spent most of our time with Master Long Hui, chairperson of the International Buddhism Sangha Association (IBSA) and Dharma Master Jue Hui, abbess of both Sanger Mission and Bodhi Monastery. In addition, there were several fellow brothers. They were all true cultivators with clear and pure moral characters. Among them were, Brother Long Zhi Tanpe Nyima (Venerable Denma Tsemang II), Brother Kuan, and a few Caucasian rinpoches. They were all very caring and helpful to us.

Life here sometimes also had a humorous side.

Because our English was not good and we were not familiar with the roads, Sister Long Hui was always the driver when we went shopping. From the times I rode with her, I deeply felt that such a high-level cultivator does not have arrogance or show status. She treated everyone equally with warmth and kindness.

Once, Sister Long Hui was going to take me to buy electronics and groceries. She said, "We will go and prostrate four times first and then we will go to a supermarket." Well, Sister Long Hui is truly different from the rest of us, I thought. She even goes to the Buddha hall to pay respect to the Buddha before going grocery shopping. She is really very pious. Since I heard what the sister said, I went to the Buddha hall first and did four prostrations. Then I spoke to her, "Sister, we can go now. I have already done the four prostrations."

Sister Long Hui was quite puzzled, "Why did you have to do the four prostrations?" I replied, "Well, didn't you say 'go to prostrate four times first'?" Hearing that, Sister laughed so heartily that she could not keep her body upright. Then she explained to me, "There is a store here called Best Buy. It is a specialty store for electronics and appliances. What I said was we would 'first go to Best Buy' and then go to the supermarket. So you did go to the Buddha hall and did four prostrations. That was also very good! Remember, during the three periods of the day (which means twenty-four hours a day), we shall keep Buddhas and Bodhisattvas in our heart!" (Note: Best Buy sounds the same as "prostrate four times" in Chinese (bai si bai).)

Every time the Great Dharma King Master came, we would immediately stand in rows to welcome Him and pay respect. In addition to our group of bhiksunis, there were two Caucasian rinpoches. One was a girl in her twenties and the other was a Caucasian female rinpoche who was a little over fifty. Some fellow brothers were also present. The Great Dharma King would always compassionately touch everyone's head to empower us all. At that time, we were not familiar with the Great Dharma King yet and all had a mind of respect and fear. Therefore, we dared not ask a lot of questions, fearing that saying something wrong would mean disrespect. In particular, the Great Dharma King spoke with a strong Sichuan accent. Moreover, words used in the spoken language can be different between Taiwan and mainland China. Many times, we were not clear about what the Great Dharma King was saying.

For instance, once the Great Dharma King Master told us to get a wiping cloth called "Pa zi". However, we simply did not understand the word "Pa zi" that He used.

On another occasion, we were told to "Kang Qi Lai" (which sounds like to carry something up). We all looked at each other and then started to guess what we were told to do. In the end, we found out that it meant to "cover" this thing up.

There was a time when the Great Dharma King told us to fetch "hua jiao mian" (which means pepper powder but sounds like noodles made of pepper). We all wondered which place sells noodles made of pepper and then reported, "We never bought any pepper noodles." The Great Dharma King Master said, "Nonsense! I clearly see it in the cabinet. How could you say there is none?" (Note: The word "mian" the powder of grains or seasoning seeds in Chinese sounds like the word "noodle" in some local dialects.)

Once we were asked for "chuang kou tie" (which sounds like a kind of sticker.) We were lost again, "What is 'chuang kou tie'?" The answer turned out to be a plastic bandage.

When we behaved foolishly, the Great Dharma King called us "Yu Gu Bang!" We really could not figure out what this meant since we had never heard of this term. I had only ever heard of the Monkey King's "Jin Gu Bang," but not "Yu Gu Bang"! Later we learned that it meant "a stick of silly bone," meaning even the bone marrow contains silly ingredients.

These types of examples were too many to mention. With us being like kindergarteners, the Great Dharma King had to give long explanations to us even though He was very busy with the matters of Buddha-dharma. We truly made it hard for the Great Dharma King Master!

Not too long after, we had another new member. This time, it was a two-month old golden retriever. Its first name was Jack. After taking refuge in Buddhism, it was given a Buddhist name of "Jie Ben" (which means a book of precepts.) It had been a monastic person in a past lifetime but, because of violating the precepts, it had descended into the animal realm in the current lifetime. The Great Dharma King Master specifically told us to take good care of it and be loving and kind to it. Jie Ben was not an ordinary dog.

Because Jie Ben was very small then, it was very fond of playing. One day, it peed inside the room on the floor. Therefore, a monastic sister wanted to educate it, so she held a rolled newspaper trying to hit the dog. The rest of us did not know about this episode and it was not reported to the Great Dharma King.

However, a few days later, the Great Dharma King came again. The Great Dharma King Master gathered all of us without a prior announcement. The Great Dharma King told everyone that a holy and virtuous one called Him to mention that some people mistreated the dog. So the Great Dharma King came to investigate who had beaten the dog. Then that sister repented right away. The Great Dharma King also taught us a lesson:

All living beings are equal. If we do not fulfill our duty and do not care for the animals due to disliking foul and stinky smells, our bodhicitta is lost. Moreover, the animals are very piteous. They are not able to speak and cannot express their needs. Then we should all the more love and take good care of them. In this residence, all living beings are equal. Even an animal is our fellow brother. In addition, the dogs here all have taken refuge in Buddhism and have been awarded precepts. They are just like us, coming here to cultivate as a result of their karmic conditions.

Sure enough, every dog here was quite spiritual. Also, quite strangely, each of them knew to prostrate to the Great Dharma King Master and listen attentively when the Great Dharma King Master was expounding the dharma without ever being taught to do so by people.

Actually the Great Danes were not the most formidable animals residing here. "Deva Beast" was raised in the dining hall. "Deva Beast" was a little squirrel that almost died at one time. The Great Dharma King saved it from an unconscious coma. Afterward, it was fed and cared for in the dining hall and grew day by day. It especially listened to what the Great Dharma King Master instructed.

Brother Kuan was playing with it one day. He put his finger into its mouth to let it hold onto the finger with its teeth. Then he lifted it in the air and its body was swirling back and forth. While holding the finger with its teeth, it knew not to apply pressure to injure the finger. However, it treated strangers quite differently. It would definitely bite people who carried impure karmas.

"Deva Beast" was very quick and nimble in motion. By leaping and jumping it could move extremely quick and fast. That was why it was many times fiercer than the dogs. Once it found its target, that person would never be able to escape and would definitely be bitten badly until falling to the ground with miserable howling. Only the Great Dharma King Master could subdue its ferocious beast nature.

Since no one other than the Great Dharma King Master could restrain it or make it listen, the Great Dharma King Master told Venerable Yundun Duojibai Rinpoche Brother to find some dry wood. He and other brothers made a big cage to house Deva Beast. When the Great Dharma King Master was not present, we dared not let it out of the cage. Otherwise someone would definitely be miserably attacked.

Not long after, we had more new companions. This time they were a color-changing lizard and a pair of white pigeons. The lizard was given the name of "Bie Long." Of course, our site became more bustling. Our work assignments, in addition to serving as religious teachers at the temple, kept expanding and were very diversified and colorful.

4

Disappointment and Sadness Tangled Together

In July 2002, a piece of shocking news came from my former worldly home. My mother was diagnosed with leukemia. This sudden and unexpected notice was like a crackling thunder in a cloudless clear sky. My heart was burning and I wished I could rush home immediately. However, the Great Dharma King Master happened to be traveling far away then. I could only beseech the Great Dharma King Master to empower my mother in a phone call. While talking on the phone, I could not control myself from crying. The Great Dharma King Master very kindly and compassionately consoled me and told me not to worry. He also promised me to empower my mother. Upon hearing the Great Dharma King Master's voice, I felt very calm without knowing why. Thus, I temporarily steadied myself.

The Great Dharma King Master was not there; so I felt that I should not ask to take time off to leave. Sister Long Hui also came to comfort me. However, at that time, my mind was filled with anxiety and could not think straight. A very strong affliction arose from ignorance. I even said angrily, "Why should I take care of the Great Danes here? I would rather go back to take care of my mother!" Due to lack of correct knowledge and view, I became irrational and my mind was filled up by distraction and anxiety. There was no power of concentration left in me. My regular practices of sitting meditation and chanting Buddha's name were all just pretense and became totally engulfed and burned away by the flame of affliction, fear, and ignorance whenever a difficult situation arose. I was very afraid of losing my mother soon and never seeing her again.

Moreover, I even started to doubt whether the Great Dharma King Master was truly a great holy one. During the long period of time since

I had come here, I had not seen any manifestation of a holy one's might and supremacy from the Great Dharma King Master. My wish of learning great Buddha-dharma was not satisfied either, since no dharma was taught. Could the teaching of cultivating loving-compassion and being prostrated to by dogs prove that a person is a great holy one? I was not able to learn what I wanted to learn. It appeared that the Great Dharma King Master did not have much to teach either. I could not stop asking myself, whether my initial choice of staying here was right. It was really hard to live like this day after day. A day seemed as long as a year. I counted and counted the days until the Great Dharma King Master finally returned. I hurriedly flew back to Taiwan after asking for a leave of absence.

My mother was already hospitalized in the Cathay Hospital. At that time, the second round of chemotherapy was about to begin. My siblings were taking turns spending time in the hospital to take care of her. I felt a deep sorrow when I saw her there. Although it had been only a little over a year since I had left her, she had thinned a lot.

While I was holding my mother's hand, she asked me, "Will you go back?" Although I wanted very much to stay at her side to take care of her, I also had the desire of learning Buddha-dharma. I did not want to give up before reaching my goal. With much hardship, I replied, choking, "Yes, I have to go back."

Having been devastated by chemotherapy, my mother turned very weak. Although her symptom was under control, I still did not want to leave her so soon. I wished to spend a little more time with her. I suddenly realized that my mother was so thin and petite and helpless. I was far from being filial and did not fulfill my duty as a daughter. Nor had I attained any accomplishment or benefit since I entered the monastic order until then. I was still entirely an ordinary person. Even if I wished to use my accomplishment of cultivation to reciprocate my parents' kindness to me, I would not be able to do so since I had not accomplished my cultivation yet.

I was very disappointed in myself and in my mind deeply blamed myself. I did not talk much about my life in America either, for fear that she would become concerned for me. Since I could not be sure whether the Great Dharma King Master possessed Buddha-dharma or not and did not discover anything extraordinary in the Great Dharma King Master, I dared not mention that I was serving as a religious teacher at the temple. What I was teaching to the students and at dharma-listening centers was related to meditation and some methods of practice, but it was all based on hollow theory. Since I myself was still at such a low level, I really could not mention that I was teaching other people.

In my heart I felt very bad about my mother and my cultivation in America. I was unable to take good care of my mother, and on the other hand, my wish of learning great dharma was unfulfilled as well. Nothing was fulfilled in either aspect. I suspected that I was really very stupid. I had been driven so much by the emotion of deciding to stay in America without considering other matters. I had now abandoned my mother to fabricate the nice dream of cultivating toward accomplishment. On the other hand, in America, I was just bitterly enduring everything that I was not used to. Even at where I was, it was not that easy to have the opportunity to meet the Great Dharma King Master! The Great Dharma King Master was very busy and would not come there easily. However, I always had the wish of having some miracle happen, so I could probe the truth of whether the Great Dharma King Master was a person of high realization or just an ordinary Buddhist. In case He was not a superior person, what could I do? I had already abandoned everything else!

While thinking about this, my heart was filled with sorrow and sadness. Tears streamed down my face. I did not know how much longer I had to endure. Thinking about the possibility of losing my mother before successfully learning Buddha-dharma and the unlikelihood of learning a truly great dharma at the time, I was almost certain that I would feel sorry for the rest of my life and never forgive myself.

I felt so much pain in my heart, as if being cut by a knife. Seeing my mother in her sleep, I wished that I could have more time to be with her. All I wanted was to cherish this time we could spend together to make up for the vacuum I had created during the past period of over one year.

Unfortunately, what happened thereafter went against my wish. I had a misunderstanding in hearing what a sister said when she called me from the home base. I thought I had heard "Hurry back." Thus, upon knowing that my mother's situation had stabilized, though I was quite unwilling and with a selfish mind, I still returned to America quickly. At that time, my mother was still in the hospital and I had only spent sixteen days with her.

After returning to America, all I could do was to check on my mother's situation by making frequent phone calls. She started chemotherapy again. One day, she fainted in the restroom in her ward and underwent an emergency physical check. Upon hearing this, I immediately beseeched the Great Dharma King Master to empower my mother. The Great Dharma King Master was very kind and compassionate. He went into the altar room to empower my mother right away and then told me, "You can take it easy. That is not a big problem. She has anemia. However, her blood supply will replenish itself."

The next day, I got a phone call from my worldly family. The results of my mother's physical check came out. Other than the numbers of red and white blood cells being low, all other indicators were normal. I felt relieved. After so long, this was the first time I realized that there was something extraordinary about the Great Dharma King Master and was also the first time I felt that it was so nice to be at this home base. This was because the Great Dharma King Master was here to eliminate disasters and remove adversity for people with His compassionate blessing.

5

Falling into a Net of Suspicion

Not long after I had returned from Taiwan, the Great Dharma King Master began to come to the home base often.

When the Great Dharma King Master came, He would be either working on Yun sculptures or paintings, or giving discourses that were recorded. The Great Dharma King Master might expound the dharma at any time. Most of the time, the dharma expounded was about the mind and the conduct, or, how to cultivate one's mind and how to cultivate one's conduct. The Great Dharma King Master was very good at expounding the dharma and was able to teach any dharma and practice of Buddhism, including lineages. However, the Great Dharma King Master represented only Buddhism, not specific sects or schools in Buddhism. The Great Dharma King Master treated all sects and schools equally without differentiation, whether they were the Lesser Vehicle, Mahayana, the Zen Sect, the Pure Land School, Esoteric Buddhism, or others. The Great Dharma King told us, "All sects and schools have their own advantages and are all good. Their teachings are applicable to different people, can correspond to different types of karmic conditions, and can generate different kinds of effects and utilizations." However, which sect was the Great Dharma King Master from and what lineage did he represent? I could not figure out the answer no matter how much I thought about it.

At that time, we could see the Great Dharma King Master creating artworks for the university almost every day. We were able to follow the Great Dharma King Master and talk to Him at a close distance to ask questions about Buddha-dharma. We were able to get more in-depth impressions about the Great Dharma King Master. The details exhibited by the Great Dharma King in His life were very common and completely the same as those of ordinary people. From the way He dealt with people and managed things, we did not see anything special either. He appeared to be just a kind person.

Later, the Great Dharma King Master began to create Yun sculptures. The Great Dharma King Master worked every day to bring Yun sculptures into being, using knives for cutting, digging, carving, drilling, and hooking, as well as various kinds of other metal tools. The tools were in different sizes. The work was very hard and tiring. In particular, the Great Dharma King Master often worked under the scorching sun and was sweating all wet as if being rained upon. Moreover, He would get very dirty all over His body, and often, even with paint, glue, and colors on His hair. However, the Great Dharma King Master was little concerned about that. To tell the truth, had He walked on the street with such an appearance, He would definitely be regarded as a dirty homeless person.

The Great Dharma King Master got up very early before dawn to do paintings for the university. There was no regular work schedule. Generally, He started to work on Yun sculptures in the afternoon and continued until almost midnight. Often, the lunch break was in the evening. Sometimes, He would even work until one or two o'clock in the early morning. While working, He would stand there for eight, nine, or more than ten hours without a break. Even the disciples who were there serving tea felt very tired, as if their legs were no longer part of their bodies due to standing for so long. Of course, it was easy to imagine that the feeling must be even harder for the Great Dharma King Master who was working laboriously.

The Great Dharma King Master often chatted while doing His work. However, after a long period of working, even the Great Dharma King Master would have difficulty to continue standing. His body would shake while walking and He would have shortness of breath and would have difficulty talking. I was somewhat puzzled. How could the Great Dharma King Master appear just like a common person and so ordinary? As a particular example, even we who were bhiksunis could carry a pail filled with water. However, the Great Dharma King Master was unable to lift a pail that was just a little over half full. That was really hard to imagine. Could it be that the Great Dharma King Master had lost His power of realization?

Although the Great Dharma King Master appeared not to have much power of realization and seemed just like a common person in His speech and behavior, His ethics and wisdom were truly very clear and pure! Because of this fact and since we had already chosen our master, we had to respect our master and value our practice. That is the basic ethical principle of a human being after all. Seeing the Great Dharma King Master's state of an ordinary person, I wondered whether the Great Dharma King had Buddha-dharma or not. However, there was something that I could not figure out. The dharma kings and venerable ones coming here from anywhere in the world were all totally respectful to the Great Dharma King Master. All questions they asked or teachings they sought were replied to or responded to by the Great Dharma King Master to fulfill their wishes perfectly. There was never a question that was not answered. That situation was unprecedented throughout history and would be incomparable for people in future generations. If the Great Dharma King truly did not have Buddha-dharma, how could He expound the dharma and the sutras so preciously and accurately? That was really an unsolvable puzzle to me!

The Great Dharma King Master often told us, "Disciples, I am really the same as you. I am not higher than you. I am very ashamed, and I am a very common person. You must know this fact in your heart. You will not learn much from me. Dharma-protectors also do not take me seriously, since I am just a humble cultivator."

The Great Dharma King Master appeared to be no different from ordinary people. So, it seemed quite strange that He was able to expound the dharma so vividly to let us reap great benefits. Often, the discourse would enlighten us on the spot. Moreover, no matter what difficult questions you might raise that might involve any topics in the Tripitaka or even be outside the realm of the Tripitaka, the Great Dharma King Master would give you the perfect answers right away without thinking. There had never been a question that was unanswerable to Him.

Examples of this kind of impromptu question-and-answer sessions could always be heard from the recorded dharma lessons. We heard from the earlier dharma lessons that the Great Dharma King declared, "You can raise questions of all types. If there is any that I cannot answer, I will leave the dharma rostrum with shame right away." In a dharma lesson recorded more than ten years ago, we also heard, "However, I only give you five years. Once this five-year period expires, I will no longer treat you this way!" People who had been present during the Great Dharma King's discourses all attested to the fact of all questions getting answered. Moreover, the facts were recorded in a number of dharma lessons, not just one lesson!

One day, the Great Dharma King Master told me to make a telephone call to a fellow brother. However, I was inexperienced in dealing with people and did not know the proper etiquette for talking over the phone. As a result, the Great Dharma King Master thought I was impolite and got really angry. He even cast my phone handset away.

At that time, I was stunned by this sudden act of the Great Dharma King Master. At the home base, this was the first time I saw the Great Dharma King Master become so angry. After reprimanding me, the Great Dharma King went to the altar. I returned to my dorm and cried with tears all over my face. I thought that I would rather return to my temple of Zhuyun Monastery to serve as the abbess there again. When I saw Sister Liao Hui, I spoke without thinking, "I really feel a lot of grievance in me!" Within only five to six seconds after I said this, the Great Dharma King Master already sent someone to call me. I wiped off my tears and went to the Great Dharma King Master in a hurry.

The Great Dharma King immediately told me, "Since you have so much grief, you should stop learning from me here. I told you long ago that I am not a holy one. Staying here will not let you learn what you want to learn. You should go quickly and find an eminent monk! It will be very good for you to be the abbess of Zhuyun Monastery! It is not too late yet. You respect me very much. I do not want to waste your time either. Otherwise I would be too sorry to you! I want to tell you today that I am an ordinary person. You will not learn Buddha-dharma by following me. I have nothing to teach you. If you leave early, you may be able to meet a true great Bodhisattva!"

Hearing that, I felt very bad. However, how could the Great Dharma King Master know this? The Buddha hall where the Great Dharma King Master sat was rather far from our dorm. How did the Great Dharma King Master know my thoughts? Without being expressed by language, how could my thoughts be known? Then, that meant my thoughts of regarding the Great Dharma King as an ordinary person all along must have been known clearly by the Great Dharma King. This matter involving the phone call must have been a manifestation purposely done to educate me. I fell into the Great Dharma King Master's setup for testing me.

At that time, I was unable to say anything but felt terrible. Oh, I was so stupid and sinful! I felt so bad that there was nothing I could say. Seeing me speechlessly stunned, the Great Dharma King Master kindly told me, "If you really do not want to leave, you can stay!" I immediately prostrated and repented. However, being ignorant, I did not notice that my impure thoughts, embedded deeply in my consciousness, were not completely corrected at that time.

Although I became aware of my impure thoughts at the time, I did not sever such mental habits completely. My opinion toward this Holy Dharma King Master who was so great was still changing back and forth and for better and for worse from time to time without my own awareness. I was even so unreasonably wrong as to regard the internal conflicts and struggles between fellow brothers and sisters as the fault of the Great Dharma King Master.

Speaking of the life within our group of monastics, getting along and interacting among fellow nuns were not simple matters. It was not always true that all monastic persons were cultivating with patience and endurance and behaved in proper manner. The reality was totally not so. Everyone had her own habits and temperament. In particular, there were two sisters whose characters were rather rude. Their relationship was like that between a nail and a hammer. Often, they quarreled with each other and neither would give in. A lot of hatred and bitterness were accumulated. The Great Dharma King Master tried tirelessly to educate us all and applied His actual practice of great compassion to guide us. The discourses were also recorded to let us listen constantly. However, not much effect was seen.

This situation was quite a big disturbance to me. Impure karmas toward the Great Dharma King Master arose in my deep mind. I kept thinking that the teaching by the Great Dharma King Master was not the Buddha-dharma that could liberate living beings. Otherwise, how could there be this situation of fellow sisters treating each other like enemies? Was this cultivation? I questioned why this group was not replaced with upper-level disciples with high levels of morality and standards, such as Venerable Denma Tsemang, Kaichu Rinpoche, Luoben Rinpoche, Layperson Kuan, and others? Why was this group of low-level people retained here? I kept thinking but could not figure out the answer. This became another reason for my intention of leaving. In addition, I simply had not learned a great dharma after following the Great Dharma King Master for so long. I doubted very much. How could I become accomplished this way? Would my current lifetime be finished like this?

6

My Experience of Meeting a Female Ghost of Wrongful Death

One day, the Great Dharma King Master told us to set up a mandala on the lawn and then make offerings to dharma-protectors. Because of the requirement by some karmic conditions, we needed to serve on different shifts to guard the site to prevent evil beings from coming or unexpected situations from rising. On that night, another monastic sister Jian Hui and I were on the shift. The evening was somewhat chilly. We were sitting in the courtyard with our bodies wrapped in thick quilts.

After three o'clock in the early morning, the color of the night was deep and heavy. The land was so quiet, as if even the sound of a needle dropping to the ground could be heard. I heard the eerie cry of an owl "Woo! Woo! Woo!" from far away in the direction behind me, and my body shivered spontaneously. I told myself to be wary of possible malevolent action, since I had once heard that some owls are manifestations of ghosts.

I held my breath to listen carefully to its movement. However, it seemed that it had already alertly noticed my attention toward it. So, after hooting a few more times, it moved closer from the direction behind me. I did not turn my head back. However, as the sound of its movement was becoming louder, I could tell that it was getting closer and closer. Eventually, it seemed to be in the midst of the tree grove about three or four feet behind me. At that time, my anxiety intensified. Suddenly, I heard the sound of leaves rustling in the trees. After a while, it seemed that the owl had flown away.

I never actually saw the owl or its shadow. However, since it no longer called out, I thought that perhaps dharma-protectors had chased this ghost away to prevent it from causing disturbance at our home base. Now I could take it easy. It was still early morning but I did not feel sleepy at all. Rather I was meditating with a clear mind. At this time, a holy scene appeared in front of me. I clearly saw an unimaginably magnificent state! I was greatly surprised and deeply felt the joy of the dharma. At the same time, I saw a tall and mighty Vajra dharma-protector standing at a distance of eighteen feet from the offering table. The Vajra dharma-protector was extremely powerful and awe-inspiring. He wore a warrior's robe and was as tall as a two-storied building. His face somewhat resembled that of Monk Ji. I immediately rose to prostrate. Now I realized that dharma-protectors stationed at the home base were working in shifts just as we were to guard our home base!

The site was continuously guarded for several days. Although some people saw dark shadows in the midst of the night, it turned out to be just a false alarm. There was nothing extraordinary. Everything was safe. All was perfectly auspicious. I prayed for Buddha light to broadly illuminate everywhere, for the prosperity and popularity of true Buddha-dharma, for expelling all disasters and hardships, and for not letting evil ghosts and demons make trouble and cause disturbance at this home base of true Buddha-dharma!

One day, when the Great Dharma King Master returned to the home base, I reported the states I saw to the Great Dharma King Master. The Great Dharma King said, "One dreams at night what one thinks during the day. All these are just illusionary perceptions and are false. These are not what cultivating and learning Buddhism are about. Don't take these seriously. You should clearly understand that I simply do not have such great ability of inviting dharma-protectors to come here."

One day in the afternoon, I drowsily entered into a dream state of bardo. Suddenly, a ghost who died from hanging manifested. She was hanging on a tree in the court with her hair covering her face. The appearance was rather frightful. She stuck her long tongue out toward me. That was very scary! I was terrified and immediately reported to the Great Dharma King Master. The Great Dharma King Master said,

"What was so scary about this? In the past, when a patriarch was gargling his mouth, a ghost was hung down from above to scare him. He was completely unperturbed and did not even think about that. As a cultivator, how could you lack the power of concentration? I have already told you that it is false and illusionary. Why do you still want to take it as real and be attached to it?" Upon hearing what the Great Dharma King Master said, I was able to remove this incident from my mind.

However, just a few days later, she appeared again. This time it was in the early morning shortly after midnight. She was right outside the French door of the living room, floating slowly from right to left and then from left to right. It was very bright outside the window, as if under daylight. I was able to see very clearly. The whole scene seemed to be blue-colored. I believed that she was the same ghost spirit hanging from the tree. She manifested her appearance before death, female and Caucasian. Her hair was golden-white. She appeared somewhat like the Caucasian rinpoche sister in her twenties I mentioned earlier (in Chapter 3) but her own age seemed to be in the forties, and she was of medium height. I had no idea as to what she wanted to do. To tell the truth, deep inside, I felt really creepy at the time. I tried my best to chant mantras. Next I saw she smiled and slowly floated away. She then disappeared.

I really could not be sure whether this was a dream, was true, or was just an illusion of my own making. Later, I reported this experience to the Great Dharma King Master. The Great Dharma King Master said, "Actually I am not quite sure whether this female ghost exists or not either. Perhaps this was an illusion and there was no such thing." Since the Great Dharma King Master said so, I also thought this experience was an illusion. However, in my mind, I felt that this home base seemed to be somewhat different from other places.

7

The Dog

"Jie Ben" was a dog that had supernatural power. It was previously called Jack. Since coming to the home base, it had been living with us and listening to the dharma all the time. As time was passing day by day, it grew up gradually. Suddenly, we discovered that it knew to make a posture similar to great prostration to pay respect. No one had taught it to do so before.

One day, Jack went in front of the Great Dharma King to prostrate by pushing its two front legs forward. It did so up and down three times and still did not want to leave. The Great Dharma King Master asked Jack, "Were you prostrating to pay respect to me?" Jack nodded to mean yes. The Great Dharma King again asked, "Then, were you asking for taking refuge?" Jack immediately sat up attentively and held its two front paws together as if holding the palms together. The Great Dharma King said, "Okay, you can sit to the side now!" Jack then sat nicely by the Great Dharma King Master's side without even moving a bit. It waited until the Great Dharma King had finished giving the discourse to the disciples and again went in front of the Great Dharma King and sat up formally. The Great Dharma King Master said, "Okay, I will hold the refuge ceremony for you right now!" Thus, Jack took refuge in Buddhism and got his Buddhist name of "Jie Ben."

Jie Ben knew human nature extremely well. It could understand completely what people were talking about. It was also extremely respectful toward the Great Dharma King. It always did three prostrations every time it saw the Great Dharma King Master.

When the Great Dharma King did not permit it to look at something, the order was, "Turn your head away. You are not allowed to look!" Then it would immediately turn its head to one side. Only until the

Great Dharma King Master instructed again, "Okay, that was over," would it turn its head back. When the Great Dharma King Master was at the back house which was quite a distance away and told someone to take a message of "The Great Dharma King Master told you to go there," to Jie Ben, even if it was asleep at the time, it would stand up right away and go through all turns by itself to where the Great Dharma King Master was. Every time it got the message, it always responded right away.

The Great Dharma King put a dog biscuit on top of its nose and told it not to move. This was for removing its greedy desire for eating to begin the training of the power of concentration. At that time, Jie Ben would hold the biscuit without moving until the Great Dharma King said okay. Then it would throw the biscuit up and catch it in its mouth to eat.

Actually, teaching a dog such behaviors should not be too difficult for dog trainers either. However, the key is that Jie Ben had never been trained by anyone. Jie Ben was able to do a number of things that people can do. One of the examples was "pretending to be dead." Normally, when people mentioned this term, it would not have any response. The same was true even when the Great Dharma King Master mentioned the term "pretending to die." However, as soon as the Great Dharma King formally gave the instruction, "Now you can pretend to be dead!" It would immediately lie on the ground without moving a bit. Even when we walked around it or pushed it, it would still show an appearance of being dead without any movement. However, as soon as the Great Dharma King Master said, "Now it is over," it would immediately roll and jump up.

Once, a monastic sister sneezed. She then casually said, "Stay away from me. Don't catch the flu from me!" Her statement did not get much attention from us. However, Jie Ben immediately took off and ran to the door, which was more than twenty feet away, to hide. Its cuteness made us all laugh heartily.

On another occasion, the Great Dharma King said that Jie Ben was having some little illness and should be fed with two almonds. Great Dharma King Master then immediately fetched two almonds for Jie Ben. Jie Ben smelled the almonds with his nose but did not eat them. The Great Dharma King fed him again but he spit the almonds out again. Then the Great Dharma King Master seriously reprimanded him and picked up the almonds to feed him again. Jie Ben reluctantly held the almonds in his mouth and slowly chewed a few times. Then he stuck his neck out and pretended to swallow with the almonds still in his mouth. People all assumed that he swallowed the almonds and the mouth made no movement after that.

About a minute later, he was given dog treats as a reward for being nice and listening to the command. Now, the secret was exposed. The almonds dropped out from a corner of his mouth. His act of swallowing the almonds had been completely faked. The almonds were hidden in his mouth while he swallowed a mouthful of saliva to deceive people. The intention was to wait until the Great Dharma King Master no longer noticed. Then he would spit out the almonds stealthily.

Figure 7-1 - The dog Jie Ben

Not long after Jie Ben had taken refuge with the Great Dharma King Master, he started to show the supernatural power of forecasting future events. When an important guest or guests was/were about to come to pay respect to the Great Dharma King, he would foretell of the arrival about five to six minutes ahead of time. He would make a kind of grunting sound while facing the front gate. When we went to open the door, no one was there. However, a few minutes later, the guest(s) did arrive. This was true every time. This ability to forecast future arrivals that Jie Ben had, could never be acquired by training with a professional dog trainer.

Once, the Great Dharma King Master had left for a long trip and no one knew the date of His return. One day, in the afternoon, Jie Ben started to voice the grunting sound again. He also prostrated toward the door. That caused us to wonder who might be coming. A while later, the door opened and the Great Dharma King Master came back. Jie Ben's ability to predict so accurately without any error made us all admit that we were not as capable as he was in that aspect!

Thinking about the fact that Jie Ben had acquired supernatural power not long after taking refuge and I was still an ordinary person, I was really very ashamed! I had cultivated for so long already. When would I attain accomplishment from cultivation and be able to possess supernatural power of various kinds just like this dog? The Great Dharma King Master used Jie Ben as an example to teach us that we must treat all living beings equally. Like human beings, all dogs possess Buddha nature. Since beginningless time, they and human beings as well as all living beings have all been parents and relatives to one another. Therefore, we must not harm any living beings. We should only love and care for them. We should never abandon dogs to make them homeless. Otherwise, evil retributions would arrive for certain.

The Great Dharma King Master's teachings and guidance truly let us learn a lot in cultivating, behaving, and developing morality. However, these benefits still did not fulfill my wish to receive and practice great dharma. This wish was still causing inconstancy in my inner mind.

8

A Cold Dead Body Even Stood Up

During the period of creating Yun sculptures, the Great Dharma King Master also encouraged all of us to create artworks. Sister Liao Hui, who was also a monastic bhiksuni, was very interested in that and was very absorbed in the work. Whenever she had time, she would devote more effort to making her artworks.

One day, she was in the yard to continue working on the artwork she created, "Hard Boulder Emanates Splendor." When the evening arrived, it was a little cold outside. At that time, she still did not come inside. Thus, Sister Shi Guang Hui of the Sanger Mission went to call her. Suddenly, she found that Sister Liao Hui did not respond and was sitting next to the artwork without even moving a bit. Sister Guang Hui felt that something was not right and reached her hand out to touch her. She found that Sister Liao Hui had already stopped breathing and her body had completely turned cold. Therefore, she immediately reported to the Great Dharma King Master.

The Great Dharma King Master came to the site, examined the situation, then said, "How could she die here!" We were all directed to take emergency steps to rescue her back. We laid her on the deck in the yard. People brought quilts and blankets to try to keep her warm. Actually, there was no warmth to be kept. The covers were really preserving the coldness. At that time, her entire body was stiff, cold, and heavy. Her pulse and heartbeat had already stopped. She had been dead for quite a while already.

At that time, the Great Dharma King Master was practicing a dharma and called out, "Amitabha Buddha, do not take this person!" It was really surprising that, after He called a few times, Sister Liao Hui slowly woke up. She was fed a few mouthfuls of warm water. We saw the complexion of her face recovering slowly. After more than ten minutes, the color of her face turned red again. After about twenty minutes, she was able to speak. In a low, listless, and in an almost inaudible voice, she told us, "My artwork was completed. I felt very happy and very satisfied in my mind. Suddenly, my mind grew tranquil. I unexpectedly entered into the concentration of dispassion and extinction."

"At that time, the empty space was full of green- and red-colored light. I thought that was the state of perfection. So I kept chanting 'Namo Amitabha Buddha' and beseeching Amitabha Buddha to come to receive me. Then Amitabha Buddha did come. Ah! Amitabha Buddha appeared extremely majestic! Just as I was reaching out to hold Amitabha Buddha's hand and my foot was about to step onto the lotus, the Great Dharma King Master arrived. I heard the Great Dharma King Master speaking to Amitabha Buddha, 'Buddha! Do not take her away so fast! Do not take her away so fast! Do not take her away so fast! Let her stay here! She still has many things to do!'"

"Amitabha Buddha retrieved the lotus, smiled, and put me back to the original spot. Then I stayed and did not leave. However, my body could not move because I had already died. Still, I was able to hear the Great Dharma King Master's voice. The Great Dharma King Master gave me a powerful empowerment and got the agreement from Amitabha Buddha. At that time, there were two columns of white light that enclosed my body and my surroundings. Then my soul returned to the body. My body temperature turned warm again."

Heavens! Just by speaking one sentence, the Great Dharma King Master was able to let a person who had died and whose body had turned completely cold stand up again. I was overjoyed. The Great Dharma King Master was really a person of high realization!

One afternoon, Shi Ding Hui, a monastic sister from the Bodhi Monastery, found a honeybee that had drowned in the swimming pool. She brought it up from the water and laid it on the floor. We couldn't tell how long ago it had died. Its body was already stiff.

At this time, the Great Dharma King Master came over and compassionately gave it an empowerment by lightly snapping His fingers. After about two minutes, the bee started to move, with its feet first. After another while, it was able to crawl again. We saw that it had only one wing left. Perhaps the other wing had been bitten off by other bees, causing it to fall into the swimming pool and drown!

Then, another monastic sister Shi Guang Hui also rushed over to look. She heard the Great Dharma King Master speaking to Himself, "Alas! Now the life has been saved but one wing was lost. That would be too piteous! What can be done? That is too sad! Too sad! It would be good to have another wing grow out!" Right after the Great Dharma King Master said so, the bee had another wing grow out! The bee then flapped its wings a few times and cleaned up its body using its mouth. In the end, it turned toward the Great Dharma King as if prostrating to pay homage. After that, it opened up its two wings and flew away easily.

By speaking just one sentence, the Great Dharma King Master was able to ask Amitabha Buddha to let a person stay. This dead person then revived! By applying an empowerment with a few mantras, He was able to let a drowned bee return to life. The Great Dharma King Master said one sentence and the bee had a new wing grow out! What kind of realization would it take to accomplish this! The Great Dharma King Master is truly a person of high realization!

9

Parting with Jun Ma Forever

After being attended by us for several years, the two Great Danes, Weis and Jin Zhong Xue were moved to a fellow brother's home. The Great Dharma King Master told this brother repeatedly that he must be sure to take good care of them and treat them like people in his family. This brother promised repeatedly that he would be sure to do so. To tell the truth, we had feelings for them, after spending time together for so long. Now it was quite hard to see them be sent off.

Compared to Weis and Jin Zhong Xue, the other Great Dane Ka Jun had better fortune in life. What happened later to Weis and Jin Zhong Xue in the new environment was that the new owner was too busy with his work to have enough time to care for them. Weis ate too much sponge filling from inside a sofa and died on the surgery table at a veterinary hospital. Jin Zhong Xue made the mistake of eating fertilizer scattered in the yard and died on the spot. We all felt very sad for their deaths.

Now the only Great Dane left at the home base was Ka Jun. He took refuge in Buddhism and got his Buddhist name "Jun Ma" (which means the handsome horse). Without being taught by anyone, Jun Ma also knew to do great prostrations to the Great Dharma King Master to pay respect.

Since he was getting old, Jun Ma became ill. We took him to the veterinary hospital for treatment. However, we did not know that he would never return home.

I still remember that Jun Ma behaved quite differently than usual before leaving home for the hospital. Normally, before going out, regardless of whether taking a trip or going to the hospital, he always very nicely followed the instruction to get in the vehicle. This time, he first went all around the yard to sniff and look everywhere. Eventually, he reluctantly got in the vehicle as if still not wanting to leave. Now I recall that scene, it seemed to have known that, once getting out of this door, there would be no return ever.

What happened next was exactly so. Jun Ma went to the hospital for treatment in the morning and died there in the afternoon. Upon hearing this sad news, we were all in tears. We brought his remains back. The Great Dharma King Master led us to chant sutras to dedicate the merit to Jun Ma. We also worked on the funeral and burial ceremoniously. The Buddhist ceremonies lasted for several days. The Great Dharma King Master conducted the dharma to elevate his spirit. We laid his body in the living room and took turns to guard him at night. One night, I was on the shift to do the chanting for him. After lighting the incense, I closed my eyes and started chanting the Buddha's name to dedicate the merit to Jun Ma.

At around 3:30am, there was a round of lightning and thunder. The room was brightly illuminated. Then it started to rain. I felt that the lightning and thunder seemed to be sudden and somewhat peculiar. However, I still focused my mind on chanting the Buddha's name. Then, Jun Ma appeared. I saw that he had turned into a tall dharma-protecting deity and stood mightily in front of me. At that time, I did not mention this scene to anyone. I was afraid that maybe my eyes were dazzled.

The next day, the Great Dharma King Master told us all, "Because of the merit he had accumulated in guarding the home base, Jun Ma reincarnated to be a dharma-protecting heavenly deity and ascended to the World of Ultimate Bliss!" Now I knew that Jun Ma truly manifested his self last night. I was not in a dream. Nor were my eyes dazzled. Also, the lightning and thunder indicated that heavenly dharma-protectors came to receive him.

We measured Jun Ma's body size and ordered a large coffin for him. Inside, there was a lot of dog food, toys, and drinking water. These were all given by the Great Dharma King Master as blessings to Jun Ma, to let him have abundant food and other necessities and inexhaustible good fortune. Although beings can get whatever they desire in the World of Ultimate Bliss, the Great Dharma King Master still wanted to provide Jun Ma a set of lasting commemoration to bring to the World of Ultimate Bliss.

Farewell, Jun Ma! The Great Dharma King Master led us to bury Jun Ma at Pet Haven in Gardena. A tombstone was erected for commemoration. The inscription on the tombstone read:

"A Great Dane whose Buddhist name was Jun Ma was born in January of 2000 in Thailand. He was moved to the west and lived in the United States. He was loyal to the Four Jewels and acquired high merit for protecting the dharma. Jun Ma has now passed away. On August 30, 2007 between 3:00am and 5:00am, the heavenly dharma-protecting deities descended upon the city of Pasadena. Thunder roared like a welcoming song and rain fell from the sky, alighting upon flowers like dew. These auspicious, wondrous, and majestic sights were fruits of Jun Ma's dharma practice. Numerous deities escorted Jun Ma to a higher realm. He now permanently lives in the Western Paradise of Ultimate Bliss, having been reborn in a lotus pedestal in one of the nine levels of that paradise. Day and night, he will be a holy dharma-protecting general. Whatever he desires to receive, he will receive. His bliss will be limitless, and his blessings will be eternally abundant. May he soon realize the great fruit of enlightenment!

This tombstone is made in his memory.

August 31, 2007 Inscribed by practitioners of the Four Jewels"

Figure 9-1 - Inscription on Jun Ma's tombstone

Figure 9-2 - Jun Ma's picture during his lifetime

10

They Did Become Big-Head Generals

After following the Great Dharma King Master for all these years, although my cultivation still leaves much to be desired, I do have my own little experience and comprehension about a well-known saying that "The appearing and disappearing of the bubbles of the three poisons are illusory. One can let go of the coming and going of the Five Skandas (the Five Aggregates) like floating clouds."

One day, fellow brother Mark Lin from Seattle and fellow brother Ming-Chi Wei from Thailand wanted to work at the home base. The Great Dharma King Master gave them a discourse, "You will not be able to do the work here because your level of realization and the condition of your physical body are not up to the task."

The two brothers respectfully asked, "Those bhikshunis can do the work even though they are thin and petite. Why can't we?"

The Great Dharma King Master expounded, "You are no comparison to them. They have no problems because they are already able to overcome the force of the three poisons. This place has an extremely powerful force and an irresistible energy of empowerment. The two of you will not be able to handle that with your physical conditions of ordinary beings."

It turned out that these two brothers purchased complete sets of protective gear covering them from head to toe. After putting their gear on, they showed up in front of the Great Dharma King Master and said, "We need not fear now. Even poisonous gas will have no effect on us. We are under full armor protection. We want to be in the holy home base, and we even want to be near the altar."

The Great Dharma King Master grinned and said, "The ones who really don't need to fear are these petite disciples of mine. You won't make it. You would be like dough men who couldn't survive even wind and waves, not to mention the powerful force of this place. In two days, we will have two generals with big heads, huge ears, and eyes that barely open!"

At that time, the two brothers said to us, "How can that be possible? You have been following the Buddha Master for so long and never had problems at the place. Could it be that we are really so inferior?"

The next day, there were more than ten of us entering the mandala. As predicted, the two laymen's faces started to deform after they worked at the mandala for three hours. Their ears became huge, their mouths were shifted in place and their entire facial features were deformed. In less than three days, their heads and faces had grown by one-third; their eyes were too swollen to open; they could barely see where they were going; and they could hardly recognize the people standing in front of them. Their body and facial features had totally deformed.

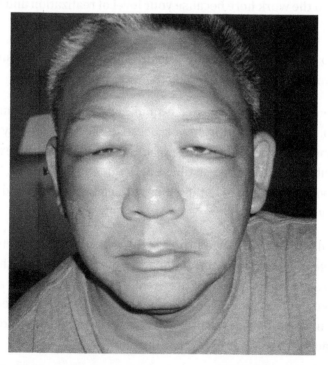

Figure 10-1 - The head of Layperson Ming-Chi Wei swelled larger and his facial features altered.

The outcome was totally as predicted by the Great Dharma King Master. Two big-head generals had appeared. In contrast, all of us who had been cultivating ourselves around the Great Dharma King Master were safe and free of any problem.

Note that the two brothers had full protective gear on including gas masks. On the other hand, what we put on was the most basic and simple things. However, the five Skandas and the demonic obstruction of poisonous gas had no effect on us at all.

This was a true account of what we had witnessed firsthand and had personally experienced.

Figure 10-2 - A recent photo, with Layperson Mark Lin on the left and Layperson Ming-Chi Wei on the right

11

Implausible to Anyone:
Not Seeking Enjoyment of Life with the Money He Has

The Great Dharma King Master never cared about Himself and was never concerned with His own interests. For instance, the Great Dharma King Master had a dedicated kitchen staff team. There were two chefs cooking for Him. They had very superior culinary skills and were able to cook whatever food the Great Dharma King Master cared to ask for.

People all know how important food and clothing are to human life. However, we never imagined that the Great Dharma King Master did not have even a slightest trace of the mentality that covets food or clothing and had never even once told the kitchen staff what He wanted to eat. When the chefs asked the Great Dharma King Master what to cook, the Great Dharma King Master would say, "You can cook whatever you feel like. I will completely rely on you on this. However, be sure to make it simple. Making it simple is good. Two or three dishes will definitely be enough. No more than that." Sister Dun Zhu who was in charge of the kitchen and the chefs all said that the Great Dharma King Master never asked for any specific food to be cooked. Throughout the years, the Great Dharma King Master always ate whatever the kitchen prepared and had never complained about anything. Just looking at this fact, who else could do so under such favorable conditions? One who pays no attention ever to food and clothing is unheard of in this world!

We saw the same fact from what the Great Dharma King Master wore. Other than wearing the special clothing and dharma robe during dharma assemblies, the Great Dharma King just wore a white shirt and a pair of dark-blue pants in His daily life. The same pair of shoes was worn all year round. The Great Dharma King Master did not wear any accessories either, not even a wristwatch. No one could believe that a person having money would give up enjoyment in life. Many people would conclude that doing so must be due to financial reasons. Actually, the reality was totally different.

The Great Dharma King is a world-famous distinguished master of art. At the British Embassy in the United States, the Royal Arts Academy of the United Kingdom awarded the first title of "Fellow" in its history of over two hundred years to the Great Dharma King Master. Paintings and calligraphies by the Great Dharma King were valued extremely high. Even one of the two-hundred limited-edition prints of a painting commanded the price of US$379,500 (including commission) in the international auction market. It set the highest record for limited-edition prints in auctions. Limited-edition prints of the Great Dharma King's artworks were valued essentially the same as that of historic Western artists such as Cezanne, Picasso, Van Gogh, and Monet. On the other hand, limited-edition prints of the artworks by Chinese artists such as Qi Baishi, Zhang Daqian, Xu Beihong, and Li Keran did not even reach the price level of US $50,000.

The Great Dharma King Master used His money from selling paintings to support monastic practitioners' living and Buddhist events. There existed some people in society who spread evil words to delude people. They lied that the Great Dharma King Master took money from people. That was really the most ludicrous lie that can only deceive foolish people. The Great Dharma King Master spent His own money to support temples and monastic practitioners. How would He still desire other people's money? We witnessed too many real examples in life. The Great Dharma King Master declined all offerings made by eminent monks, dharma kings, and great rinpoches who came to pay respect. Some of the offerings were over one hundred million CNY (over 16 million US dollars). Moreover, many achievements from His own research were donated for free without receiving any compensation.

One such example was Fa Bi Sheng (Hair Must Grow, a powerful ointment that stimulates hair growth), which was the No. 1 product approved by China's Ministry of Health. Another example was a tea named Bi Yu Chun. It received the highest grade of 101.5 on a scale of 0 to 100 and was ranked as the No. 1 tea product of China. The Great Dharma King Master donated this product to a company more than ten years ago and has never asked for any money from the company since then. If the Great Dharma King Master wanted to collect the royalty from this product, it would be an endless source of income. However, the Great Dharma King Master did not take any money or compensation of any form. In fact, the Great Dharma King Master no longer had any contact with the company.

The Great Dharma King only benefits others and people in society but does not care about Himself. We can all think over this fact. The Great Dharma King did not even accept the legitimate incomes that He was fully entitled to. Could He be interested in scamming other people for money? Therefore, those slanderous attacks were obvious evil rumors spread by evil masters and swindlers.

While contemplating about these deeds of such nobility, wisdom, and greatness, I asked myself: how could any ordinary person do so? As a result, I started to inspect my own wild imagination. I deeply repented. However, I had no way to realize that my remorse was superficial. I did not know this at all!!!

Figure 11-1 - A document issued by the Ministry of Health of China mentioned that Mighty-Power Hair Nurturing Ointment was previously named Hua Kang Fa Bi Sheng.

Figure 11-2 - Mighty-Power Hair Nurturing Ointment (Fa Bi Sheng) was named as the No. 1 product in this document issued by the Ministry of Health of China.

Figure 11-3 - News reports about the Bi Yu Chun tea at the time

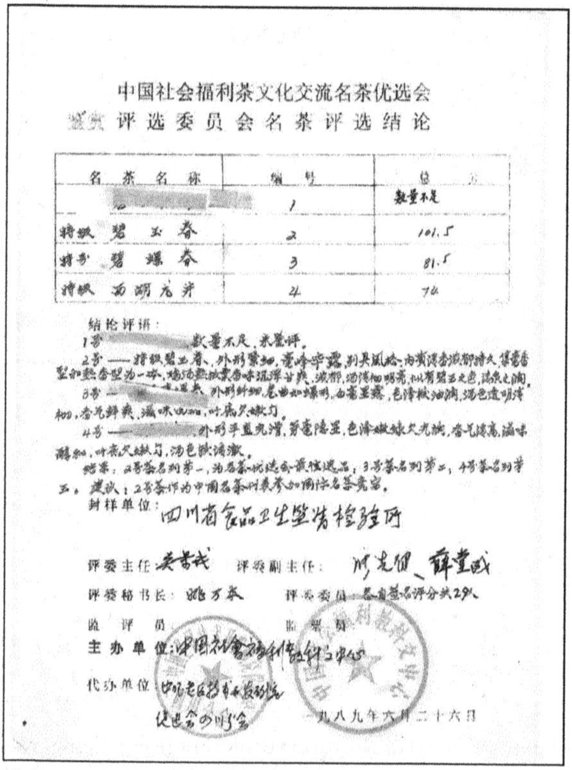

中国社会福利茶文化交流名茶优选会

评选委员会名茶评选结论

名茶名称	编号	总分
	1	数量不足
特级 碧玉春	2	101.5
特级 碧螺春	3	81.5
特级 西湖龙井	4	76

结论评语:

1号——数量不足,未量评。

2号——特级碧玉春,外形紧细,毫峰毕露,别具风格,内质清香浓郁持久,滋味香甜如熟香型第一味,场汤醇爽如香羊味,浓醇,汤清如明亮,以有碧玉色,汤亮七润,汤色透明清

3号——外形卷曲,毫毕如螺形,白毫显露,色泽银油润,汤色透明鲜,香气鲜爽,滋味浓甜,叶底尽嫩匀。

4号——外形手卷完净,叶电隆显,色泽嫩绿大光润,香气清高,滋味浓醇,叶底尺嫩匀,汤色欣清淡。

然后,2号参样列第一,为名茶优选之首候选, 3号参样列第二,4号参样列第三。建议:2号参评的中国名茶优样参加两际名茶竞容。

封样单位: 四川省食品卫生监督检验所

评委主任: 吴志武   评委副主任: 刘光倜 薛重威

评委秘书长: 姚万芬   评委委员 各自签名评分共29人。

监评员

主办单位: 中国社会福利促进会文化

代办单位: 四川名优名茶发展会

优选会办公室   一九八九年六月二十六日

Figure 11-4 - Bi Yu Chun tea received the highest score of 101.5 and was ranked as the No. 1 product in China.

12

Poisonous Artemisia Made Several People Fall

One day, a monastic sister at the home base, Jian Hui, joyfully held a bunch of wild vegetable greens and told us, "Look! Here are fresh wild greens that grew in the yard, Chinese kale. There is no pesticide on them!" Because this sister had studied Horticulture in school, people tended to believe whatever she had to say about plants, and everyone thought that we would have fresh wild greens to eat that day!

Because it was my turn to cook that day, Sister Jian Hui handed the wild greens to me, hoping that they would be cooked for dinner and everyone could taste this wild version of Chinese kale. However, I felt that it was not appropriate to do that. I said, "It may not be good. What if it tastes really bad and no one wants to eat it. What can we do?" I did not start to cook it. Then, this sister said firmly, "Don't worry. You can just cook it. If nobody wants to eat it, I will eat it all. There will be no leftovers." Therefore, I reluctantly cooked the wild vegetable greens.

In the early evening shortly after five o'clock, this course of wild vegetable was cooked and put on a plate. Its color was fresh green like emerald. The vegetable was emitting flashing green light and a delicious smell. What would this beautiful dish taste like? There was still some doubt in my mind as to whether it was edible. However, out of curiosity, I picked up a small piece the size of a thumbnail to sample it. Uh, it tasted so bad! It was bitter and astringent! How could it be Chinese kale! It tasted terrible!

Because I did not feel hungry at that time, I decided to do the practice of chanting Buddha's name first. Perhaps it was due to the small amount that I ate, I felt no toxic effect at that point. After I finished the practice and opened up my eyes to stand up, things went quite wrong. Both the sky and the ground were swirling around me. I could not even walk and had to hold on to the wall for support. I walked staggeringly and slowly to return. I did not know then that it was due to my eating the very poisonous Artemisia. I thought that I must have caught a cold while sitting there chanting Buddha's name. Thus, I hurriedly went back to my room and lay down on the bed. While I was lying down, I heard other people's yelling, "This vegetable has some problem! Don't eat it!"

Within a few minutes, those who ate it all felt powerless in their arms and legs. Their eyes were fuzzy and heads spinning and dizzy. All fell to the ground. A brother immediately brought the leftover portion of this dish to report to the Great Dharma King Master. The Great Dharma King Master told him, "This is Gelsemium elegans, also called Artemisia. Even a little bit can be deadly. You go there quickly and check to see if they died! Clearly report how many of them died and whether any are still alive. Do not miss even one. Report their names so I will notify the Yama King not to accept them. Be quick! Save them fast! The faster, the better!"

Five people were present at the time, Acarya Xuan Hui, Acarya Hui Zhu, Dharma King Muya Jiongzha, Layperson Ming-Chi Wei, and I. Those who ate the cooked Artemisia were pale and grey in the face. Their complexions were as ugly as that of a dead person without showing any trace of blood. Their minds were dazed and not functioning. Brother Muya Jiongzha was also cramping. Brother Ming-Chi Wei was breathing hard with his eyes opened very wide.

The Great Dharma King Master saw the scene and told everyone to vomit and throw up what they ate. Since I only ate a small piece, I did not spit out anything. Some other people could not throw up either.

The Great Dharma King Master immediately flipped His fingers to empower everyone and announced to the sky, "Dharma protectors in all heavens come quickly to protect my disciples. Let them spit out the poison and have their souls return!" Strangely, right after this proclamation, people all wanted to throw up. They went to the restrooms to vomit and could not stop. Everyone threw up multiple times and went to the restroom repeatedly after only a short while. The sound of vomiting was heard continuously inside, making people who did not eat the poisonous vegetable also want to vomit.

The five of us repeated this cycle of vomiting many times. Eventually, the stomach was emptied completely clean with nothing left. We were also totally exhausted.

The Great Dharma King Master instructed us to have some rice congee and then go to bed to rest. Because the poison of Gelsemium elegans is neurotoxic in nature, one who ate it would immediately feel numbness in the head and the four limbs would palsy as if paralyzed. Even an energetic strongman would be unable to support the body and fall to the ground.

Thanks to the Great Dharma King Master's blessing, the five of us returned safely from our trip to the boundary of the Yama King's territory. It was so fortunate that the Great Dharma King Master was present at that time and immediately instructed dharma-protecting heavenly deities to save us. Otherwise, the consequence would have been too disastrous for us to imagine!

No one could have anticipated that a small plate of vegetable could cost five human lives. Sigh! The human life is a phenomenon of impermanence. A person's life can be lost on any day. We all should work hard and diligently, with the urgency of putting out a fire burning on our hair. We should caution ourselves not to grow lax and indulgent!

Here, we saw with our own eyes that the Great Dharma King Master no longer had any appearance of being ill. Rather, in an audacious and powerful manner, He loudly gave this solemn decree, "Dharma protectors in all heavens shall listen to this decree. Save these poisoned Buddhist disciples now!"

At this time, we all realized and understood everything. I imagined that even the famous Monk Ji in history or another great Bodhisattva in the same rank would not have such power of authority. Then, who is our Great Dharma King Master? We could only speculate that He was too high for us to imagine! The truth was definitely not as the Great Dharma King Master's modest claim, "I am a humble one and an ordinary person. I am the same as you. I do not have Buddha-dharma to teach you. Dharma-protectors do not like me either." Good Heavens! I, Zheng Hui, was too naive and ignorant for my age. It was now obvious that the Great Dharma King Master had been casually giving this type of test to us in daily life to hone our mindsets! However, I was still too ignorant to completely recognize what a great holy and virtuous one the Great Dharma King Master was!

13

Severe Bleeding from a Deep Cut Healed in Three Hours, as Seen by Eye Witnesses

The Great Dharma King Master worked laboriously almost every day. The artworks of Yun sculpture were created one by one very quickly. On this day, the Great Dharma King Master once again had been standing for more than ten hours. What was different was that the Great Dharma King Master felt more and more pain in His feet and could not even walk properly.

Eventually, the Great Dharma King sat down and took off His shoes and socks in front of us. We were dismayed to discover that a thick layer of callus had grown on His feet. The callus was about as wide as an egg. We all felt very upset to see that.

The Great Dharma King Master asked us, "Who has a very thin blade?" Sister Jue Hui went back to her room and brought a very thin razor blade. The Great Dharma King Master used the blade to cut the thick callus from the foot. We all got very close and were ready to collect the callus parings for worshipping. Our eyes focused on the parings that dropped on the ground. Suddenly, one cut went in too deep. A piece of flesh attached to the callus was cut off. Blood immediately flew out and dripped down. Because the wound was on a lateral cross section, the bleeding was very hard to stop. We were all scared and in panic. Some went to get cotton balls. Some were looking for hydrogen peroxide or alcohol. Some of us started to chant "Namo Amitabha Buddha!" Some others prayed to "Namo Kuan Shi Yin Bodhisattva!"

However, the Great Dharma King Master was not afraid at all and remained extremely calm. He pressed thick gauze onto the wound. Blood soon permeated through and the gauze became red. The Great Dharma King Master just took away the gauze and poured hydrogen peroxide liquid on the wound. A lot of white bubbles formed on top of the wound. The Great Dharma King Master then again applied a thick layer of gauze and tape to wrap the wound tightly. At this time, we started to pick up the callus parings from the ground. I took very few of them and was thinking: Is this stuff valuable? To tell the truth, these are just callus parings from the foot. What is the special reason for worshipping them? Actually, other people were not too much interested in the callus parings either. There were still a few pieces left on the floor. Usually, people would have grabbed them all in a hurry!

We tried to persuade the Great Dharma King Master to discontinue working, but it was in vain. We could not stop Him. Strangely, He could still stand with such a serious wound. The Great Dharma King Master actually stood for another three hours. Then, as the sky turned dark, the day's work was called off.

The Great Dharma King Master got in the vehicle that Brother Kuan was driving. We respectfully saw the Great Dharma King off. However, in less than ten minutes, we saw the vehicle returning and immediately welcomed the Great Dharma King Master in again.

Brother Kuan told us, "While in the vehicle, the Great Dharma King Master wanted to see how the wound was. After turning on the lights and taking off the sock, a strange thing happened. That big bleeding wound could no longer be found. We only saw the newly grown flesh. Even the wrapping gauze in the sock had disappeared. I asked the Great Dharma King Master to return here immediately to let you witness this fact. The Great Dharma King Master did not want to do that. I said, 'They might have already had the thoughts of impure karma and could devolve to a lower state.' The Great Dharma King Master said, 'Okay, helping them remove bad karma is good.' So we came back here. You all come over and take a look!"

All of us formed a tight circle to look at the Great Dharma King Master's wound. It was now flat and completely healed with new flesh grown there. The newly grown flesh could be seen in great detail. The color was pink and tender and the skin was fine and smooth and looked just like the tender and clean skin of a baby. It was only three hours since the beginning of this whole incident. The large cross-sectioned wound had now totally disappeared, with new flesh taking its place. What did this mean?

The Great Dharma King Master was absolutely not an ordinary person and must be a truly great holy and virtuous one! If not, how could the knife-wound disappear and new flesh grow completely after only three hours!

At this time, people all paid attention to one important matter and crawled on the floor to look for the callus parings cut off from the Great Dharma King Master's foot. A fellow sister was not able to get any and asked for what I had. However, I only had two pieces. How could I give any to her? If she had asked twenty minutes earlier, I would definitely have given one to her because the callus parings were not valuable to me then. As of now, the callus parings from the Great Dharma King Master's foot were no longer the same. They had become invaluable treasures.

Because she did not get the callus parings from the Great Dharma King Master's foot from me, that sister did not talk to me for quite a few days.

Our mindsets as ordinary people were really sad and piteous! I felt that my conduct was just like that of an animal. To tell the truth, as I write now, I feel that a cultivator like me is truly piteous. I regarded myself as smart—having graduated from my studies in law and logic, and perceived myself as very special. I even used my ordinary person's mindset to speculate about the mind and conduct of a holy one! Recalling those experiences made me realize that I was a big fool, being tested while indulging in the thought that I had correctly observed and concluded that the Great Dharma King was no different from an ordinary person. I feel that I am so terrible. However, I want to truly repent and to speak from the bottom of my heart. I will not tell lies because I want to attain liberation and accomplishment. My master is a great holy and virtuous one. I will definitely seize this opportunity to repent for my sins and bad karma!

14

It Transformed As Was Told

Yun sculptures are a kind of sculptural artwork invented and created by the Great Dharma King Master. The Yun sculptures made by the Great Dharma King Master are too good to be described in words. They represent the ultimate summit of the true Vidya of Craftsmanship and the incomparable art of Buddha-land. The miraculous features and beauty of Yun sculptures are not comparable to any art or treasure of the human world. At a special exhibition held by the Congress of the United States in Washington, DC, Yun sculptures were praised as a present given by God to mankind and extraordinary treasure gifted from the World of Ultimate Bliss. Some people gave this most appropriate comment without the slightest exaggeration, "Since the appearance of the Yun sculpture artworks, all splendid pearls, jade, and gemstones become pale and have lost their luster in comparison, like the stars in the sky being dimmed by a clear moon. How beautiful is it? Its beauty can keep people absorbed in heart and soul!"

In several thousand years of human history, no such miraculous and beautiful form of art has ever appeared. Therefore, we can conclude that Yun sculptures are not what common holy ones and Bodhisattvas can create. Thus, I came up with the description of, "This is not an object of the human world. Rather, such a treasure of all times can only be found in heaven." Then, what is the real fact? How were the artworks created from the hands of the Great Dharma King Master?

One day, fellow brother Ven. Yundun Duojibai Gadu Rinpoche came to pay respect to the Great Dharma King Master. At that time, the Great Dharma King Master was about to start working on Yun sculptures as usual. Gadu Rinpoche asked the Great Dharma King Master, "How many years would it take to make this artwork?" The Great Dharma King Master replied, "Only one to two hours." We were all shocked to hear that on the spot with our eyes and mouths wide open. How could that be possible!

The Great Dharma King Master told Brother Gadu Rinpoche to leave his mark on that piece of material and then let people move it into the small meditation room. Of course, no one would dare to go in and disturb it. We stayed outside to guard the room while doing our practice of chanting Buddhas' names or sutras.

Time passed by in seconds and minutes. We heard the sound of ping, ping, and pong, pong, as if a large army was in action inside the small room. We also smelled an extremely fragrant scent. Very beautiful and wondrous clouds of various colors appeared in the sky. The main color was a peach pink. The clouds descended very low and were so beautiful that they were beyond description. After about two hours, the room was once again open. We saw that the floor was full of remnants and particles of the material. A brand new artwork of Yun Sculpture came into our sight.

It did only take two hours. The artwork was crystal-like bright with extremely fine details. Its beauty was more than eyes could capture. With the glass-like transparency, it was unbelievably touching and striking to see and the countless forms and variations within the structure were indescribable by words. Actually, the Yun sculpture was made from carving an acrylic material and then applying colors. We all stared at it and were speechless at its beauty. We now completely knew a fact. This could not be done by human beings. It was a masterpiece made by heavenly beings and Bodhisattvas. This is the treasure art from the Buddha-land and the heaven realm without a doubt. In terms of manually carving, not one percent of the work could be accomplished even after spending one hundred years. The Great Dharma King Master gave this artwork the name of "A Pillar Holding Up Heaven."

On August 18, 2004, at about eleven o'clock in the morning, we took this Yun Sculpture out to take photographs of it.

This artwork was more than three meters tall. We planned to lift it onto the wooden baseboard of a showcase equipped with lighting boxes. This wooden baseboard was specially ordered based on the measured size of the artwork. At the time of setting it up, the size was exactly right. This time, however, something extremely surprising and beyond imagination happened when we applied our forces at the same instant signaled by a verbal cue to lift up and lay the artwork onto the baseboard. The position of the bottom of the artwork on the baseboard had greatly changed. The artwork had grown by two inches in one dimension. However, it also became significantly smaller than the baseboard in the direction of the other two sides. No matter how we rotated the artwork to adjust its position to fit, there were always two sides that went beyond the boundary of the baseboard. The artwork had grown bigger. In particular, its upper part had become too wide. The top lighting box of the showcase could not cover it. Simply speaking, the artwork could not fit into the showcase.

The Great Dharma King Master seriously criticized us, "Why didn't you do the measurement right earlier? Wouldn't this display cabinet costing thousands of dollars be useless now? Oh! It would fit in if the baseboard is a little larger!"

However, it was a fact that the artwork had grown bigger for no reason. What could we do? Still, in order to take pictures, the Great Dharma King Master let Brother Qi Pengzhi (aka, Brother Kuan) to use a black pen to draw a contour of the artwork's bottom on the baseboard. This was for determining the positions of holes to be cut on the lower lighting box for illuminating the artwork from below when taking photos.

More than ten people, including the six or seven of us who were monastics and rinpoches and laypersons, held the artwork to keep it from moving while Brother Kuan was drawing the contour. At this time, the Great Dharma King Master spoke to Himself, "It would be nice if you could become a little smaller!" Then, the Great Dharma King Master felt that the color of the artwork could still be improved and decided to do a little coloring. So we lifted the artwork off the baseboard to let the Great Dharma King Master apply colors. The Great Dharma King Master then started to use acrylic-based color paint to paint and polish.

Approximately five hours had passed and it was already four o'clock in the afternoon. After the Great Dharma King Master patched the color, we then lifted it onto the baseboard and tried to place it according to the contour that Brother Kuan had drawn earlier. At this time, we surprisingly found that this artwork could in no way be set according to the contour drawn by Brother Kuan. The outline and shape of the artwork had changed completely!

The two sides of the artwork's upper part that had gone beyond the boundary of the baseboard shrank, while the direction of the other two sides that had been significantly smaller than the baseboard grew. Measurement with hanging strings showed that the artwork changed its shape entirely. The two sides that had been wider than the showcase shrank by four inches. On the other hand, the two sides that had been narrower than the showcase grew by two inches. Now the artwork could be put into the showcase in an optimum fitting. There was a space of one inch at all four sides of the showcase. We all shouted cheerfully and our excitement was beyond description.

At this moment, Brother Qi Pengzhi traced a red line around the bottom edge of the artwork once again on the same baseboard. Now, we could clearly see both the black contour drawn at about eleven o'clock in the morning and the red contour drawn after four o'clock in the afternoon of the same day when the artwork was found to have transformed its shape.

This artwork was as hard as a stone. It did not change in any way from the time of its creation until now. How could it change as desired within the five hours after the Great Dharma King Master blamed it as being too big and should have been a little smaller? It did not only shrink. It also grew in the dimension that had been too narrow. The transformation it underwent was in exact accordance with the size of the showcase.

During these five hours, none of us had ever left the site where the showcase and the artwork stood. We were all present to watch the Great Dharma King Master color the artwork. Also, there were many birds around the place. For fear of the birds perching on top of and polluting the artwork, we did not leave.

With a sentence spoken casually by the Great Dharma King Master, changes took place as asked. The artwork altered its outline and shape, manifesting the fact that non-sentient objects could be transformed according to the Great Dharma King Master's thoughts. How great is such realization? We once again saw and experienced the Great Dharma King Master's unimaginable true state!

However, the Great Dharma King Master said, "This is too miraculous! What has happened? It is truly eye opening for me. Who has made this artwork shrink? That must be a person who hides his or her abilities very well. You talked about learning the dharma from me. It seems that I should learn from you. Thank you very much. You have saved me several thousand dollars on this showcase!"

Figure 14-1 - A photo of Layperson Kuan taken with the baseboard of the showcase. The text within the baseboard was written by Layperson Kuan to record this true story (See Appendix A - The Account of a Holy Incident.).

15

A Forecast Was Made to Predict the Coming of a Million Poisonous Bees; They All Arrived on Time to Catch the Karmic Opportunity

Often, many eminent monks and great virtuous ones of the Buddhist circles would come to pay respect to the Great Dharma King Master. Examples were Wangzhe Rinpoche, Mozhi Rinpoche, and even one who was the reincarnation of the great patriarch master of the four major sects of Tibetan Esoteric Buddhism. Within the realm of exoteric Buddhism, there were Ven. Elder Dharma Master Wu Ming, Ven. Elder Monk Yi Zhao, and others. The Great Dharma King Master was always very humble and treated them with a normal mentality. Nor did He publicize whom He taught. Moreover, regardless of whom that person was and how much money or wealth was offered, the Great Dharma King Master never accepted any offering from anyone. This is what I saw from my personal experience after all these years. The Great Dharma King Master made His vow on this issue.

Fellow brothers at the home base told me about an event that could cause people to ponder deeply.

At that time, Ven. Elder Dharma Master Wu Ming, Ven. Elder Monk Yi Zhao, Master Long Hui, Bodi Wentu Rinpoche, Luosang Zhenzhu Geshe, Dharma Master Guang Hsin, and others received the empowerment and initiation of Buddha-dharma conferred by the Great Dharma King Master. I am not going to say much about the magnificence of the dharma here.

Many people know about a species of bee called the Yellow Jacket, which is a type of aggressive and very poisonous and vicious bee. Its venom is neurotoxic in nature, similar to that of the cobra. Just one or two stings can be fatal. Before the start of this ceremony of empowerment and initiation, the Great Dharma King Master announced, "In just a short while, there will be over a million Yellow Jackets coming to make trouble." At the beginning of this dharma assembly, over a million Yellow Jackets appeared at the scene, exactly as the Great Dharma King Master had forecasted.

The Great Dharma King Master told everyone, "The Yellow Jackets will definitely sting people today. However, you do not need to fear. They will not sting you. Some of you are at the age of eighty to ninety years old. You will not be able to bear the sting. They can just sting me only. I will bear the pain and suffering on your behalf."

As soon as the Great Dharma King Master started to chant mantras, the million or so Yellow Jackets covered up the sky over the eminent monks and great virtuous ones like a huge dark cloud. Some of them were shuttling swiftly back and forth within the attending crowd. People were chanting mantras loudly. The place was quite noisy. However, not even one Yellow Jacket stung anyone to cause injury.

Figure 15-1 - Over one million Yellow Jackets covered up the sky.

Experts said that it was absolutely impossible, particularly under daylight and in a very loud and noisy situation that over a million Yellow Jackets did not sting and injure anyone. This is just absolutely impossible.

However, just as was told by the Great Dharma King Master, the Yellow Jackets did not sting other people. Instead, they all went toward the Great Dharma King Master. The Great Dharma King Master told them, "You are not allowed to sting too many times!" Sure enough, after making a few stings, the Yellow Jackets dispersed. At that time, the Great Dharma King Master was stung on the face and the forehead and large swollen lumps appeared right away. However, these swollen wounds disappeared completely the next day. Just this one event revealed the fact: how could this incident possibly happen to an ordinary person?

Figure 15-2 - The eminent monks attending the dharma assembly were chanting mantras loudly under the one million plus Yellow Jackets.

Also, I now recall another event. The Great Dharma King Master has a layperson disciple Guo Ruyu. He was the Director of Creativity and

Research, Department of Poetry, Calligraphy and Painting Institute in Sichuan Province and the Associate Dean of Chengdu Fine Brush Painting Academy. Once, he bought two oil paintings in Chengdu and mailed them to the Great Dharma King Master as an offering. The Great Dharma King Master looked at them and said, "These oil paintings were very well done and have very high values to collectors." Then He told Brother Denma Tsemang to inform Layperson Guo Ruyu, "These two oil paintings were poorly done. There is nothing good to speak of. The ancestors of oil painting were not in China, but in Western countries, in the United States. Don't buy these things anymore."

We were all puzzled after hearing that. Since the oil paintings were apparently very good, why should Brother Guo be told that they were not good? I then asked the Great Dharma King Master, "Why should Brother Guo be told so?" The Great Dharma King Master replied, "The paintings are good, of course. However, if this situation is told to your brother, what can I do if he continues to spend money and buy paintings for me? To keep him from spending money, we can only tell him that the paintings are not good."

At this moment, I once again felt the Great Dharma King Master's holy and pure nobility. The conduct of benefiting His disciples truly made us feel ashamed!

16

Buddha-Bathing Dharma Assembly

It had been several years since the Great Dharma King Master started to make Yun sculptures. At one time, I asked myself, "Could viewing artworks of Yun sculpture lead to accomplishment?" Of course, artworks of Yun sculpture were truly miraculous and magnificent. However, could that make me become liberated from samsara? In addition, there still existed serious conflicts and tit for tat behavior in the mutual relationship of fellow sisters within our monastic group. Although I already knew that the Great Dharma King Master was truly a great holy and virtuous one, the tangled knot in my heart still could not be untied. Occasionally, impure thoughts as well as the idea of leaving would emerge in my mind.

One day, the Great Dharma King Master told us that we were going to make a Buddha-bathing lotus pond by hand, as there would be a Buddha-bathing dharma assembly coming soon. Moreover, this dharma assembly was going to be "holy," not "worldly."

I had attended Buddha-bathing dharma assemblies held in temples before. However, there had been no preparations of this magnitude on those occasions. This time, even the Buddha-bathing pond had to be brand new. Therefore, we had to make it ourselves. Moreover, we had to make a heaven-bathing pond and apply colors to the statues of the eight types of celestial beings. Other works of preparation included a Vajra dharma rostrum, Vajra foundational pillars, the Ground Wheel for dharma protectors to practice the dharma on the ground, a document of petition to be sent to the heaven realm, Vajra seed characters, thangkas (Tibetan scroll paintings), and so on. The process was tedious and complicated, and was definitely not like the "worldly" Buddha-bathing dharma assemblies commonly held at other temples.

The Vajra foundation pillars had to be planted deeply into the ground and be very firm and sturdy. The Great Dharma King Master said, "Although you do not see the wind when the dharma assembly begins, at the time of practicing the dharma, gusty winds will suddenly roll into the site. If they are not firm and sturdy, the Vajra foundation pillars will be pulled out and fall. Then, the entire curtain wall will fall with the Vajra foundation pillars. The Buddha-bathing dharma assembly can't continue in that circumstance."

It was very troublesome to make the Buddha-bathing lotus pond. It had to be made with wood materials of the best quality. Then many layers of paint had to be applied, using various colors. Making the lotus that stood at the center of the Buddha-bathing pond was even more difficult. After the Buddha-bathing lotus pond was finished, it weighed about seven hundred pounds.

The Great Dharma King Master said that we should fill it with a small amount of water as a test. We poured more than thirty pails of water into it. The Great Dharma King Master told us to lift the pond up to pour the water out. At this time, the Great Dharma King Master wanted to lift it with us. However, we all refused to let the Great Dharma King Master take part in the lifting, because the Great Dharma King Master was very tired already. Then, the Great Dharma King Master stood on the opposite side of us to let us pour the water to rinse the Great Dharma King Master's feet. In the end, the seven nuns and two fellow brothers exerted all our strength and made five or six attempts. Eventually one side was lifted up a little bit. However, we were not able to raise it high enough to pour the water out.

Then we inserted our legs and feet into the space below the bottom, in order to use both arms and legs for support and lift. Some of us had already laid the edge of the pond onto their thighs. At this time, some people became exhausted. Then the Buddha-bathing pond weighed down heavily. Our feet could no longer bear it. Worse yet, we could not apply any force upward to withdraw our feet. We felt that our legs were about to break. The pain was extremely hard to endure as the heavy pressure did not allow us to pull our feet out. We all screamed out of fear.

At this extremely critical moment, the Great Dharma King standing at the other side gave a loud shout and pressed His hand on the side of the Buddha-bathing pond closer to Him. This Buddha-bathing pond was then tilted up by the Great Dharma King Master's light pressing. Our feet now could easily work with our hands to apply the force together. The Buddha-bathing pond was raised and the water was poured onto the Great Dharma King Master's feet. This way, the pond was emptied at once.

The side to which the Great Dharma King Master applied force was the most unfavorable position. Such miraculous power was simply unheard of. Just pressing by hand He lifted the Buddha-bathing pond from the other side. According to the principle of leverage, where He pressed was the least powerful position. At this critical moment of rescuing His disciples, the Great Dharma King Master once again exposed the fact that He was not an ordinary person. How could it be possible that He could not lift even a half-filled pail of water! Had the Great Dharma King Master not done so, I could imagine that quite a few fellow disciples would have had their feet crippled.

At this time, I recalled an incident that fellow brothers had once told me. One day, a group of people including Brother Gadu Rinpoche, Brother Kuan, and Sister Xuan Hui Acarya went to the Big Bear Lake. Inside a room, there was a big bar-shaped wooden antique dining table. It was very heavy. Four people were not able to lift it away from the ground. However, the Great Dharma King Master casually grabbed one side and the whole table was lifted from the ground. People who were present all said this was unimaginable and showed that the power of Buddha-dharma was boundless!

That night, I could not fall asleep at all. I kept thinking, "The Great Dharma King Master is too profound. People like us would never be able to see the Great Dharma King Master's true nature from His appearance."

However, in spite of the apparent facts, the Great Dharma King Master still said that He had only given us encouragement to let us have confidence. The lifting was completely done by us, and He simply did not have the power to shake or help lift up the Buddha-bathing pond. What the Great Dharma King Master said now was no use to us at all. We could never believe that. This was because we clearly remembered that, when the Great Dharma King Master pressed with His hand, our hands could suddenly lift up the Buddha-bathing pond.

On May 26, 2004 (April 8 by the lunar calendar), the holy Buddha-bathing dharma assembly was held. The Great Dharma King Master started the dharma. To prevent the invasions of heretics and evil dharmas, the four types of Buddhist disciples present including dharma kings, venerable ones, rinpoches, dharma masters, and laypersons were told to chant the Heart Sutra, the Diamond Sutra, Namo Avalokiteshvara Bodhisattva, Mahakala, Ucchusma Vajra, the Great Compassion Mantra, and the Shurangama Mantra. All chanting was done following the methods of true Buddha-dharma.

At this time, a jacaranda tree in front of the mandala immediately started to drop flower petals. The flower petals spread the mandala everywhere. In the sky, auspicious clouds were flipping and rolling. The flowing of flower petals from the tree lasted three hours from the start of the dharma assembly. The flower petals were coming down continuously without any interruption. When the dharma assembly ended, the shower of flower petals also stopped. At that time, the Buddha-bathing pond was full of flower petals. The scene was a great eye-opener for me and the attending crowd. It filled us with dharma joy.

At the same time, the whole sky was boundlessly clear. The splendid sun was shining from the sky. However, there was one small auspicious cloud floating over the mandala. The shadow of the cloud covered the statue of Prince Siddhattha like an umbrella. Throughout the entire process of the dharma assembly, the cloud was always blocking the sunlight for the dharma prince statue of Sakyamuni Buddha.

The Great Dharma King Master began to empower the fragrant water in the Buddha-bathing lotus pond. All of us altogether had poured ninety pails of water into it. Each pail contained about forty pounds of water. The Great Dharma King Master threw a white dharma wheel into the Buddha-bathing lotus pond. Miraculous transformations started to occur. People saw that several Vajra beings appeared inside the Buddha-bathing pond. They wore colorful golden helmets and body armor as well as silk clothes that were transforming into colors of red, green, yellow and others. The Vajra beings moved forcefully and quickly and manifested countless transformations. They were mighty, brave, and formidable. The manifestation of this holy scene blew away all kinds of dark karmas. People were all sighing out of surprise. We could not express enough praise toward the Great Dharma King Master. At that moment, the Great Dharma King Master was no longer the Great Dharma King whom we saw in our daily life. Rather, He must be the Number one extremely great holy and virtuous one in the whole world. Whose reincarnation was the Great Dharma King? We thought He must be Avalokiteshvara Bodhisattva, if not Manjushri Bodhisattva!

It was a cloudless sky with the sun shining brightly when people started to respectfully chant the prayer. Then, a series of rolling thunder cracked in the sky. The thunder struck one after another, shaking the sky and moving the ground. The bombardment of thunder was accompanied by the howling of wind. Suddenly, a gusty wind came from the west. People were all very surprised. The indescribably auspicious and propitious dharma joy immediately filled up the entire site of the mandala. The World-Honored Sakyamuni Buddha and dharma protectors of all heavens arrived at the sky above the mandala, manifesting a holy scene in front of us! The roaring thunder and howling winds all diminished at once after about half a minute!

The Great Dharma King Master led us in practicing the dharma. After the solemn ceremony of bathing the Buddha, people had to respectively move the water inside the Buddha-bathing lotus pond into the adjacent heaven-bathing pond to bathe the heavens. This was the holy state that the holy Buddha-bathing dharma assembly must manifest. Otherwise, the word "holy" could not be in the name. Furthermore, this ritual would determine whether this dharma assembly was truly a holy Buddha-bathing dharma assembly or not. According to the stipulation of the dharma, it was not permissible to use pails to scoop the water up from the Buddha-bathing pond and then pour it into the heaven-bathing pond. The Buddha-bathing pond must be lifted to pour the water into the heaven-bathing pond. That was the legitimate way of fetching the water.

This square-shaped Buddha-bathing lotus pond had a net weight of about seven hundred pounds. After adding the ninety pails of fragrant water for bathing the Buddha, the total weight reached 4,260 pounds. At that time, fourteen big men came forward to join their forces to lift it. However, there was not even the slightest movement. Other people also took their turns to try. However, all attempts were futile after people exhausted their energies with everyone's veins showing while exerting the force. The Buddha-bathing lotus pond did not move at all. We were unable to pour water from the Buddha-bathing pond into the heaven-bathing pond. At this time, there was no indication of success of the dharma assembly. The situation was terrible. The dharma water could not be fetched to bathe the heavens. With all our energies, we still could not handle the Buddha-bathing pond of over four thousand pounds.

While we were all at a loss, Master Long Hui, who was serving as the announcer of the ceremony, was also very worried. She asked the rest of us, "Which one of you can come up and fetch the water?" There was no reply from anywhere. People all lowered their heads without speaking. Then, Master Long Hui called Great Rinpoche Akou Lamo by name, "Great Rinpoche! Can you come up and fetch the water?" Great Rinpoche Akou Lamo asked for and got the permission from the Great Dharma King Master. She then said, "I thank my Great Dharma King Master for permitting me to fetch the water. However, I still need another person to help." Then she asked Dharma King Gar Tongstan to join her.

Now these two people were going to do this job. People were still very nervous. Could it be lifted up successfully? We heard that the two of them shouted loudly, "Ohm, Ah, Hum!" Following the sound of the mantra, this Buddha-bathing pond was lifted up at once. Along with the water-splashing sound of "Hua! Hua! Hua!" they poured the water from the Buddha-bathing pond into the heaven-bathing pond. People were awed in great admiration and extreme excitement. They shouted "Wah!" "Hey!" "Good Heavens!" and "Oh! My God!" The continuous sighs and praises broke the quiet and still atmosphere prevailing just a moment ago. Everyone appeared joyful with a broad smile!

The key ceremony of fetching the water through realization in the dharma assembly was now accomplished. We were all surprised and amazed with heartfelt praises and extreme excitement and joy for this superior and holy Buddha-dharma. Right at this moment, the dharma manifested this real scene that could not be matched anywhere else in the world. We were all completely knocked out by this manifestation of true dharma of Tathagata and could not keep from feeling the utmost admiration.

Now people saw the Buddha-bathing pond being lifted by two persons. We all went forward and joined our forces together to try again. However, no movement resulted. We did not want to accept this result, so we scooped about half of the water out of the Buddha-bathing pond and tried again. We still could not lift it even a bit.

After respectfully fetching the clean water for bathing the heavens, the Great Dharma King Master began to practice the dharma of bathing the heavens. We all chanted the heaven–bathing verse once. Suddenly, a strong wind arose. The curtained dharma tent was shaking and the hanging thangkas were flipping up and down. The supporting frame of the dharma tent was making squeaking sounds due to the wind and appeared unable to withstand the force and was about to break.

At this time, we heard a wave of low, heavy, and extremely loud dragon roars, accompanied by the approaching rolling thunder. The thunder exploded loudly above our mandala, indicating the arrival of the eight types of celestial beings at the site of the Buddha-bathing mandala. The celestial beings happily received the dharma bathing bestowed to them by the Buddha. The holy scene was propitious and auspicious.

After the dharma assembly had ended, we fetched the dharma water from the Buddha-bathing pond. At this time, we were surprised and delighted to discover that the brown-colored fragrant fluid with various scented spices added had now become clear water again. The Buddha had already accepted and removed the merit devoted into the fragrant fluid. The merit achieved in this dharma assembly was magnificent and perfect.

After the dharma assembly, the Great Dharma King Master promised to use the dharma wheel to give a special empowerment to me and other sisters. I was extremely happy. My previous thought of leaving was now thrown to nowhere. I remembered the impure thoughts that I had before and had a lot of regret and sorrow. However, I did not realize that such bad mentality and thoughts had already turned into seeds of sin and evil and had left me a regrettable cause of disaster with the sinful karmic retribution!

The next day, the Great Dharma King Master empowered the other sisters in front of the Buddha-bathing pond located outside of the house. I would be the next. I was waiting quietly inside the house by the door with a hada and offering in my hand because I should not stand too close to the mandala. As soon as the sisters ahead of me finished receiving empowerment, I would step forward immediately.

At this time, two sisters who were not on the roster of people receiving empowerment this time were in my vicinity. They saw me waiting and holding a hada in my hand and then started to whisper to each other as if discussing something. A while later, these two sisters suddenly rushed out of the door and stood in front of me and blocked me. In the end, when the Great Dharma King Master finished the prior empowerment and called me, I was kept inside the door by these two sisters. The Great Dharma King Master immediately left, in another direction. I was kept inside the house and simply had no time to rush out and call the Great Dharma King Master not to leave.

"Great Dharma King Master! Great Dharma King Master! Please do not leave!" I anxiously went around within the house to the door of the room that the Great Dharma King Master entered into. Then I waited outside and dared not leave. After a long while, the Great Dharma King Master came out from the room. I immediately knelt down to beseech for empowerment over and over again. The Great Dharma King Master said, "It's too late. My dharma wheel is no longer here! Maybe you can have an opportunity next time!"

I was speechless at the time. I felt so sad that I could not find anything to say. I knew this was the retribution I deserved. It was too serious to be resolved by repentance. It was caused by my sin and bad karma. It was my own fault because I was cranky and had all those wrong ideas and I could not bear even a little bit of hardship. I should have known that one should give up one's life rather than the dharma!

At first, I loathed the two sisters. Why should they block me and try to steal the opportunity? However, I realized later that I should not blame them. Of course they also wanted the opportunity of receiving empowerment. Everything was due to my own causes and effects! Buddha-dharma could only be acquired with genuine sincerity. There could not be even a tiny bit of opportunistic mentality mixed in. Moreover, my experience was definitely not comparable to the ascetic practice that Master Milarepa had undergone! Of course I felt extremely sorry. However, time had passed already. No matter how disappointed and regretful I was, the great opportunity had been lost already. There was nothing I could do anyhow!

Sometime later, it seemed that the Buddhas and Bodhisattvas already knew that I was aware of my faults. One day in the evening while I was organizing and filing newspaper clippings, the Great Dharma King Master summoned me. At that time, I replied with, "Amitabha Buddha!" This was actually quite strange because my normal response would always be, "Yes, I, the disciple, am here!" How did I reply with "Amitabha Buddha!" without thinking today?

The Great Dharma King Master said, "It seems that your karmic condition for receiving this empowerment has now matured. Come with me!" Wow! I was extremely happy and grateful. The Great Dharma King Master led me and Sister Xiao Ping to the Buddha-bathing pond and then told us to stand still on the spot. At this time, the Great Dharma King Master summoned a great holy and virtuous one and told him to fetch the water. The great holy and virtuous one immediately followed the order and lifted up the Buddha-bathing pond weighing 4,260 pounds to pour the water onto the two of us. So we received this great empowerment.

Who was this great holy and virtuous one? Was this great holy and virtuous one male or female? We still did not know because the great holy and virtuous one wore a cone-shaped bamboo hat to cover his or her face so we could not recognize who he or she was.

The scene was video-recorded live. The video recording has been saved and is still available now. Moreover, this Buddha-bathing pond is currently housed at Hua Zang Si in San Francisco. Just as Master Long Hui said, "Whoever you are, you won't be able to lift up the water with the Buddha-bathing pond with a weight of 4,260 pounds. It is also impossible to have two people to do this together to pour the water into the heaven-bathing pond. If you do not believe this fact, I, as the chairperson of the International Buddhism Sangha Association and the abbess of Hua Zang Si, formally make this announcement today. We will bet with this temple. If any party is able to pour the water from the filled Buddha-bathing pond into the heaven-bathing pond using two persons, we will gift this temple to them. The reason is that such people must be great holy ones and should enjoy the use of this temple to propagate Buddha-dharma and benefit living beings. However, we believe that, other than people who were present at the holy Buddha-bathing dharma assembly, such people are non-existent. In this world, you cannot find people who can lift 4,260 pounds with the combined force of two persons."

I was extremely grateful to the Great Dharma King Master and all Buddhas and Bodhisattvas in the ten directions! Though a Buddhist disciple who had committed sin, I once again received an opportunity! As a bhiksuni, my mind and conduct were absurd. I was truly a stupid bonehead and was very low! I even absurdly regarded some totally irrelevant observations such as the non-unity and conflicts among fellow sisters, the evil knowledge and views of people in society, the conflicts and struggles between some brothers, and the non-conformity to the dharma and not carrying out the teachings of the Great Dharma King Master in our cultivation, as excuses to blame the Great Dharma King Master. This mentality of mine was similar to regarding the mistakes and sins committed by those naughty Arhats and the Buddha's disciples who did not listen to and did not follow the Buddha's teachings in their cultivation as Sakyamuni Buddha's faults, and consequently concluding that Sakyamuni Buddha was not a holy one. This meant I was too irrational. Seriously speaking, I had a rubbish mind and was just a person filled with dark karma wearing monastic clothing.

I also thought about the fact that there were plenty of people with the same mentality among the four types of Buddhist disciples. They also regarded the mutually incompatible conduct among fellow brothers and sisters as the Great Dharma King Master's fault. This type of person was as low as I was and not worthy of being mentioned. Now I fully recognized that we were just a bunch of idiots. What could we do other than repent? To tell the truth, we were not even up to the standard of a human being!

Everything I mentioned about the holy Buddha-bathing dharma assembly is true. There is nothing that is not based on true facts. Many people attended that dharma assembly, including Dharma Master Ruo Hui, Long Zhou Rinpoche, Chijiang Dorje Rinpoche, Jimei Zhuoga Rinpoche, Queji Gyatso Rinpoche, Nuola Jianzan Rinpoche, and others.

At that time, many news media organizations also reported on this dharma assembly. An original news article published in a newspaper is included here.

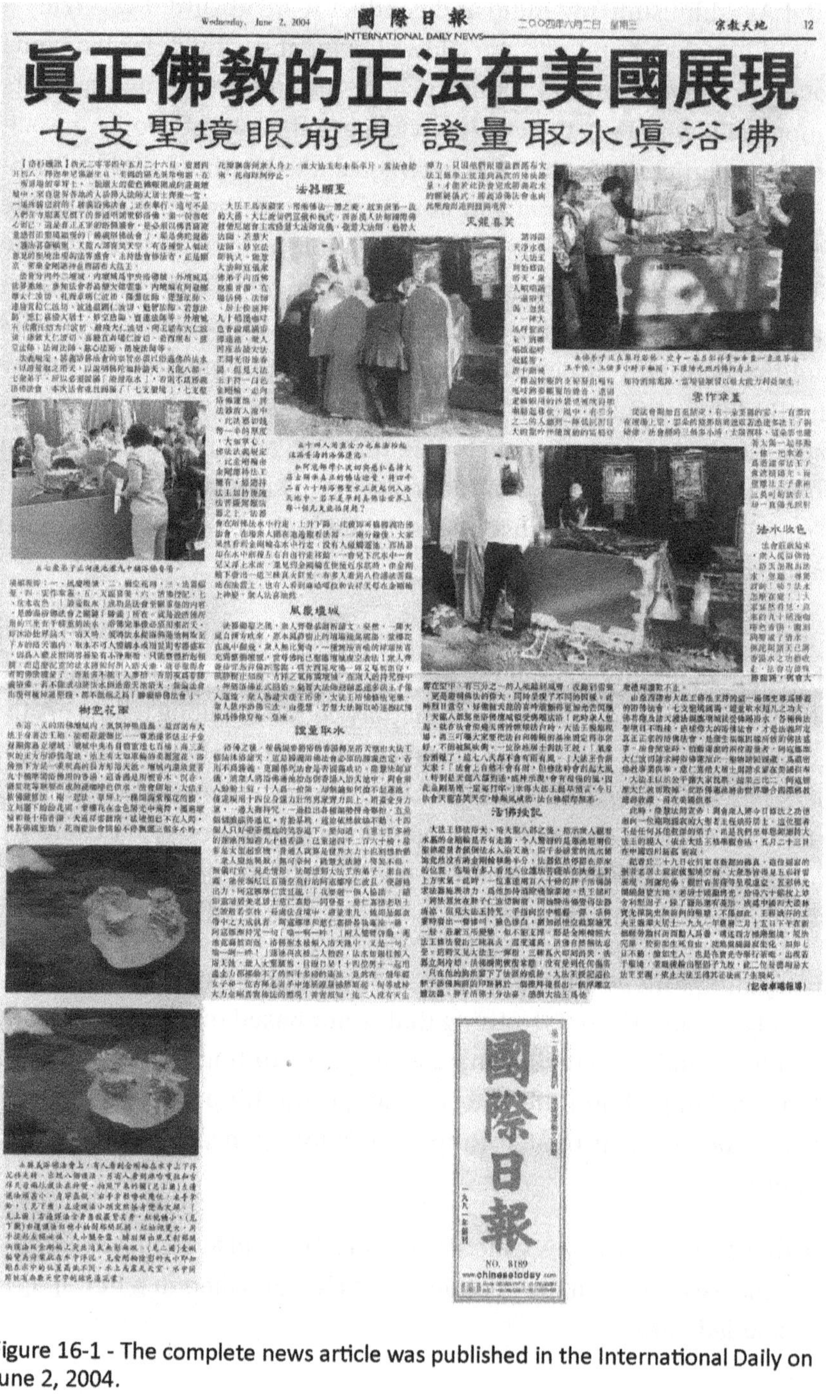

Wednesday, June 2, 2004 國際日報 INTERNATIONAL DAILY NEWS 二○○四年六月二日 星期三 宗教天地 12

眞正佛教的正法在美國展現

七支聖境眼前現 證量取水眞浴佛

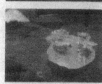

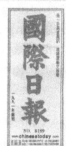

Figure 16-1 - The complete news article was published in the International Daily on June 2, 2004.

17

What Nectar Is This?

Now I am going to tell what happened when I came to the United States to attend the dharma assembly in the year 2000. This event returned perfectly to my memory on the third day after the holy Buddha-bathing dharma assembly. The scenes and states had been wiped clean and totally forgotten but suddenly reemerged in their entirety. I now clearly remembered everything.

The day of attending the dharma assembly was when I first saw the Great Dharma King. After prostrating to pay homage, I forgot proper manners and carelessly stared at the Great Dharma King without moving my eyes away. The Great Dharma King had a pair of big eyes that were very large and profound, as if being able to see through the state in one's inner mind. The Great Dharma King's voice was heavily accented. He spoke in a firm tone that could inspire and assimilate the audience. The Great Dharma King's countenance was audaciously impressive and solemnly majestic. His forehead was broad and plump. His solemnity imparted a sense of peace, auspiciousness, and kindness and was absolutely not what any ordinary person's worldly appearance can resemble. His movements revealed self-confidence and a disposition of nobility and grace. Although the Great Dharma King looked so majestic and different from common people, I was not able to tell which Bodhisattva He was. At that time, my attention was completely absorbed in looking at the Great Dharma King. I did not want to move my eyes away. I wanted to discover something.

At this time, a dharma master spoke to the Great Dharma King while kneeling on the ground, "Today, we come to pay our homage to Great Dharma King Dusongqianba!" Another one tried to correct, "No, we come to pay our homage to the Great Dharma King Vajradhara!"

The Great Dharma King replied, "You all took a long trip to fly here from the other side of the Pacific Ocean. What a trip! Do you come to see Dharma King Dusongqianba, or Dharma King Vajradhara? If you come for the purpose of seeing either one of these two dharma kings, you will be disappointed because I am neither of the two dharma kings in your mind."

"Take the Great-Jewel Dharma King Dusongqianba of the Kagyu Sect for example, He left long ago. People can only see the books He wrote, stories about His life, and His teachings of the dharma. Even seeing Bodhisattva Dusongqianba in person is just a superficial phenomenon, not the intrinsic nature. Was Master Marpa really the person Marpa? That was just a name. His spiritual consciousness or tantric practice of the three karmas or the fact of which Bodhisattva was in the body was another matter. Master Tsongkhapa absolutely was not the Master Tsongkhapa by appearance. Rather, this extremely great holy one was Manjushri Bodhisattva. That is to say, He had the appearance of Tsongkhapa but essentially the three cultivations or fundamental nature of Manjushri Bodhisattva. Simply speaking, He was the holy Manjushri Bodhisattva. As to Master Padmasambhava, there are various speculations. The truth of who Master Padmasambhava was is only known to the heaven. In other words, only extremely great holy ones would know this fact."

"Talking about the reincarnations of holy ones, it is generally perceived as one generation following the previous one and how many generations or incarnations there are in total. In reality, the previous Bodhisattva has not been in this person long ago. That is to say, although being recognized as the same person, the truth is that this reincarnation is typically not the original holy one. In terms of the external and superficial recognition, appearance, identity, and lineage, there are the first incarnation, the second incarnation, the third incarnation, and so on. However, in terms of the mind consciousness, realization, structure, and the three cultivations that cause the inner quality, movement, and cognition, essentially another Bodhisattva is using this body to propagate Buddha-dharma."

"You all should pay attention to one question, which is related to the true facts often seen in our life. Say, a rinpoche in his or her first and second incarnations was very capable with extraordinary realization and broad supernatural powers. However, the third reincarnation did not have much capability and had no realization to speak of, showing very low levels in all aspects. This situation has been seen very often, putting the answer to the question right in front of you."

"Let me ask you to do some thinking. Could cultivation degenerate from one incarnation to the next? If so, how could such regressive causes lead to the supreme and perfect enlightenment? If the incarnation were a Buddha or Bodhisattva, could it be possible that each reincarnation would reduce and lower the capability of practice by quite a bit? Therefore, this is not the real situation. The truth is not like this."

"For example, Dusongqianba was very capable and manifested extraordinary realization in the first generation. However, there were regressions of various degrees from the second to the sixth reincarnations. Then, the seventh and eighth reincarnations were also very great. This fact makes the answer very clear. In one sentence, though all were called reincarnations of Dusongqianba, they were not the same holy ones with the same fundamental nature."

"If anyone insists that they were the reincarnations and the returning of a so-and-so, then let me ask you. Why would His realization retreat from before? Could the realization, cultivation, and conduct of a Buddha or Bodhisattva regress?"

"You all should know clearly that Buddhas and Bodhisattvas uphold the principle of great compassion. They would benefit living beings with great bodhicitta at any time. They all are willing to come and stay with a reincarnated rinpoche to serve as this rinpoche or dharma king bearing the title of the lineage. Doing so can facilitate the endeavor of propagating Buddha-dharma and benefiting living beings."

"Of course, on the contrary, there have also been situations of an ordinary child being recognized as a reincarnation with the identity of a so-and-so great rinpoche or great dharma king. That is why people often see some famous reincarnated dharma kings and rinpoches die at a very young age, before beginning to propagate Buddha-dharma. Some of them even died before finishing learning and understanding the sutras. You should think about this carefully. If this person were a genuine reincarnation of the great rinpoche of the last generation, how could he or she die ahead of time without becoming fully proficient in the sutras, saving living beings, and carrying out the endeavor of Buddha-dharma? Isn't it ridiculous that a holy one took such a trip without taking care of living beings? There can be no such thing, right?"

"So, I now tell you. Dusongqianba of the first generation left here long ago. Then, which Bodhisattva was Dusongqianba of the first generation? Do you know? For each reincarnation of the Great-Jewel Dharma King Dusongqianba, only great Bodhisattvas and Himself would know which Bodhisattva or which ordinary cultivator took the place."

"That is why I have to tell you now. Since the recognition document said that I once took over Dusongqianba's position in Buddha-dharma, you think that I am Dusongqianba or Dharma King Vajradhara. That is okay either way. Actually, this is just a superstition of superficiality. Then, who am I in reality? I can only tell you that I am a humble one. I am nobody. However, you must believe that all dharmas I expound belong to true Buddha-dharma. As to my appearance that you see, it is untrue and illusory. Judging from external appearance, there is no certainty of who I am. I can only tell you the same answer regarding whether I am Dusongqianba, Dharma King Vajradhara, or Dharma King Yangwo Yeshe Norbu. Only Bodhisattvas with universal enlightenment or wonderful enlightenment and Buddhas know who this reincarnated one really is. Of course there is a true and real me. However, I cannot tell you now. It is useless to say that. You will not believe what I say, just as you will not believe in your mind that I am a humble one as I said. Therefore, in the highest level of Buddha-dharma, the most accurate way of recognizing reincarnated rinpoches is the holy method of recognition by selection. That is the only exact method. After a while, I believe that you will see the fact of whether I am Dusongqianba or Dharma King Vajradhara."

After the Great Dharma King gave this discourse, He suddenly, right in front of us, turned into an elder dharma king about one hundred years old. Everything about Him changed, including all His clothing. In a mighty and powerful Vajra voice, the Elder Dharma King asked, "Would you say whether I am Dusongqianba, or Dharma King Vajradhara, or Yangwo Yeshe Norbu, or a one hundred year old Elder Dharma King? Remember! I am none of them! External appearance is not what I truly am. Who am I after all? The karmic condition is not mature yet to reveal that. I can only tell you that I am a humble one. If today's dharma assembly can be perfectly successful, you can just regard me as a humble one. The reason is that I am not any Bodhisattva or Arhat. I am just someone who expounds the true dharma of Tathagata. I do not have an appropriate title now. If today's dharma assembly is unsuccessful, you will see the true nature of an ordinary person."

To be honest, I and all others present were already filled with respect and admiration by this shocking transformation. Manifesting a transformation right before us, how great that was! However, after hearing what the Great Dharma King said, I felt like I was inside clouds and mists. The assertions could be interpreted as both affirmative and negative. I seemed to understand the words but did not get the meaning. However, I did see the facts. This middle-aged dharma king transformed into an elder dharma king about one hundred years old, right before our eyes. Later, He transformed back. Moreover, He was able to summon Mahakala Vajra. This fact already manifested the genuine and highest realization of a Buddha or a Bodhisattva. It was strange that He denied that He was a Bodhisattva. I was quite mystified and did not know what to think.

The dharma assembly then began on that day. People all opened their eyes to watch closely. Master Long Hui washed clean the dark-red dharma bowl made of copper and put on the lid to cover the bowl. People had to stare at the empty bowl with attentive eyes. After a period of practicing the dharma, several rays of flashing red light descended from the sky and penetrated directly into the bowl. The light was very bright. At this time, the Great Dharma King said, "Amitabha Buddha has arrived! The nectar has descended into the bowl! You can have several people go outside and look. There are too many people here today. Do not have everyone go out. Having a few people go out is enough. See whether the Buddha is in the sky or not."

Figure 17-1 - When the dharma assembly started, Dharma Master Long Hui washed the empty dharma bowl clean in front of all the attendees.

Dharma Master Jue Hui and a few other dharma masters and laypersons went out to look at the sky. They saw that Amitabha Buddha appeared in the sky and was walking step by step with each step on a lotus. People at the site could not control their excitement. The atmosphere was boiling with excitement.

When the announcement was made to open the dharma bowl, nectar was inside, bestowed by the Buddha. What kind of nectar was it? Needless to say, this was the genuine and precious nectar bestowed by Amitabha Buddha and was not substitutable by any material or object in the human world because the nectar was jumping, possessing spirit and vitality. Also, it was accompanied by an extremely nice scent. At the same time that the nectar was bestowed, more than one hundred colorful shariras descended into the bowl.

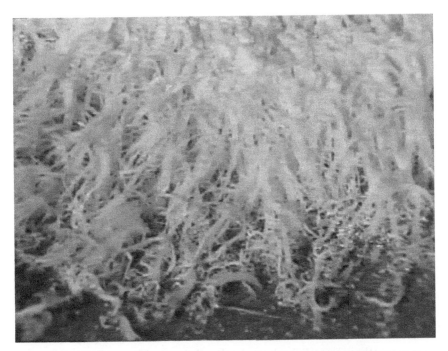

Figure 17-2 - The genuine precious nectar bestowed by Amitabha Buddha

The Great Dharma King was even able to transform Himself into a completely different elderly man during the dharma assembly. He turned into an elder eminent monk with white hair and long beard. Moreover, He was able to invoke Amitabha Buddha to appear in the empty sky. If He were not a truly great Bodhisattva with extremely high holiness, how could all these be accomplished by man-made efforts? He was truly very great and must be an outstanding one among superior persons, an extremely great holy one, and a great holy Bodhisattva without doubt!

However, soon after I returned to Taiwan, I forgot everything about the dharma assembly. All memories of it were completely wiped out. I only remembered the Elder Dharma King's solemnly majestic demeanor and voice. That was truly miraculous and strange! On the third day after attending the holy Buddha-bathing dharma assembly in 2004, the scenes of this dharma assembly in 2000 reemerged. That is why I wrote my experience here in this section.

18

While Hiding in the Dark, I Discovered the Great Dharma King's True Identity

After becoming a monastic practitioner, I have always respectfully worshipped Kuan Yin Bodhisattva (Avalokiteshvara Bodhisattva.) I love to learn and practice the dharma gates of Kuan Yin Bodhisattva. I chant the Great Compassion Mantra very often.

One day, the Great Dharma King Master was very happy. He said that He was going to visit and pay respect to a dharma king. This dharma king once served as the supreme leader in charge of the four major sects of Tibetan Buddhism. He was Great Bodhisattva Tangtong Gyalpo, who was a greatly accomplished one in the dharma of Kuan Yin Bodhisattva and was widely regarded as the reincarnation of Kuan Yin Bodhisattva. The Great Dharma King Master said He was going to beseech teachings from this great Bodhisattva. We even prepared a present for the Great Dharma King Master to bring when He went to pay respect to Great Bodhisattva Tangtong Gyalpo. To tell the truth, I also wanted very much to have Great Bodhisattva Tangtong Gyalpo as my master. This was because Great Bodhisattva Tangtong Gyalpo was a greatly accomplished one in Tibetan Buddhism's dharma of rainbow body. He was the father of medicine, ferryboats, bridges, and operas in Tibet. Within the Tibetan nation, in addition to worshipping Buddhas and Bodhisattvas, Master Padmasambhava, and Master Tsongkhapa, people mostly worship four most important Buddhist leaders as the highest holy ones. These four are Great Bodhisattva Tangtong Gyalpo, Panchen, Dalai Lama, and Great-Jewel Dharma King Karmapa. It was this Great Bodhisattva Tangtong Gyalpo who brought to the living beings of Tibet limitless good fortune and blessings. To this day in Tibet, Great Bodhisattva Tangtong Gyalpo is worshipped in temples and at people's homes.

Upon hearing this news, I was very happy. The Great Dharma King

Master was already a very great Bodhisattva. Now a Bodhisattva who was even higher and greater than the Great Dharma King Master also came to the world. Moreover, this Bodhisattva was a greatly accomplished one in the dharma of Kuan Yin and was a reincarnation of Kuan Yin Bodhisattva. Even the Great Dharma King Master was going to seek teaching from this great Bodhisattva. I had to seize this opportunity to learn the great dharma. This was what I had been waiting for day and night! It was so hard to get a human life. Even if it meant losing my life, I was still going to quest for the dharma!

I made an all-out determination. After our Great Dharma King Master had left, I brought an audio recorder with me and went by myself to Hua Zang Si in San Francisco on an airline flight.

After arriving at the temple, I waited for a long time in a car outside the temple. I did not see the great Bodhisattva coming. Eventually, I heard the message that the great Bodhisattva had arrived. Sure enough, I saw many people coming. However, only some eminent monks and great virtuous ones were allowed to enter the hall. I was not concerned about anything. While people were swarming to enter, I mixed into the crowd. At that time, I did not get noticed.

The dharma platform in the great hall on the first floor had already been set up. It was very large. Behind this dharma platform there was another dharma platform that was the offering table to Sakyamuni Buddha. After a while, people had to be all cleared out of this place and moved to the small room on the right side. Thus, I was plotting in my mind as to what to do. While people were all crowdedly moving toward the small room on the right side and no one was noticing, I pretended to make an offering and then hid stealthily under the offering table at the rear of the great hall. In front of me were a dharma platform and a dharma throne.

At that time, I did not even know how I got the courage to do so. This was the one and only time in my current lifetime I had done something like this. I was nervous as well as excited. What made me nervous was the possibility of being found out. Then the outcome could only be described with one word, "miserable!" I was excited about the soon-to-come opportunity to learn a great dharma. Meanwhile, I was also very curious about this great Bodhisattva with outstanding fame and reputation. What dharma was the Great Dharma King Master going to learn from Him?

I waited under the offering table for at least one hour and more. My feet became numb. Suddenly, I heard the sound of steps. Several people came in, and some sat on the dharma platform. However, I could not see anything from under the table and could only try to listen with full attention. Many dharma kings and rinpoches from Tibet, India, Bhutan, Sikkim, and Nepal came in and were going to hold a dharma assembly for manifesting their realizations. Unfortunately, these people eventually all went to the Amitabha Buddha Hall upstairs. Dharma masters were dispatched to guard here. So I could not get out and be present for that occasion.

Several more hours passed. Suddenly, there were people coming in. I heard the Great Dharma King Master's voice saying, "Dharma masters should withdraw immediately. Dharma King Tangtong Gyalpo is coming in!" My heart was beating strongly due to excitement, as if it would jump out of my chest. I was happily shaking my fists and putting up funny faces while hiding under the table. I imagined my lucky opportunity had come and I now would have the karmic condition of this lifetime with the dharma!

Again, more than ten minutes passed. I heard someone announcing, "Come in!" Due to curiosity, I quietly lifted open the curtain of tablecloth. However, because of the position of the dharma throne with its back toward me, I still could not see anything. I got a little worried. Then I heard the voices of two rinpoche brothers with whom I was acquainted. After a while, the Great Dharma King Master let them leave and only an interpreter from Taiwan stayed. Her name was Hehui Chen. She had been a professor of law at Soochow University in Taiwan.

After a while, I heard the steps of some people walking in. At this time, the interpreter said, "Tangtong Gyalpo is paying homage to Great Dharma King Vajradhara. First prostration! Second prostration! Third prostration!"

Hey, how could it be like this? I was stunned at that time. This was not what the Great Dharma King Master described, that He was coming to beseech the dharma from this Great Bodhisattva Tangtong Gyalpo. Rather, it was this great Bodhisattva who was coming to beseech the dharma from the Great Dharma King Master! Heavens! I was so foolish! At this time, I was so excited that I was almost going to cry. I used my hands to cover up my mouth and hold my nose to not be heard. However, my body was still trembling.

After Great Bodhisattva Tangtong Gyalpo finished his prostrations, the Great Dharma King Master asked an apparently deliberate question, "What is your name?"

"Tangtong Gyalpo."

The Great Dharma King asked, "What is your purpose of coming here today?"

"I come to beseech the highest Buddha-dharma from Great Dharma King."

The Great Dharma King asked, "Is it true that you once were the supreme leader of the four major sects of Tibetan Buddhism?"

"Yes."

The Great Dharma King continued to ask, "Are you a disciple of Master Padmasambhava?"

Great Bodhisattva Tangtong Gyalpo replied, "I am a disciple of Master Padmasambhava. Today, Master Padmasambhava sent me to beseech the highest great dharma from Great Dharma King Vajradhara."

This Great Bodhisattva replied in English. Then the interpreter translated sentence by sentence. The Great Dharma King said, "Because of Master Padmasambhava's recommendation, I accept you as my disciple!"

At that time, my whole body became numb with astonishment. Hiding in the dark, I discovered the true identity of the Great Dharma King Master. I finally became aware that I was really the most stupid idiot in the whole world. After all, all I had done was to turn away from the easiest shortcut and take an unnecessary long path instead. I was a big fool who threw away the diamond to pick up a piece of brass!

The Great Dharma King Master was completely feigning about coming to pay homage to Great Bodhisattva Tangtong Gyalpo. The Great Dharma King Master was not just at the level of "Great Dharma King" and was in reality a truly topmost extremely holy great Bodhisattva. Common people tended to boast of their own status as very high. However, the Great Dharma King Master described Himself as being very ordinary. Ah ha! Great Dharma King Master, now You could no longer hide from the fact. Only You were the greatest Vajradhara Bodhisattva at the level of universal enlightenment or wonderful enlightenment in the dharma realm! You said that You were a humble cultivator and also You were coming to pay homage and learn the great dharma! All these were pretenses! You could no longer dissimulate anymore.

When the conversation turned to transmitting the dharma, I thought that now the dharma would finally be transmitted, so I could learn the great dharma. I was about to be successful! However, who knew that the Great Dharma King would then say, "This is not the right place for transmitting the dharma. Let's go to the Amitabha Buddha Hall." Hey, why was the place changed? There was no way for me to go upstairs. People were standing guard there. My heart was burning with anxiety. However, there was nothing I could do. Hearing the sound of steps indicating that several people were leaving, all I could do was to stay under the offering table with anxiety and desperation.

After the dharma had been transmitted, the Great Dharma King Master and the Great Bodhisattva returned. Great Bodhisattva Tangtong Gyalpo did His prayer and presented an offering of a big red envelope (containing money). The Great Dharma King Master did not take any of that. The Great Dharma King told Him, "I will not accept this big red envelope. I only keep a hada and a thangka portrait of the Four-Armed Kuan Yin."

After finishing everything, the Great Dharma King Master announced, "There is no need to guard the door of this hall. Video recording can also be stopped. You all can now leave!" After people had all left, the Great Dharma King said, "This shameless person! You are so insincere!

The one who tried to steal the dharma should come out now!" I was wondering whom He was talking about. Could He be talking about me?

The Great Dharma King continued, "You still do not come out. Do you want to wait until there is no oxygen and can no longer move to let people carry you out? How can there be such a way of learning the dharma? This is stealing the dharma. Do you understand?" I still did not move. The Great Dharma King spoke seriously, "Zheng Hui! You are too bold!" Now I was scared. I crawled out quickly and immediately knelt in front of the Great Dharma King Master. I repented, "Great Dharma King Master! I, your disciple, am guilty. I was wrong. I am sinful. I deserve to die ten thousand times for my sin!"

The Great Dharma King Master said, "You also made the audio recording. Why didn't you take it out?" I handed up the audio recorder and repented, "For the sake of Buddha-dharma, I, the disciple, made the recording without permission. I am sinful! However, Great Dharma King Master should not insult me as 'shameless.'" The Great Dharma King Master said, "If you want to save your face (opposite to shameless), why did you hide your face? Why did you crouch underneath?" I was dumbfounded and had nothing to say.

The Great Dharma King Master spoke kindly with a smile, "This was too offensive and too ridiculous! Your thought of questing for the dharma is understandable. However, how could you steal the dharma? Seeing your mentality, you just need to always benefit living beings in the future! I will not publicize this matter to people. On the other hand, before the karmic conditions become mature, you are also not permitted to tell anyone about my accepting Tangtong Gyalpo as my disciple and his coming to beseech and learn great dharma from me!"

At that moment, I was extremely embarrassed. I replied, "I, the disciple, will obey! I am guilty. I repent. I will establish merit to offset my sin. I will certainly benefit living beings! I will definitely benefit living beings!"

The Great Dharma King Master said, "Don't mention this anymore!"

Although I was not able to learn the great dharma on that day, I finally learned a fact. In all those years, my mind had flipped back and forth like that of a villain. I regarded the untrue appearances that the Great Dharma King Master manifested for the purpose of observing and testing His disciples as the reality. Actually, these were just the Great Dharma King Master's masks. Only the Great Dharma King Master was truly the highest and greatest Bodhisattva at the level of universal enlightenment or wonderful enlightenment in the dharma realm.

Speaking to the point, if the Great Dharma King Master did not intend to present Himself as a common person to test us all to select qualified candidates for the dharma, this event of the Great Dharma King Master accepting Great Bodhisattva Tangtong Gyalpo as a disciple would not have been described by the Great Dharma King Master as His going to beseech and learn the dharma from Great Bodhisattva Tangtong Gyalpo. That was obviously contrary to the fact. This actual fact was what I personally experienced.

After accepting Great Bodhisattva Tangtong Gyalpo as a disciple, the Great Dharma King Master still never mentioned the fact that Great Bodhisattva Tangtong Gyalpowas was a disciple of His. Rather, He praised how great this Great Bodhisattva Tangtong Gyalpo was and told people to learn from this great holy and virtuous one. He also instructed many temples to set up offering tables and statues of Great Bodhisattva Tangtong Gyalpo for worshipping. Only after Venerable Khu-ston brTson-'grus g.yung-drung Henghsing Gyatso Rinpoche and I had carelessly revealed that Great Bodhisattva Tangtong Gyalpo was a disciple of the Great Dharma King Master, this fact became known publicly. Then, in the treasure book of *H.H. Dorje Chang Buddha III*, the fact was clearly explained — Great Bodhisattva Tangtong Gyalpo was a disciple of the Great Dharma King Master.

Rinpoches, Dharma Masters, and Venerable Ones Were Defeated; the Youngest Ones Manifested True Holiness

After knowing the Great Dharma King Master was the highest and greatest holy one in the dharma realm with perfectly proficient and unimpeded wisdom and completely free of attachment to self, I recalled many occurrences. These events were replayed one after another in my mind. The more I thought, the more unimaginable they appeared to me.

There were two youths who completely deserved the status of great holy and virtuous ones. They did not wish to reveal their names. Therefore, their names are not publicized here. One of them was a female youth who was able to make Yun sculptures when she was only eleven years old. She had never made artwork and actually had never had anything to do with art before then. However, she dared to be interviewed publicly by news reporters to declare that she would become an internationally famous artist in six months.

Once she made that announcement in public, she immediately began to learn the dharma of the Craftsmanship Vidya from the Great Dharma King Master. Great wisdom was opened up in her. Within five months, she created many exquisite and beautiful sculptures. We actually saw her sculpting and coloring. In only five months, less than the six-month time she had declared, she became the youngest world-class artist in the whole world. The dean of the New York Academy of Arts and other experts appraised her artworks and issued a certificate to her. Thus, she became the youngest world-class artist in the whole world. She also published a book at that time.

You all can think about this fact and what it means. Is this something that ordinary people can accomplish? It is simply impossible! You might think this is fantasy. However, this is fact after all!

Rinpoches, Dharma Masters, and Venerable Ones Were Defeated   99

Another occurrence was even more incredible. During an examination to determine levels of realization, a couple of dharma kings, rinpoches, and dharma masters took the exam. Each of them drew a mandala with sands on a big stone slab. However, no one was able to cause the mandala to penetrate through the stone slab. After the examinee drew the mandala with sands on the stone slab, Bodi Wentu Rinpoche and Henghsing Gyatso Rinpoche would lift and remove the stone slab to show the result. Each time, no mandala was manifested below it. Not a single grain of sand went through the stone slab.

After everyone had scored zero, this young lady arrived. Like everyone else, she also grabbed a handful of sand and drew the seed word(s) representing the mandala on the stone slab. All of a sudden she said, "I have already drawn it underneath!" When Bodi Wentu Rinpoche and Henghsing Gyatso Rinpoche once again lifted the stone slab away, people all shouted with one voice, "Wow!" Everyone was greatly astonished. The mandala drawn above the stone slab penetrated through the stone slab and formed the seed word mandala underneath the stone slab. It would be inconceivable that one who possesses such a holy realization to create a mandala through the stone slab above it is not a Mahasattva!

Figure 19-1 - At the dharma assembly, dharma kings, rinpoches, and dharma masters took an open exam to create a mandala underneath a slab of stone and were also proctoring other exam takers.

Figure 19-2 - This was the mandala constructed with five-colored rice. In the center were multi-colored sands that represented a number of yidams. Around the multi-colored sands were sands of light-green color. Five-colored sand surrounded the inner container in the center.

Figure 19-3 - Two rinpoches lifted this big blue-colored stone slab to cover up the plate of the mandala. Each examinee would then apply the sands from above the stone slab to draw a diagram of mandala underneath. However, the result seen when the stone slab was removed was always a failure.

Figure 19-4 - After they had failed the exam, dharma kings, venerable ones, and dharma masters were watching with humility the female youth dharma king taking the exam. What was the outcome going to be?

Figure 19-5 - After the female youth dharma king had practiced the dharma, the stone slab was removed. Now, the randomly scattered multi-colored sand had disappeared and actually flew into a bowl located above the dharma platform. In addition, the sand that had been on the surface of the stone slab penetrated through the stone slab and created a mandala with a seed character. The surrounding audience including dharma kings, venerable ones, and the four types of cultivators were all in awe.

Figure 19-6 - The surrounding audience saw in person that the female youth dharma king had successfully manifested a Mahasattva's holy realization of creating a mandala through a stone slab. A holy mandala with a seed character was created under the stone slab.

Then my thoughts turned to a male youth, who was the master of recognition for Kaichu Rinpoche. He normally appeared to be among the category of youths in society known as a "handsome brother". He loved having fun and was particularly fond of collecting automobiles. Since he was very talented in sculpting and painting, he was awarded the title of "Youth Artist" by the Royal Arts Academy of the United Kingdom. His artwork has since entered the art markets, which provided him the financial means for his hobbies.

After selling his paintings, he did not buy books of Buddhism. Rather, he bought brand-name goods and luxury cars. In his daily socializing and communications, he did not talk at all about Buddhism. He only talked about life, sports, travel, and enjoyment like a common person. How could such a youth be a person of high realization or a great virtuous one? However, Kaichu Rinpoche and Venerable Xiangge Qiongwa (who was also a monastic dharma master) and others all talked about how great he was. He was even appointed to be the honorary dean of the Los Angeles Buddhist Academy. After accepting this appointment, he did not go there even once. How could such behavior be associated with treating Buddhist work as more important? Naturally I could not agree with such views. A strong impure opinion arose in me. However, I also thought about the fact that even his disciple Kaichu Rinpoche was already so great and that Great Dharma Master Xiangge Qiongwa was also very proficient in sutras. At the time, I was at a loss as to what was right. I was not able to resolve this conflicting mentality of mine.

On one occasion, some rinpoches and great dharma kings in the world were participating in an examination of holy realization. This was equivalent to a contest of selecting someone for the Golden Dharma Throne. The winner's status was to be claimed by the realization that would reveal which level of an Arhat or which Bodhisattva stage one was at. I was present at the dharma assembly as a member of the audience that day. Many people attended that dharma assembly. They were some famous great rinpoches, great dharma masters, and dharma kings. Each had some impressive background. Some of them were even great figures who were reincarnated from patriarch masters. Many people dared not take the exam, and those who did failed to invoke the Vajra.

At this time, people found and asked this youth to come. To tell the truth, my heart was chilled when he walked in. I would assume that other people at the site had the same feeling as I did. Just the way he dressed could reveal what a low level he was at. He did not wear a rinpoche's red robe or a dharma king's gown. Nor was he in the traditional clothing of exoteric Buddhism. He did not even wear the formal attire of a suit and tie. Rather, he wore the name-brand casual clothing preferred by youths with a kind of cowboy taste. That appearance was too mundane and too ugly and totally looked like that of a worldly dandy!

He did not say anything. It also appeared that no one respected him either or regarded him as an important figure. He walked to the dharma rostrum by himself and took out a set of dharma robes to put on. A tall hat with a pointed tip was now on his head. At that moment, his entire appearance and body figure changed. All of a sudden, he looked completely majestic!

He sat down facing everyone and immediately entered the state of concentration. His eyes were open. He did not move at all. The great virtuous ones closest to him at the front proctoring the exam were only about three to four feet away from him. People said that his appearance while in concentration was definitely not ordinary, completely resembling a sculpted statue. There was not even the slightest trace of spiritual mind consciousness.

At this time he manifested his holy realization. A Vajra was invoked by his call. Non-sentient objects were turned into sentient beings, with extremely mighty power. People were all astonished with admiration.

Behind a separating board at a distance of about fifteen meters behind him, a written number indicating a forecast was rolled and wrapped into a piece of hada. Then the package was shook open toward the sky and dropped to the ground. Every time, he was able to tell the written contents with complete clarity. The number he gave matched the wrapped forecast exactly without any discrepancy.

There was another way of testing him, Before you drew three from the one hundred completely different written letters of petition, he had predicted which three you would take out. The three written petition letters you actually drew out afterwards were certain to show complete agreement, no matter who you might be. His demonstration of the utilization of the Vajra force was even more unimpeachable. A small Vajra pill the size of a mung bean was placed inside a covered transparent crystal bowl. As soon as he started to exert his realization power from a distance of about six to seven meters away, people saw the Vajra pill flying and dancing inside the crystal bowl. It pinged and bounced on the wall of the bowl repeatedly back and forth extremely fast. Suddenly there was a loud cracking sound. The Vajra pill even penetrated through the crystal bowl and directly flew to the center of the Supreme Peace and Bliss Master White Vajra Long-Life Mandala (The greatest and highest dharma in the Vajra division.) It then settled there firmly without any movement. The center area of the mandala was just the size of a ping pong ball. The audience was stunned with astonishment. However, an even more miraculous scene was seen when they went forward to take a look. There was no hole or any break in the crystal bowl.

Such a power of utilizing the dharma was truly extraordinary and indescribable by words. According to what I know, after all these years, with the exceptions of this youth and the Great-Cross Justice Dharma King, no other holy and virtuous ones in this world possessed such strong and abundant Vajra dharma powers.

Of course, such capabilities are naturally possessed by the top-class extremely great holy and virtuous ones having the status of Four Sun-Moon Wheels or Five Sun-Moon Wheels. This is because, they are the genuine incarnations of Manjushri Bodhisattva, Samantabhadra Bodhisattva, Kuan Yin Bodhisattva, or the Tara so that they have the realized level of Four or Five Sun-Moon Wheels. By passing the rigorous examination and verification, this young man captured the throne of the golden dharma rostrum.

These two youths were the youngest but they manifested true holy realizations and completely deserved the status of being great holy and virtuous ones. Other dharma kings, venerable ones, rinpoches, and dharma masters were all defeated in the contest. Thinking about this series of unimaginable occurrences, I now understood the saying, "A first-stage Bodhisattva does not understand the acts of a second-stage Bodhisattva." Now I realized that I had been truly stupid in the past! I was so stupid that I was swayed by superficial false phenomena and became a "silly-bone" bhiksuni through those tests.

For a period of time, the Great Dharma King Master suddenly became ill. He almost could not walk and had to be assisted by my fellow brothers using a wheelchair to move around. Also, He was not able to remember anything. Even a matter that was handled moments before or something that was just put down would be completely forgotten. We had all become very used to these experiences and such manifestations would not have any effect on us. We had already received too many tests. Now we knew this truth. Regardless of whether the Great Dharma King Master was ill or not ill, and whether He was physically strong or not strong, whatever phenomenon manifested on the surface by an extremely holy one, it was always a state of holy realization to us.

20

A Book's Entrance into the Temple Caught the Attention of a Magnolia Tree; the Power of Utmost Buddha-Dharma Was Mysterious and Difficult to Measure

In 2008, the Buddha Master's identity was finally published in the treasure book of *"H.H. Dorje Chang Buddha III."* The Buddha Master's true identity is the third incarnation of the primordial and highest Buddha in the dharma realm, Dorje Chang Buddha.

On June 21, 2008 in San Francisco in the United States of America, in a solemnly majestic atmosphere, the world's first ceremony to welcome the treasure book *"H.H. Dorje Chang Buddha III"* was held at Hua Zang Si by the International Buddhism Sangha Association (IBSA). More than one hundred Buddhist organizations came from various places in the world to attend this grand ceremony led by the IBSA.

When the banner welcoming the treasure book *"H.H. Dorje Chang Buddha III"* was hung above the door of Hua Zang Si, a giant Buddha light appeared in the sky above Hua Zang Si. It was gorgeously bright and auspicious. This was what is called a celebration taking place in both the human world and the heavens. This supremely magnificent event let us all witness with our own eyes unprecedented holy manifestations.

On that day, the dharma assembly began with a dragon-lion dance. Three dancing lions paid respect to the Buddha amid the heated rhythms of drums and gongs. Amid the sound of dharma drums and dharma horns, monastics conducting the ceremony proceeded in columns into the grand hall, led by the leading pennants. The seven types of Buddhist disciples presented offerings. Rinpoches, dharma masters, and great virtuous ones from all over the world practiced the dharma, made offerings, and gave speeches to celebrate this treasure book. Everyone could perceive and receive the auspiciousness.

Figure 20-1 - The seven types of Buddhist disciples were respectfully welcoming the treasure book of "H.H. Dorje Chang Buddha III" at the Grand Hall of Hua Zang Si.

Since Dorje Chang Buddha is the supreme leader of Buddhism in the dharma realm, could this ceremony be just a celebration held in the human world? We knew that this was the first dharma assembly to welcome the treasure book about His Holiness the Buddha! As people were all pondering, Buddhas and Bodhisattvas lifted off the curtain of Their celebration. The most precious gift from Buddhas and Bodhisattvas was presented, nectar from the heavens.

"Nectar is descending! Nectar is descending!" People shouted while rushing out to watch. At this time, from the clear and blue sky totally free of any cloud, thunder rolled continuously. The uninterrupted sounds of the torrent of thunder had never been heard before, as if fireworks were launched in the heavens.

Now people saw the densely descending nectar appearing from nowhere coming through the tree branches. We could neither see where it came from nor how it eventually disappeared. Floating like goose feathers and flocs, the nectar was rolling and dancing in the space between the tree branches. Sometimes going up and sometimes coming down, it flew and danced back and forth with total freedom, without any effect of being attracted by the Earth's gravity. Drops of nectar, one after another, drifted and fell upon people's faces and bodies. The nectar was extremely fragrant and sweet. Hundreds of hands reached toward the sky. People all wished to get a share of this great fortune.

Figure 20-2 - The packed crowd under this holy tree at Hua Zang Si was happily receiving the empowerment of being bathed by the fragrant nectar descending from empty space.

In contrast, right outside the perimeter of Hua Zang Si, it was dry everywhere under the cover of a completely fine summer sky, with the bright Sun shining. The temperature on that day was as high as 86°F. There was not the slightest trace of rain or snow. However, as soon as one stepped into the area covered by the holy tree inside the temple courtyard, nectar came down in waves, imparting unusual fragrance.

It was most miraculous to see that the nectar never fell to the ground. Anytime you saw it falling almost to the ground, it suddenly disappeared. This was a true manifestation of the legend that "holy objects do not touch a worldly ground." People dared not believe their eyes but the fact was right before them and was seen by all in the packed crowd. They were enchanted with all kinds of benefits and enjoyment. Some had pain from illnesses completely removed; some felt a relaxing numbness throughout the body; some entered a state of lightness, peace, and bliss; and some even entered into states of holiness. At this time, Hua Zang Si was entirely enveloped by light rays of seven colors. The sounds of fireworks in the heavens were continuously heard through the torrent of cracking thunder, presenting the most magnificent gift to the treasure book of "*H.H. Dorje Chang Buddha III.*"

Holy nectar rained continuously for two days and two nights. Buddhas and Bodhisattvas used this holy and pure congratulating present to welcome the treasure book and inform people in the world that H.H. Dorje Chang Buddha III is the utmost supreme Buddha. Throughout the history of Buddhism of more than 2,500 years, the wisdom of the Five Vidyas of the Buddha is now truly manifested in perfection. Dorje Chang Buddha is the greatest supreme leader of Buddhism in the dharma realm.

Our eyes had been blindfolded. We had even mistakenly regarded the Buddha Master as a Great Dharma King Master. We had been truly very stupid and too ridiculous! We had even addressed the Buddha Master as "Master". We had lacked basic awareness and manners. We had even compared some great dharma kings or great venerable ones with the Buddha Master in terms of their status. How could they be in any position to be remotely comparable? No wonder Master Padmasambhava had sent Great Bodhisattva Tangtong Gyalpo to beseech and learn the great dharma from the Buddha Master.

Dorje Chang Buddha has come to this world twice. The first time was in the form of the holy and venerable Vimalakirti, who was Dorje Chang Buddha II. The second time is now in the form of H.H. Dorje Chang Buddha III.

Dorje Chang Buddha is also called Buddha Vajradhara or Ruler of Vajra Beings. In the entire universe, Dorje Chang Buddha is the first Buddha with form and is the supreme and unsurpassed Buddha. That is, the highest leader of Buddhism in the entire universe came into being in the form of Dorje Chang Buddha. It was Dorje Chang Buddha who began transmitting dharma and saving living beings in the dharmadhatu. As a result, Buddhism was born and the Buddha-dharma began spreading and being propagated. In all of Buddhism, regardless of whether in exoteric Buddhism or esoteric Buddhism, the original ancestor of all Buddhist sects is Dorje Chang Buddha. The teaching of all Buddha-dharmas was started by Dorje Chang Buddha, for Dorje Chang Buddha is the sole primordial ancestor of Buddhism.

Dorje Chang Buddha had transformed into the ancient Buddha Dipankara, Vajrasattva, and others. The ancient Buddha Dipankara taught dharma to Sakyamuni Buddha. Sakyamuni Buddha was the first to teach the dharma in the earthly realm (this Saha World). However, all Buddha-dharma originated from the original ancestor of Buddhism, Dorje Chang Buddha.

The dharma expounded by H.H. Dorje Chang Buddha III transformed many into eminent monks, great virtuous ones, and great laypersons, as well as great dharma kings and great rinpoches, and enabled them to attain the accomplishment of becoming liberated. The holy states they realized included: being free from birth and death, leaving firm relics after the cremation of the body, emitting light from the corpse, having a state of body that does not decompose after passing away, and being notified of the time of passing and then passing away in a sitting position in a state of liberation.

In some instances, His Holiness the Buddha even transmitted the dharma to the disciple first and forecasted the time of the disciple's attainment of accomplishment. The disciple was sent on a tour to visit the World of Ultimate Bliss ahead of time and then returned to this world to wait until the predicted time to ascend to the World of Ultimate Bliss. In addition, the Dharma of "Xian Liang Great Perfection" transmitted by His Holiness the Buddha can let the disciple accomplish the rainbow-body state within two hours and be able to personally see and stay in the Buddha-land.

Those who became accomplished in these ways were too numerous to list. Two examples mentioned here are Ven. Elder Dharma Master Wu Ming and Ven. Elder Monk Yi Zhao.

Throughout his entire life, Ven. Elder Dharma Master Wu Ming strictly abided by the precepts and cultivated himself in a concrete and thorough manner. His fundamental practice was the Kuan Yin Dharma, which he penetrated deeply. He edified countless people and was praised as "the incarnation of Kuan Yin Bodhisattva in Taiwan." At a Buddha-Bestowed Nectar Empowerment Initiation conducted by H.H. Dorje Chang Buddha III, Ven. Elder Dharma Master Wu Ming manifested his two-faced and two-armed nirmanakaya

form. This revealed that he was a holy monk who was the incarnation of a Bodhisattva.

Figure 20-3 - Ven. Elder Dharma Master Wu Ming manifested his nirmankaya with two faces and two arms.

Figure 20-4 - After entering parinirvana, Ven. Elder Dharma Master Wu Ming left an uncorrupted body in a sitting pose.

Ven. Elder Monk Yi Zhao was the successor to H.E. Dharma Master Xu Yun. He was one of the two patriarch leaders of the Zen School. The southern patriarch was Elder Dharma Master Ben Huan. Ven. Elder Monk Yi Zhao was the northern patriarch and also the holder of the highest dharma lineage of the Zen School.

Ven. Elder Monk Yi Zhao was truly a great holy and virtuous one who had extirpated long ago all roots leading to birth and death and had realized the supreme fruit of bodhi. In order to save living beings in the six realms from suffering, the elder monk emulated Ksitigarbha Bodhisattva by making the following vow: "As long as there is any living being in the earthly realm, I vow not to become a Buddha." He was praised as being the nirmanakaya of Ksitigarbha Bodhisattva by the Buddhist circles. On June 8, 2000, the elder dharma master received a Nectar Empowerment Initiation from H.H. Dorje Chang Buddha III. He was praised by H.H. Dorje Chang Buddha III as being a rare, outstanding, and enlightened monk who abided by the precepts.

Figure 20-5 - Ven. Elder Monk Yi Zhao entered parinirvana in the afternoon on January 5, 2013; the Buddhist world suffered the loss of a great pillar (reported online by ifeng.com on January 17, 2013).

H.H. Dorje Chang Buddha III is also the primordial Buddha with the most manifestations of holy feats. His Holiness the Buddha only benefits others and does not accept any offerings. Wherever He went, dragon deities, birds, and animals all came to take refuge and listen to the dharma. At the same time, demons, evil spirits, and swindlers were very much disturbed and angered. H.H. Dorje Chang Buddha III's acts of only serving people and not accepting offerings made those who always collect offerings very upset and furious because H.H. Dorje Chang Buddha III's speech and conduct essentially cut off their sources of income. The impact on them was not just embarrassment. More importantly, they could no longer openly and boldly reach out their hands to people for money. Therefore, under utter exasperation, various such big figures could only use the tactic of baselessly fabricating accusations to defame H.H. Dorje Chang Buddha III. Doing so was the only fig leaf they could find to cover up their greedy acts of grabbing money from people. Of course, this was quite understandable. Otherwise, how could they cover up their ugly nature? How could they make a living and support themselves without collecting offerings!

H.H. Dorje Chang Buddha III is the holiest primordial Buddha who received the largest numbers of recognitions and congratulations from the topmost great holy dharma kings and rinpoches in the world in the history of Buddhism. Actually, His Holiness the Buddha does not need recognitions. The most evident recognition comes from the thirty main categories of accomplishments that H.H. Dorje Chang Buddha III has solely created. Throughout history, with the exception of the dharma expounded by Sakyamuni Buddha, there has never been any holy and virtuous one who could have attained half of such accomplishments. Moreover, organizing His Holiness's accomplishments in thirty main categories is simply a matter of name and form. In fact, His actual accomplishments have far exceeded thirty main categories. The accomplishments manifested by H.H. Dorje Chang Buddha III are truly unprecedented. His Holiness' unprecedented accomplishment is the true factual recognition.

In the treasure book, *H.H. Dorje Chang Buddha III*, the dharmas of *"What Is Cultivation"* and *"Sutra of Definitive Truth"* expounded by

H.H. Dorje Chang Buddha III are the grand hall of genuine Buddha-dharma, the fundamental principle of liberation, and the origin of the great dharmas of the dharma realm. Of course, discourses and teachings of many other great dharmas were not published in the treasure book, such as *The Supreme and Unsurpassable Mahamudra of Liberation* and *Expounding the Absolute Truth through the Heart Sutra* that are the ultimate genuine sutras and dharmas for attaining liberation. By following and entering deeply into these teachings, cultivators can become completely enlightened and quickly realize the three stages of accomplishment, which are the generation stage, the stage of perfection, and the stage of unattached application. Consequently, they can derive infinite benefits from the dharma, receive perfect good fortune and wisdom, and expediently attain great accomplishment of liberation and become holy ones. This is because H.H. Dorje Chang Buddha III is not just a Buddhist; rather, He is a Buddha and the great guiding master to all Buddhists in the three spheres. His Holiness the Buddha not only commands the teaching of the faith of Buddhism (knowing Buddhism as the truth), but also brings the perfect and complete system that includes Buddha-dharma and the study of Buddhism. That is why we are not just learning a single subject of the faith of Buddhism or the study of Buddhism. In addition to learning the faith of Buddhism and the study of Buddhism, we can learn the genuine Buddha-dharma that cannot be encountered anywhere else. This genuine Buddha-dharma can bring us the holy realization of entering deeply into the holy states on the spot.

21

A Vicious Demon and Formidable Beast

There was a rinpoche brother who claimed that he was a reincarnation of Buddhas and Bodhisattvas and cheated living beings everywhere he went. He deluded many people to put up everything they had as offerings for him, causing problems in many families. Since he had seriously violated the precepts, the Buddha Master sternly reprimanded him a number of times. However, he ignored all that and even dared to lie to the Buddha Master.

Because his conduct of swindling and bluffing was so bad that it caused many living beings to suffer, eventually dharma protectors had to inform him that he was going to meet with a miserable and menacing retribution. He was then captured by order of the Yama King and died miserably. He became a blood-flashing vicious ghost.

In order to lessen his sins and dark karmas, and also for the purpose of educating and transforming two persons who were masters and had the same behaviors, a group of people who were involved in the endeavor of propagating Buddha-dharma and saving living beings including dharma kings, rinpoches, dharma masters, and others were asked to confront this blood-flashing vicious ghost, evil demon Nuori, to gain practical experience. Therefore, the Buddha Master ordered dharma protectors to arraign this evil demon to the home base to be educated and transformed. After that, what had been a very auspicious backyard became a gloomy dark forest. Its horror was beyond description.

In the afternoon of that day, the Buddha Master was setting up an altar in the backyard. Out of curiosity, I stayed right by the Buddha Master's side. When the Buddha Master took out a photo of this vicious ghost taken after his death, I was very scared, "Ah! That is so horrible!" The eyes in the photo had been closed originally but were now insidiously and ruthlessly opened into a slit. The eyes were also moving and he gave me a treacherous cunning smile, as if he were about to eat me. I hurriedly diverted my eyes away and dared not look at the photo anymore. My whole body was trembling with goose bumps swelling up all over. If you just took a look, the formidable image would immediately be imprinted onto your memory and could no longer be removed.

The Buddha Master was going to tell dharma protectors to send Nuori's spirit to the home base. I hid myself behind the Buddha Master, because that was the only safe place.

The Buddha Master suddenly spoke, "Attention! He is coming!" Right after that, a round of gloomy, miserable, and terrifying ghost howling was heard from a distance of about two or three miles and then arrived with unimaginably fast speed right in front of me at the next instant. Meanwhile, a strong gloomy wind blew over, causing tree leaves to drop down all over the place. Now this vicious ghost was captured and brought back. The eyes in the photo were blinking, and I felt as if some accomplice of his had arrived as well!

At this time, the temperature had a big sudden drop of more than ten degrees. This garden that had previously been filled with warmth, comfort, elegance, auspiciousness, and peace changed completely. The shadow of the ghost emitting blue light with the after-death desolation, terror, and gloom appeared in the backyard garden every night. Only the Buddha Master could walk there freely. No one else dared to get close. From then on, we formed groups when walking in there and dared not move around alone. When the evening was about to come, we would withdraw from the backyard spontaneously. Even during daytime, no one dared stay there alone. There was a strong gloomy and pressing air that made people feel suffocated. That atmosphere tended to make people want to run away immediately without staying for even one moment.

Even the dog Jie Ben who had used to love playing in the backyard garden day and night now dared not go there during the day. Additionally, every time the Buddha Master called it to get in there, right after the Buddha Master finished talking, he would run back to the front living room immediately. Then he would hide his tail while his limbs trembled at a very high frequency.

The photo of that vicious ghost was put on the altar set up within the gloomy dark woods. It was very startling that the horrible eyes seemed to be staring at your beating heart, as if he was ready to assault you with his claws reaching out to scoop out your heart.

The Buddha Master intended to use this reality to educate and transform venerable ones, dharma kings, rinpoches, and dharma masters into abstaining from everything that is evil, doing everything that is good, and using correct understanding and views to cultivate, learn Buddhism, and to treat cultivators. Of course, it was also for educating and transforming me. Therefore, some people were arranged to go to this altar in the evening to meet with the ghost and obtain an experience in person.

The blood-flashing vicious ghost made a vow at the time of his death. He was going to find those disciples who violated the precepts like him and did not listen to the Buddha Master's teaching to let these people know the eventual outcome of violating the precepts. This would be his way of creating merit to offset his sins.

When the Buddha Master led a disciple walking to the front of the altar, a golden leopard with a body length of more than two meters suddenly appeared from where the photo was on the altar. It opened its mouth to show its sharp teeth and put up a pose to launch a leaping assault. The Buddha Master gave an order, "Bad beast! Don't go wild!" Immediately, a black leopard appeared by the Buddha Master's side. It was even fiercer. The two leopards then confronted each other. Step by step, the black leopard eventually forced the golden leopard to go away.

This scene was already scary enough. What happened next was even tenser because, after the Buddha Master led the disciple to the altar, the Buddha Master would leave the site. The disciple would be left there alone to practice the dharma. The Buddha Master would not be with the disciple.

When dharma assemblies were held in the past, people would all try to get ahead to secure an opportunity to attend. This time, however, no one volunteered to go. People all wanted to shy away from this event and were afraid of hearing their names called to confront the ghost.

Even the phrase "rounds of merciless gloomy winds" was not sufficient to describe the atmosphere at the site. The originally calm woods now suddenly had gusty winds everywhere, blowing tree leaves with the sounds of "Shua! Shua!" The photo of the the blood-flashing vicious ghost that had been laid flat there jumped up all of a sudden and stood upright. Even the sound of opening a coffin could be heard. Amid the crying and howling of ghosts under a sky without the moon and stars, a shrill yelling was heard. The next moment, the blood-flashing vicious ghost was walking out of the photo.

People who had participated in this event all said that it was really very dreadful. Some were so terrified as to pee their pants wet. Some were too scared to walk and were shivering all over.

When Brother Gongla Rinpoche saw the ghost walking out of the photo and leaping toward him, he used the Vajra rice empowered by the Buddha Master to shoot at the ghost with a form called "Scattering Blooms by a Heavenly Lady" that he learned while he was still in high school. That did beat the blood-flashing vicious ghost to the ground. The brother then went forward to check if the ghost was dead. While he bowed down to look at the ghost's face, this vicious ghost unexpectedly spit out a mouthful of poisonous corpse water that was extremely foul smelling. The brother's facial features immediately became deformed and dislocated. Seeing his deformed and dislocated facial features, other people were also very scared.

When her turn came, Sister Huei-Chin Yang wanted to console the demonic ghost. She prepared a big piece of fried crispy pork chop to offer to him. She thought that the outcome might be a little better. As soon as the pork chop was put down, the ghost quickly rushed out of the photo and swallowed the pork chop with bone in one gulp. Sister Huei-Chin Yang was scared and trembling all over. Moreover, she was not forgiven either. The ghost blew a mouthful of poisonous corpse vapor toward her, distributing the fetid smell all over her body. She immediately started to wash herself with water from the swimming pool. However, the stinking smell could not be washed away.

There was also Brother Venerable Xirao Jiebu. He carried the Vajra rice empowered by the Buddha Master and entered the site by himself. The photo of the the blood-flashing vicious ghost suddenly jumped up to stand on the ghost's platform and began to walk forward. Brother Xirao Jiebu threw the Vajra rice toward him and loudly chanted the Buddha Master's mantra. The Buddha Master knew that the situation was dangerous and rescued Brother Xirao Jiebu right away. Then the Buddha Master drew a circle on the lawn and told Brother Xirao Jiebu not to get out of the circle. At this time, the vicious ghost transformed into a golden leopard at a distance of a little over three meters from Brother Xirao Jiebu and was getting ready to eat him. At this extremely crucial moment, Brother Xirao Jiebu sat up inside the circle and threw the Vajra rice toward the outside. As the situation was becoming extremely dangerous, the Buddha Master appeared again. Then the golden leopard got scared and fled in panic.

Dharma king brother Muya Jiongzha also gave this testimony, "The blood-flashing vicious ghost was really scary. I clearly heard his miserable howling coming from a place very, very far away. Then he came before me very quickly in just one or two seconds. Gusty winds were blowing with sands flying and rocks rolling. The picture stood up and walked. Even the image on the picture suddenly became bigger with a cunning and creepy smile. The eyes opened and blood was flowing down from the corner of his mouth. He suddenly leaped towards me. If I had not had the Vajra rice to resist him, I could definitely have been eaten alive. I can say that no one could have kept himself or herself from being extremely horrified in such a situation."

In addition to the others mentioned, Great Dharma Master Xiangge Qiongwa had a confrontation with the ghost as well. He and Venerable Xirao Jiebu and Dharma King Muya Jiongzha were all highly capable masters of the Nyingma Sect. However, they were all defeated.

Fellow brothers and sisters who had confronted the blood-flashing vicious ghost also included Dharma King Palden Lodoe, Master Long Hui, Baima Dorje Chuomu Rinpoche, Jiangjia Rinpoche, Luoben Rinpoche, Gacong Di Rinpoche, Layperson Weicheng, and others. They all said that the horror of the ghost could not be described in words! His demonic power was too strong and too vigorous. If not protected by the Buddha Master, I thought none of them would have been able to get out of the gloomy dark forest alive!

At one night during this period, the Buddha Master suddenly told us to bring flashlights and led us to the backyard. Using the flashlights, we unexpectedly discovered many wild beasts there. Because they were somewhat far away, the animals seemed to be mountain lions, leopards, sable wolves, and nine-tailed foxes. When they saw us coming, they all jumped out of the swimming pool to the ground. In such a situation, we had to be led by the Buddha Master. Otherwise, with a probability of eight or nine out of ten, we would have been eaten by the wild beasts.

At this time, we used flashlights to illuminate the surrounding trees. Doing so made us terrified. Actually the beasts did not leave. Rather, they were not far from us and were on the trees, on the wall, on the ground, and on the roof. In different types of body profile and as fierce as tigers and wolves, they were peeking at us. We decided to set up video cameras there during the day so these animals could be videotaped at night.

When we played the video recordings, what actually appeared in the videos were snow leopards and panthers. There were many of them. They were happily inhabiting and playing on the deck. However, it was strange that they were completely out of sight during the day. Where did they come from and where did they go? None of us knew.

After the arrival of the leopards, we closed the door to the backyard garden rather early before dusk every day. However, at night, we could still hear them jumping from the roof to the deck. One day, a leopard even showed up in the front yard before dark. Several brothers saw it on the roof above a room. It was a little after five o'clock in the afternoon, before the sky had turned dark. That made us very scared. Every time we went to the front yard to get something, we had to look around in all directions and were still terror-stricken.

This situation, keeping us in fear, lasted a few months. Eventually, the time came when the vicious ghost was to be sent away. Before entering sleep that night in a half-dream and half-awake state, I saw a large iron-fence cage drop down from above to cover him completely. At the same moment, I also heard the sound of his forceful struggling and yelling, "Buddha Master! I, the disciple, will correct myself. I will be a good ghost who does not harm people! I will definitely cultivate myself!" To this day, I am still unable to forget his voice.

The next day, the Buddha Master led us to hold a ceremony for the demonic ghost, to see him off. I sensed that he was restrained with handcuffs and fetters. He was escorted onto a prison van and left.

Alas! Abstain from everything that is evil and do everything that is good. Brother in the past and vicious ghost at present, I wish that you rest in peace and cultivate well after paying for your retributions.

After sending away the blood-flashing vicious ghost, mountain lions and leopards also vanished. However, they left lots of urine and feces in the backyard for us to clean up. Also, one or two of them had died there because we found their skeletons in the corners one or two years later.

The home base finally returned to its prior auspiciousness. However, not long after that, we found five newborn infant leopards inside a tent in the backyard garden. Good Heavens! A female leopard gave birth to five infant leopards here. Now we would be in misery! None of us had the experience of taking care of leopards!

Fortunately, this was a false alarm. They were five newborn black kittens.

Since the mother cat was too weak, the kittens suffered malnutrition. In the end, only three survived. One female was sent to another place. The other two were named "Xiao Ding Mao" and "Black Rose" respectively. They were kept at the home base and became members of our family.

The dharma kings, rinpoches, and dharma masters who underwent the confrontation also wrote about their personal experiences at the site in order to bear witness to the truth of these events. Those who participated include Dharma King Palden Lodoe, Ga Chong Di Rinpoche, Great Dharma Master Xiangge Qiongwa, Venerable Xirao Jiebu, Great Master Long Hui, Baima Dorje Cuomu Rinpoche, Layperson Yang Huei-Chin, Dharma King Muya Jiongzha, Jiangjia Rinpoche, Luoben Rinpoche, Layperson Weicheng, and Gongla Rinpoche. Their hand-written manuscripts are still kept. I personally read the hand-written manuscripts they wrote. What I wrote in this chapter was just a brief account. Their writings were very complete. To prove their truthfulness, they all took oaths against very severe consequences. Actually, their oaths were not even necessary. I myself experienced this event too.

The experience of this event gave many people a good education. However, based on what I knew, two of them still did not learn from this lesson and could not correct much of their bad habits. The Buddha Master already made the greatest effort to educate and transform them and was also very concerned about the difficulties they faced for liberation and accomplishment. Actually, this fact was quite normal. Among the disciples taught and transformed by Sakyamuni Buddha at that time, some cultivated correctly but others degenerated.

This dharma assembly made me deeply understand a fact. Throughout thousands of years, only my Buddha Master, H.H. Dorje Chang Buddha III, and Sakyamuni Buddha could be regarded as utmost supreme. Which of the dharma kings and venerable ones of esoteric Buddhism or foremost masters of exoteric Buddhism in history had such capabilities? There were no extremely great holy ones who had such truly great Buddha-dharma among them!

Dharma King Palden Lodoe

Ga Chong Di Rinpoche

Great Dharma Master
Xiangge Qiongwa

Venerable Xirao Jiebu

Great Master Long Hui

Baima Dorje
Cuomu Rinpoche

Layperson Yang Huei-Chin

Dharma King Muya Jiongzha

Jiangjia Rinpoche

Luoben Rinpoche

Layperson Weicheng

Gongla Rinpoche

Figure 21-1 - Photos of people who had confrontations with the blood-flashing vicious demon (arranged in the order of submitting their reports documenting what they experienced).

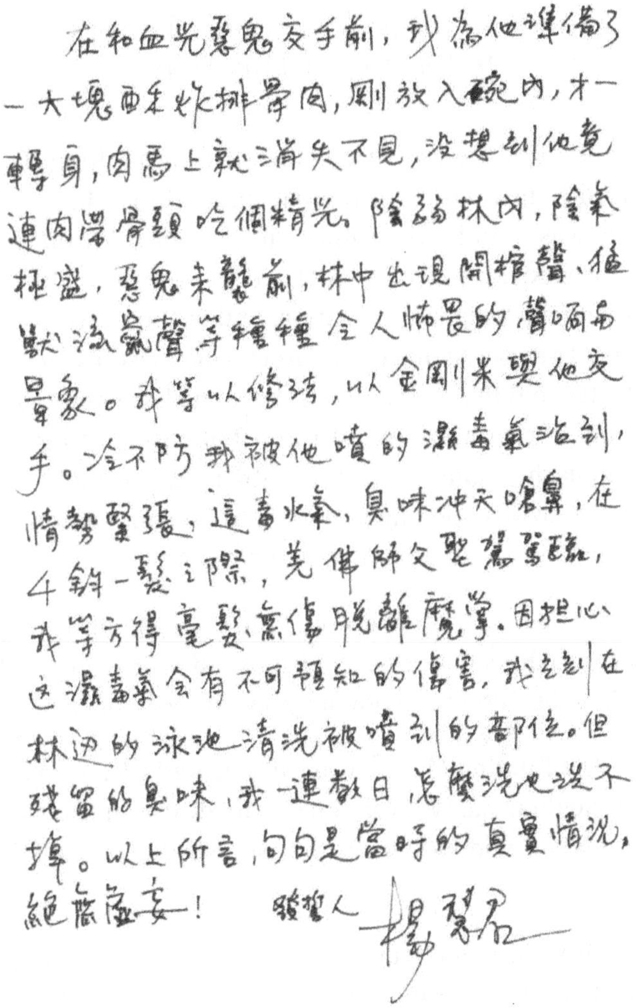

在和血光惡鬼交手前，我為他準備了
一大塊西年炸排骨肉，剛放入碗內，才一
轉身，肉馬上就消失不見，沒想到他竟
連肉帶骨頭吃個精光。陰弱林內，陰氣
极盛，惡鬼來襲前，林中出現開棺聲、猛
獸嘶氣聲等種種令人怖畏的聲響而
景象。我等以修持，以金剛米與他交
手。冷不防被他噴的瀨毒氣洛到，
情勢緊張，這毒水氣，臭味冲天嗆鼻，在
千鈞一髮之際，羌佛師父聖駕等臨，
我等方得毫髮氣傷脫離魔掌。因擔心
这瀨毒氣會有不可預知的傷害，我立刻在
林边的泳池清洗被噴到的部位。但
殘留的臭味，我一連數日怎麼洗也洗不
掉。以上所言，句句是當時的真實情況，
絕無虛妄！　　發誓人　楊琴君

Figure 21-2 - The hand-written testimony by Layperson Huei-Chin Yang documenting her experience at the scene (See Appendix B.)

Clouds in the Sky Suddenly Dropped to the Top of This Tree

The examination of the crown opening of Dharma King Palden Lo-doe, the third reincarnation of the patriarch of the Macang Sect Hsi Jao Seng Ge, was held by the United International World Buddhism Association Headquarters (UIWBAH) and was proctored by the International Buddhism Sangha Association. At that time, I was considered to be selected to serve as one of the proctoring masters. However, the Buddha Master told the monastics at the home base not to attend. As a result, none of the monastics at the home base participated in or were present at the exam. To tell the truth, I really wanted to see this examination of crown opening in person to find out what miraculous and mighty power would be shown in the exam.

The Buddha Master was not present at the exam either. Though dharma masters and rinpoches beseeched over and over again, the Buddha Master said, "I absolutely will not attend your event of examination."

On that day, the Buddha Master was with us and gave us a discourse to expound the dharma. We were facing the direction toward the site of the examination and looking at the sky, wishing to see something in the sky.

This pious wish did come true. In the sky above, toward the direction of the site of the examination, there were lumps of white clouds. The biggest miracle was that a five-colored light ring appeared in the clouds. Then, an instant later, the white clouds suddenly dropped down from the high sky and descended to the height of a treetop. I was so astonished that I almost lost my breath. I also was very terrified and thought it was an explosion of an atomic bomb. While I was astonished and terrified, a blue light flashed and the Sambhogakaya form of Dorje Chang Buddha I appeared from the rolling clouds on top of the tree. Then, it was blended with the blue light, transformed into a five-colored long rainbow and disappeared. We were completely stunned by this exciting scene, and tears gushed out of our eyes. Our hearts were thumping as hard as the beating of a gong. The only feeling we had now was: "This is the realm of Buddhas; this is the Buddha-land! This is our Buddha Master, H.H. Dorje Chang Buddha III!" We were completely unable to control our emotions and feelings.

At this time, we heard the Buddha Master saying, "What are you doing! Why are you still not listening to me? Why should your thoughts go astray?"

I said, "Buddha Master, the greatest holy scene of Buddha-dharma appeared! I saw Your Holiness in the clouds. The clouds suddenly dropped down from the sky. It lasted only three to four seconds. Dorje Chang Buddha was sitting inside and then left by transforming into a rainbow body!"

The Buddha Master said, "You are now listening to my discourse. Do not let your eyes be dazzled. Even if Dorje Chang Buddha was there, that was Dorje Chang Buddha I. I am a humble one."

Dharma King Palden Lodoe passed the exam proctored by seven monastic masters and ten witnesses on the spot. He truly realized the accomplishment of Vajra Body Substitution Meditation and was able to let his spiritual consciousness exit and re-enter his body freely. According to the descriptions given by the proctoring masters, many figures of mandalas and dharani appeared in the crowd at the site. It was most magnificent!

Brother Palden Lodoe had already passed the examination of the crown opening proctored by seven monastic masters and ten witnesses for three years in a row. This year's exam was his second annual re-examination. At this annual examination, he demonstrated a mighty Vajra force across empty space before the seven monastic masters and ten witnesses.

Figure 22-1 - After Dharma King Palden Lodoe (sitting at the front) passed the exam proctored by seven monastic masters and ten witnesses, the proctors and the onlookers came forward to congratulate him.

It was definitely not easy for him to receive the genuine great dharma transmitted by H.H. Dorje Chang Buddha III. Since he had become a disciple of H.H. Dorje Chang Buddha III, he had always been very pious. More than ten years earlier, a book titled *The Fruit of Pious Devotion* was published. The book described that disciples of the then Great Dharma King Vajradhara—H.H. Dorje Chang Buddha III as we now know—were all superior persons and also introduced the true stories about Brother Hsi Jao Ken Teng Palden Lodoe's quest for the dharma. For the details of how Brother Palden Lodoe quested for the dharma with a sincere and devoted mind, I invite you all to read the book *The Fruit of Pious Devotion*. Here, I only tell a short story which is an abbreviated version of what is on Page 7 to Page 34 of the book.

Brother Hsi Jao Ken Teng Palden Lodoe was very pious in learning the dharma. During his quest for the dharma at that time, the Great Dharma King Vajradhara Master (not publicly known as H.H. Dorje Chang Buddha III at that time) once led more than thirty people to go to the Jinghui Mountain. On the way, they met a beggar-like figure named Yun Zi who was also a disciple of the Great Dharma King Vajradhara. He resembled so much the famous monk "Ji Gong" of Chinese history. He stood on the road to stop Great Dharma King Vajradhara's vehicle.

A fellow brother named Wen Zhongxia pointed at him and scolded him as a low-class beggar. Brother Yun Zi started to chase the vehicle from behind. He was running like mad, with his shabby clothing waving in the wind.

To prevent him from chasing further, the vehicle was accelerated to a speed of fifty miles per hour. The road leading to the Jinghui Mountain Villa was more than one hundred miles long, and was also very narrow. Vehicles passing or meeting could all be clearly seen. No one saw any vehicle or Brother Yun Zi passing by. In less than one hour, the vehicle starting out from Chengdu arrived at the Jinghui Mountain Villa.

At this time, a loud yell suddenly came from the side of the mountain, "Master, I am here to welcome You!" People saw that Brother Yun Zi was sitting on a tree trunk with his legs crossed. Upon seeing the Great Dharma King Vajradhara Master, he immediately came down to prostrate on the ground. He very respectfully performed the full etiquette. People saw that he had already finished his tea in the cup. The tea he had prepared for the Great Dharma King Vajradhara Master had also turned cold already. Local people said that this crazy monk had been there for almost one hour. That means he had spent only two or three minutes to travel this distance of one hour's drive.

People realized that he really had great supernatural power and all knelt down respectfully to pay respect to him. Fellow brothers from Taiwan and Hong Kong had never met with Brother Yun Zi before, but he called out their names one by one without any discrepancy! Brother Hongquan said, "Let's pay attention to see how he leaves!"

Finally when Brother Yun Zi was about to leave, dressed in shabby clothing and shoes, he carried the tea set and a plantain-leaf fan and walked in a shaky, drunkard-like manner. After walking away for about thirty feet, people heard a sound of "Shua." He disappeared in one leap.

Perhaps most people will have trouble believing this event. However, it was factual and witnessed by dozens of people. Recalling that an article titled "Special and Miraculous Power Lost Its Function, with Half of the Body Stuck in the Wall" was published in the Chengdu Evening

News on February 14, 1995, the person reported in the article was probably a figure like Brother Yun Zi. However, Brother Yun Zi seemed to have superior abilities than the man in the article because he was just trying to penetrate through a wall and got stuck in it, whereas Brother Yun Zi entered the ground and disappeared.

成都晚报　　1995年2月14日

星期二　　第十二版

特异功能失灵　半身陷入墙内

六十九岁的印度教圣人克里沙·拉瓦尔而对二百多名科学家和研究人员，成功地穿过了印式超自然现象研究院的两道钢筋水泥墙，令在现场的科学家大为惊讶。但当他穿越第三道一百八十二厘米的厚墙时，超自然现象研究员加雅因注意力分散而被卡在墙内。博士在答记者问时说，他的大半个脸和左手已经出现在墙的那一面，其余部分还在墙内。我们试图与他沟通，但他不能讲话，现在唯一的希望是看他能否再创奇迹。这是一个壮丽的悲剧，现在唯一穿出墙来。

（摘自《扬子晚报》）

Figure 22-2 – A copy of a newspaper report published in the Chengdu Evening News on February 14, 1995 (in Chinese), about a Hindu holy person who tried to penetrate through a steel-reinforced cement wall and ended up getting his body stuck in the wall.

Near the end of 1992, Brother Palden Lodoe once again went to quest for the dharma from the Great Dharma King Vajradhara Master. The Great Dharma King Vajradhara Master said that He did not have abilities. Learning from Him would be a waste of time, and only eating and wearing clothing could be learned. Brother Palden Lodoe was told to go to the train station to find a highly realized person. However, this brother mistook a madman for a superior person. He even slept on a street in open air near the train station and experienced extraordinarily bad feelings that could not be described in words.

The coldness of the frigid winter made his body shiver all over after lying down for only a few minutes, as if he were sleeping in an icy cellar. As he was thinking, the brother felt much sorrow in his inner heart. Without having learned any skills, he even fell to the dire situation of wandering on the icy cold street. At this time, the brother truly experienced the suffering of those people who had to endure cold and hunger while sleeping on the street. The brother thought, "Still, where is that person with high realization? I am longing for him to be my master. When will my wish come true?"

Later, the brother told this story to his wife, also a fellow sister of his. The sister laughed heartedly, "You met a madman. In the alley next to the Manjushri Temple, there is also a psychiatric patient who sleeps on the street all year round. The Great Dharma King Vajradhara Master wants you to experience empathy for others. What differences are there between sleeping in a hotel and on the street? People who are wealthy and powerful must not forget people who are stranded in hunger and cold. Don't forget people who are enduring hunger and cold. We should have a loving heart for living beings. Where do you go to find a person with high realization? Our Great Dharma King Vajradhara Master is the utmost highest superior person! You are too silly! Even people like Brother Yun Zi are disciples of the Great Dharma King Vajradhara Master. You regard an eel as a dragon. You should think carefully to realize." It suddenly dawned on him what she said was true.

Later, the brother saw that the Great Dharma King Vajradhara Master's left lower leg suffered from vasculitis. It swelled red and was even discharging pus in some places. The left foot became twice as big as the right one. At the same time, there was a high fever of 39.9°C. However, the Great Dharma King Vajradhara Master did not even care and still expounded the dharma to the disciples every day. Five days later, when the brother returned from the Er-Mei Mountain and went to visit the Great Dharma King Vajradhara Master again, he saw that the Great Dharma King Vajradhara Master was teaching physical exercise to people. The vasculitis had already disappeared without even a trace left.

Brother Hsi Jao Ken Teng Palden Lodoe had witnessed many holy feats of the then known as Great Dharma King Vajradhara. Thus, he made up his mind to quest for the dharma. Of course, he learned many dharmas. However, he did not become a true holy and virtuous one until he had successfully practiced this dharma to have his crown opened. Now, because of his pious devotion, he finally learned the true dharma of Tathagata and became a true holy and virtuous one. If this were not true, the primordial Buddha and supreme leader of Buddhism in the dharma realm Dorje Chang Buddha would not have dispatched clouds to the treetop to manifest the holy state at the time of his taking the exam.

Since Hsi Jao Ken Teng Palden Lodoe had already realized the generation stage of Vajra Body Substitution Meditation with the practiced accomplishment of opening the Great Bliss Gate (on the top crown of the head) to allow the spiritual consciousness to exit and make external utilizations, could this fact mean he did not need to care about the precepts and did not have to abide by the precepts in his cultivation and daily conduct? The answer is, resoundingly and completely, No! Any practitioner who has not attained realization at the level of Three Sun-Moon Wheels is at risk of regressing from already-attained accomplishment and becoming an ordinary person again. A holy and virtuous one, such as Hsi Jao Ken Teng, who is only at the level of Three Sumeru Wheels definitely cannot be an exception.

In the recorded dharma teachings, H.H. Dorje Chang Buddha III taught and cautioned everyone many times that any great holy and virtuous one who has not attained the rank of Golden Button Grade Three (i.e., the realization at the level of Three Sun-Moon Wheels) can possibly regress from his or her already-attained accomplishment and become an ordinary person again. After having his crown opened through practicing Vajra Body Substitution Meditation to become a holy and virtuous one with the rank of Blue Button Grade Three (i.e., the level of having Three Sumeru wheels), Palden Lodoe suddenly had a great change in his nature and committed malicious sins of the five turbidities. Additionally, even after H.H. Dorje Chang Buddha III had inculcated him many times, he continued to be duplicitous without repenting and correcting earnestly. Consequently, he met with the retribution of a shortened lifespan and died. Moreover, even before Palden Lodoe received his retribution, H.H. Dorje Chang Buddha III had already told everyone in the recorded dharma teachings that Palden Lodoe was certain to meet with the most severe retribution since the law of cause and effect never errs.

It was at the last moment of Palden Lodoe's life that his son Songjie Rinpoche played the recorded dharma teaching expounded by H.H. Dorje Chang Buddha III next to his ear and told him that he had only this last hope to remove his sins by completely and thoroughly repenting. At this time, true repentance developed in him. At the very moment when he was about to be captured by the Black and White Ghosts of Impermanence (sent by the Yama King to arrest a person's soul when the person was about to die) and to be sent to the hell realm, brightness rose in his genuine mind with true repentance. He was received and guided by Kuan Yin Bodhisattva (Avalokitesvara) to ascend to the World of Ultimate Bliss. Therefore, Palden Lodoe's real example further reminded us that all cultivators must abide by and follow the Buddha's teaching and cautions, cultivate oneself in concrete steps, benefit living beings, not deceive others, not do even a little bit of a bad thing, and not fall into the 128 Evil and Erroneous Views. Only by doing so can we attain accomplishment and become liberated.

Common people might think that the descriptions about Brother Yun Zi's supernatural power were too implausible and could not possibly be true. To tell the truth, when I read the stories of Brother Yun Zi from the book *The Fruit of Pious Devotion*, my first impression was that the stories were made up. Later, when I arrived at the Buddha Master's location, I beseeched the answer about this from the Buddha Master. The Buddha Master said,

"Yun Zi is a common person. How could he have such abilities! Did you see that happen? Whatever that was not seen in person is not plausible. Do not be attached to and pursue these baseless things at any time. Even if we clear up all the doubts to believe this was true, he and you are two separate individuals. These things have nothing to do with your cultivation and learning Buddhism."

"Remember. One who is learning Buddhism must study and understand 'What Is Cultivation'. When the opportunity comes in the future, you should listen to Expounding the Absolute Truth through the Heart Sutra, which I teach. That is truly important, is the goal for becoming liberated and accomplished, is the precious essence of the entire teaching that the Buddha produced, is the true understanding about human life as well as everything in the universe, and is the only truth of no arising or ceasing!"

"Many people are very stupid. Some dharma kings, venerable ones, great rinpoches, and great dharma masters seem to have some realization from outer appearances, but are actually so foolish that they do not know they are deceiving themselves. Perhaps some people may ask, 'Don't they have Buddha-dharma? Among the dharmas taught by the Buddha, except 'What Is Cultivation' and Expounding the Absolute Truth through the Heart Sutra, aren't there other Buddha-dharmas?' The answer is yes. Of course there are other dharmas. Sakyamuni Buddha expounded 84,000 dharma methods. However, Prajna is the highest. As to other dharma methods, those are not for people who are not sincere in learning. That is why I can only teach you all cultivation. When your cultivation becomes good, you will treat Buddhas and Bodhisattvas sincerely and will benefit living beings sincerely. Regardless of whether you are a dharma king, venerable one, great rinpoche, or great dharma master, if you do not treat Buddhas and Bodhisattvas sincerely, it is absolutely impossible for you to learn the true Buddha-dharma."

Since the Buddha Master told me not to be attached to such stories of Brother Yun Zi, the image of Brother Yun Zi gradually faded from my mind. However, now these stories seemed to be returning to my mind.

Actually, the stories of Brother Yun Zi were heard from others after all, and were not seen by me in person, so I could not be certain that these were true facts. On the other hand, I did experience a fact that was an even greater feat than the legends of Brother Yun Zi.

One day, the Buddha Master was practicing the dharma of empowerment to eliminate disasters and beseech good fortune for us. The dogs as well as the birds and animals at our home base were also to be empowered. Because Dharma Master Jian Hui was in charge of feeding and raising these animals, she was responsible for their dharma affairs too. Therefore, she held a letter of petition to be used for beseeching good fortune and eliminating disasters for these animals.

During the dharma assembly on the day when these animals were to be empowered, she realized that this letter of petition had been lost. She was very scared and could not keep herself from crying. We all helped her search for it, but it could not be found. The most critical matter was that the dharma assembly had already begun and was formally in session, and it must not be paused in the middle. The only option she had was to go to the temple located in another city called Monterey Park to fetch another copy of the letter of petition. However, it had been quite a while after Dharma Master Jian Hui had left and the dharma assembly proceeded to the step for burning that letter of petition. She still did not come back. The situation was really urgent! I had to make a phone call to ask her when she could return. The call was answered by Dharma Master Zheng Xue at that temple. She handed the phone to Dharma Master Jian Hui.

Dharma Master Jian Hui told me that they were practicing a dharma. She asked me not to delay her with calls right now and said that she would be back as soon as possible. However, our hearts became hopelessly chilled upon learning that she was still at the temple practicing a dharma. Even if she came back immediately by driving very fast, it would take more than twenty minutes and she would not arrive in time for the scheduled program of the dharma assembly. It seemed that this dharma assembly would have to be aborted. However, such an outcome would bring very, very bad dark karmic hindrance to all of us.

Not only would we not be able to beseech good fortune, but also our disasters and hindrances would be increased. This is a matter of insulting the yidam and dharma protectors. It would be like inviting the most honorable guests to a banquet and when the guests were all seated, the host announcing, "Sorry! All the things that I prepared for you to enjoy are gone!" Wouldn't it be an insult to Buddhas and Bodhisattvas?

Even if she could come back in twenty minutes by driving like racing, she would still not make it in time for the dharma assembly because the letters of petition had to be presented one after another without a pause, and it was about the time to burn the one with the animals' names on it. From the temple in Monterey Park to the site of the dharma assembly in Pasadena, two other cities must be passed through and the traveling distance is about eleven to twelve kilometers. Because of the many traffic lights on the way, it would usually take more than twenty minutes and sometimes even forty minutes to drive the distance.

I was so worried that I called the temple again. Dharma masters at the temple said, "Dharma Master Jian Hui just left a little over three minutes ago." It was a little after 4:50pm in the afternoon during rush hour. Dharma Master Jue Hui said that she was most afraid of coming back to the home base from there during this time of the day when it often took more than forty minutes. However, to our great surprise, Dharma Master Jian Hui arrived at our site only a little over three minutes after hanging up my call. We were all stunned and speechless!

After further investigation, it turned out that, after having the phone conversation with me, Dharma Master Jian Hui also went to the Hall of Five Buddhas to teach people to chant the Six Syllable Great Bright Mantra before leaving. This was confirmed by all dharma masters at the temple. Based on a calculation that subtracted an estimated two minutes for practicing the dharma and getting into the car, she traveled this distance of eleven kilometers in only a little over one minute.

If anyone said that Dharma Master Jian Hui had the ability of flying, I really could not agree. The reason was that all she did at the home base was to deal with the animals, including dogs and cats as well as wild ducks and birds. She tended to stare at the sky when having nothing to do. We had known each other for more than ten years. I personally felt that she was not different from any ordinary person and did not have any miraculous or extraordinary qualities. I truly could not understand what had happened this time.

However, I had to accept this subtle and wondrous holy feat as a fact because I also asked in person Dharma Master Zheng Xue, who took my call and gave it to Dharma Master Jian Hui, to confirm the fact. Dharma Master Zheng Xue was at the temple at that time and handed the phone to Dharma Master Jian Hui. I spoke to her in person. Moreover, there were six or seven dharma masters who were present at the temple and witnessed this event. They testified that Dharma Master Jian Hui was at the temple at that time. She even taught them how to chant the Six Syllable Great Bright Mantra by heart. At the moment when Dharma Master Jian Hui returned to our home base, I called the temple and verified that she had still been at the temple only about three minutes before.

Regardless of how Dharma Master Jian Hui did this, whether she had the supernatural power of flying or was brought back by other holy forces, this event was a fact that we and other people at the temple all experienced. I had the experience of making the phone calls in person. Dozens of people including dharma kings, venerable ones, rinpoches, great dharma masters, and great virtuous ones experienced this event at the dharma assembly site. I now list the names of eighteen people who gave their testimonies. One of them is Dharma King Gar Tongstan, who was at the temple at that time. He stated that Dharma Master Jian Hui was chanting the Six Syllable Great Bright Mantra with other people and then showed up at the site of the dharma assembly a little over three minutes later. He also mentioned that Buddha-dharma is solemn and dignified and should not be talked about casually. Other witnesses were Kaichu Rinpoche, Akou Lamo Rinpoche, Great Dharma Master Miao Kong, Great Dharma Master Long Hui, Bodi Wentu Rinpoche, Great Dharma Master Xiangge Qiongwa, Baima Dorje Cuomu Rinpoche, Henghsing Gyatso Rinpoche, Xuan Hui Acarya, Dharma Master Zheng Ci, Jimei Zhuoma Rinpoche, Layperson Gui Zhen, Layperson Qu Zhen, Hui Zhu Acarya, Fa Hui Acarya, Layperson Jin An, Layperson Jun Feng, and others. They all confirmed with their own experience and what they saw with their own eyes the fact that Dharma Master Jian Hui had traveled at the speed of a fast-flying airplane and this was completely true. Even if what was said about Brother Yun Zi were not true, this event was still an ironclad fact because it happened to us and was experienced by all of us.

I asked Dharma Master Jian Hui, "When did you realize such a great ability?" Dharma Master Jian Hui replied, "How could I have such a great ability? All were your illusions." Then I reported this matter to the Buddha Master to seek response and confirmation. The Buddha Master said,

"You are crazy! You and your gang of people are only interested in such illusory and groundless things. I would not believe that Jian Hui is such a great and superior person. Even if she truly has such abilities, demonstrating them carelessly would have the consequence of death or at least a serious illness. You should focus your mind on cultivation. Only true cultivation is what I want you all to do. Although I do not have such abilities, I do not believe that this wondrous but questionable thing has happened."

The Buddha Master's words made me speechless. Could something that I dare to bet and take an oath on against severe consequences be untrue? If it were not true, would I dare to take the oath? However, the Buddha Master was not interested in this. What could I do? I could not oppose what the Buddha Master said. I can only tell you all about this simple and ironclad fact. Stories of Shariputra's action power by wisdom, Mahamaudgalyayana's supernatural power of going a long distance in a short time, Master Mi Hong's trip from Shigatse to Chengdu, and the miraculous and wonderful legends about Brother Yun Zi were halfway between the plausible and the dubious to me. However, I had to believe this event even if I did not want to because it was an ironclad fact that I saw with my own eyes and experienced in person.

The next day, I went to the temple at Monterey Park and met with Dharma Master Zheng Xue and other monastics there. I once again asked her about where she was when she handed the phone to Dharma Master Jian Hui when I called. Dharma Master Zheng Xue was very annoyed to hear this and replied, "I clearly told you yesterday that I was at the temple. Why do you still want to ask today?" She told me to go with her to the Hall of the Three Holy Beings of the West right away.

As soon as we went into the Hall of Three Holy Beings of the West, she immediately knelt down in front of the statues of Amitabha Buddha (Buddha of the Western Paradise of Ultimate Bliss), Avalokitesvara (Kuan Yin) Bodhisattva, and Mahasthamaprapta Bodhisattva and raised her hand to take this oath against poisonous consequences.

"I, Buddhist Disciple Shi Zheng Xue, now at the Hall of Three Holy Beings of the West, seriously take an oath in front of Amitabha Buddha, Kuan Yin Bodhisattva, and Mahasthamaprapta Bodhisattva, as well as all Buddhas, Bodhisattvas and Dharma Protectors. During the entire process of yesterday's dharma practice, Dharma King Gar Tongstan, six monastics including Dharma Master Jian Hui and myself, and a layperson were present. From the beginning to the end of this process, no one ever left the temple in the middle of the practice."

"Dharma Master Zheng Hui called me and asked me to look for Dharma Master Jian Hui to answer the phone. I answered the call right inside the temple. I handed the phone to Dharma Master Jian Hui in person. I also heard Dharma Master Jian Hui telling Dharma Master Zheng Hui that she would return as soon as possible."

"If there was a little bit of a lie in what I said above, Shi Zheng Xue will definitely descend into the Uninterrupted Hell and experience all kinds of sufferings. If what I said has any merit, I dedicate it to all sentient beings in the six realms. May living beings have the opportunity to listen to the true Buddha-dharma and cultivate to attain liberation! Amitabha Buddha!"

I realized that I should not have asked her such an unreasonable question. I felt very bad that Dharma Master Zheng Xue suddenly took this oath against severe consequences. I also knelt down in front of the Three Holy Beings and took an oath,

"The reason I asked that question again was because some people had raised doubt about you and Dharma Master Jian Hui possibly not being present at the temple when I called you. I now must seriously make a statement."

"You gave the phone to Dharma Master Jian Hui. Dharma Master Jian Hui had the conversation with me. After I had talked to her, she returned to our site in a little over three minutes. This was witnessed by tens of people. If I have lied, I will definitely descend into the Uninterrupted Hell. Amitabha Buddha!"

Although the Buddha Master did not approbate this event and was not interested in this matter at all, it was a fact after all. Dharma Master Jian Hui's super-fast flying was undeniable. Even a common disciple of the Buddha Master was so great. You can imagine, how could the dharma kings, venerable ones, and great dharma masters in society possibly bear some resemblance to the true dharma of Tathagata brought by H.H. Dorje Chang Buddha III?

23

This Great Holy and Virtuous One Left Quietly without Leaving His Name; In Contrast to Some People Who Have Little Realization but Love to Boast of Their Own Background

Among the dharmas of decision by selection, "the Dharma of Selection in Dark Confinement" is an upper-level great dharma. This dharma is superior to the "the Dharma of Inquiry by a Flying Lot," "the Dharma of Selection with Mani Stone," "the Dharma of Lot Drawing from a Golden Vase," and "the Dharma of Card Drawing Across the Curtain." It is even higher than "the Dharma of Vajra Selection" and is ranked only below "the Dharma of Divine Forecasting."

However, holding a ceremony of "the Dharma of Selection in Dark Confinement" for someone does not necessarily mean that this person's status and identity are high. Whether one's status and identity are high or low should be determined from the decision by selection. "The Dharma of Selection in Dark Confinement" can determine by selection one's true identity with one hundred percent accuracy.

I attended this dharma assembly in person. It was carried out by an anonymous great holy and virtuous one to confer an initiation of Selection Made in Dark Confinement from One-Hundred Dharmas to Choose the Door toward Enlightenment to Dharma Master Zhengda (Awang Deji Rinpoche). This great holy and virtuous one entered the dharma assembly wearing a cone-shaped bamboo hat covered with a black veil, just like a kungfu hero in a movie. His face was completely covered. He quickly went into a small Buddha hall. The door was guarded by several rinpoches. No one knew who he really was. H.H. Dorje Chang Buddha III, Whom people all were most eager to see, also came to the hall of the dharma assembly.

First, dharma masters presented a manuscript containing all one hundred letters of petition to this great holy and virtuous one who would practice the dharma for this dharma assembly. The great holy and virtuous one circled three of the one hundred letters of petition using a pen with red colored ink as the predictions made ahead of time for publishing at the conclusion of the dharma assembly. When the disciple who was subject to the decision by selection drew three letters of petition, the three circled ones would be verified that they all matched the letters of petition actually selected by the disciple. These three then represented this disciple's correct karmic conditions at that time. The other ninety-seven letters of petition did not match karmic conditions of the disciple receiving the initiation this time and were all crossed out, indicating they were at least irrelevant if not untrue.

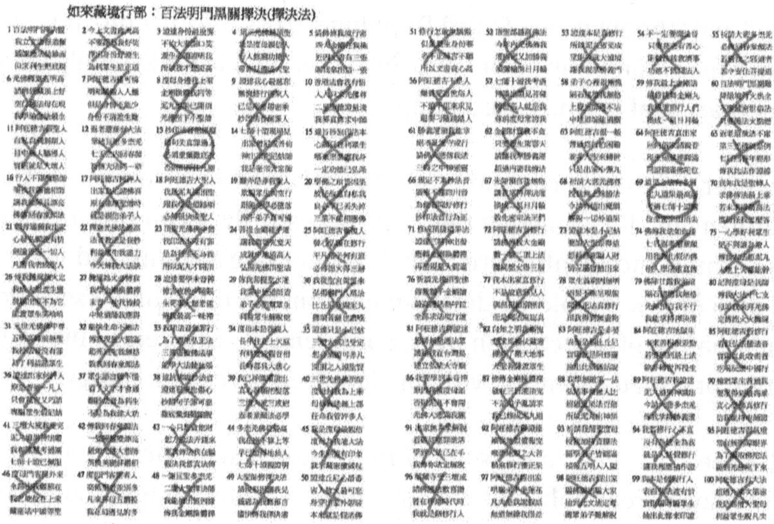

如來藏境行部：百法明門黑關擇決(擇決法)

Figure 23-1—The anonymous great holy and virtuous one selected three out of the one hundred letters of petition. These three marked with circles were numbered 4, 13, and 69. The other ninety-seven letters of petition not matching the karmic condition of Dharma Master Zhengda were all crossed out with an X. (See Appendix C for the complete contents of all these one hundred letters of petition.)

Additionally, a required procedure was to make a seal on the spot. This was very rigorous and was done by dharma masters in person. An uncarved stone seal was rested on both of its ends and unsupported in the middle. With a strike by a hammer, the seal was broken into two pieces. The uneven face of one of the two pieces was ground slightly with sand paper, while still preserving enough lines and contours from the break. A seal made this way could never be duplicated, even if you attempted to do it ten thousand times. Once the seal was made, it was used at the scene to stamp the one hundred letters of petition written by hand by the disciple. Every letter of petition was stamped so no one could make any falsification.

Dharma Master Zhengda drew three letters of petition by herself in complete darkness. Later with lights on, dharma masters opened them up to verify them. As expected, they all completely matched the three that were circled by the great holy and virtuous one earlier. Then the three were rolled and squeezed again into nubs in front of the public and put together with the other ninety-seven nubs with the same appearance. After mixing them together by shaking the golden vase, they were sent to the great holy and virtuous one for selection. In less than one minute, the great holy and virtuous one selected three. Dharma masters again opened them in public. They were the same ones that Dharma Master Zhengda had drawn earlier. Moreover, they were all stamped by the seal made on the spot.

Figure 23-2 - Great Dharma Master Miao Kong (standing in front of the desk at the front) was publicly opening up the small nubs of the three letters of petition drawn by Dharma Master Zhengda (kneeling at the center) in the dark.

To verify that the other ninety-seven pieces did not have the same contents, dharma masters opened them all to verify. They were all stamped with the seal made on the spot. Each one was read out by the dharma masters. There wasn't any repetition at all. All were unique and agreed with the contents in the common manuscript. This fact proved that the Dharma of Selection in Dark Confinement conducted by the great holy and virtuous one was completely carried out by perfect holy realization.

These one hundred letters of petition were all written by the person undergoing the decision by selection, Dharma Master Zhengda. The most important fact was that Dharma Master Zhengda had to take an oath against severe consequences, in front of the offering table and before all people present, to all Buddhas and Bodhisattvas in the ten directions, the eight types of celestial beings, and deities in all heavens. Her oath swore that these one hundred letters of petition were written by her and kept by her; all letters of petition were never touched by the great holy and virtuous one; the drawing of the three letters of petition was done by her in complete darkness without any visibility and were arbitrarily picked; and there was not any falsification from the beginning to the end. If what she said were false, she would definitely descend into the Vajra Hell to suffer forever without any chance of being saved.

Figure 23-3 -Dharma Master Zhengda (kneeling at the front), took an oath against severe consequences before people at the dharma assembly, to all Buddhas and Bodhisattvas, the eight types of celestial beings, and deities in all heavens.

This dharma assembly determined for certain Dharma Master Zhengda's karmic conditions. The numbers and contents of the three letters of petition selected were respectively:

No. 4: H.H. Dorje Chang Buddha III is the holiest. I am a trusted aide of the Tara. A cultivator building temples has great merit. You will be brought to see the Buddha and become a holy one.

No. 13: Transcribing and copying the recorded dharma lessons was a foolish violation. Making errors in sentences to cause the loss of true meanings made me a person of guilt. I must repent earnestly and correct completely. Otherwise the outcome would be being detained in the mundane world.

No. 69: The dharmas of Lamdre have many levels. The Dharma of Mud-Pill Lamdre is the highest. Having passed the exam proctored by seven monastic masters and ten witnesses, my status is at the summit of esoteric Buddhism.

The selections made by the Dharma of Selection in Dark Confinement concluded that Dharma Master Zhengda was a reincarnated holy one and a trusted aide of the Tara. Her status of the dharma was extremely high, at the upper level representing the summit of esoteric Buddhism.

Figure 23-4-These were the three original nubs drawn randomly by Dharma Master Zhengda in the dark, corresponding to her letters of petition No. 4, No.13, and No.69, selected by the great holy and virtuous one.

H.H. Dorje Chang Buddha III conducted "the Dharma of Divine Forecasting" using a golden vase for an anonymous great holy and virtuous one who did not reveal his identify. The forecast was repeated three times without discrepancy, proving its correctness. "The Dharma of Divine Forecasting" showed that this great holy and virtuous one possessed master's qualifications at the middle level of holy realization with Three Sun-Moon Wheels. That represented a truly rare great holy and virtuous one. Even Dharma King Gar Tongstan who is the chairperson of the United International World Buddhism Association Headquarters, Kaichu Rinpoche, and Holy and Virtuous One La Zhen possessed just master's qualifications represented by One Sun-Moon Wheel. Even Mozhi Rinpoche's realization was only at the level of Two Sun-Moon Wheels. He surpassed the status of Mozhi Rinpoche and truly deserved the title of great holy and virtuous one. To achieve the status of "Great Holy and Virtuous One," one must possess master's qualifications at the middle level of holy realization with Sun-Moon Wheels.

The United International World Buddhism Association Headquarters issued a document for receiving the certificate of Three Sun-Moon Wheels to the great holy and virtuous one on the spot. After the dharma assembly had ended, people were all very excited and thought that they would have the opportunity of paying respect to the great holy and virtuous one in person and knowing who He actually was. However, the great holy and virtuous one did not leave his name and did not meet with people. He left quietly without accepting the document. People were very disappointed. So far no one knows who He really was. People only learned that this was a selfless great holy and virtuous one possessing master's qualifications with Three Sun-Moon Wheels. The demeanor of a true Mahasattva and a true great holy and virtuous one was definitely not what those who chased fame and gain, those who faked being holy ones by boasting and self-promotion, and those dharma kings, venerable ones, and great dharma kings who used false initiations to cheat believers for money and property could even slightly resemble.

Master's qualifications with Sun-Moon Wheels are very amazing and indicate the levels of realization and status of master's qualifications.

Regardless of what dharma king, venerable one, rinpoche, or dharma master one is, as long as one is not at a level of Sun-Moon Wheel(s), one does not possess master's qualifications with holy realization and can at most be a holy and virtuous one with Sumeru Wheel(s). Even Dharma Master Zhengda whose status is at the summit of esoteric Buddhism and who was a trusted aide of the Tara still does not have the realization representing master's qualifications with Sun-Moon Wheel(s). This fact can give people an idea about the kind of amazing realization a great holy and virtuous one with Three Sun-Moon Wheels possesses. (To learn more about the levels of master's qualifications with Sun-Moon Wheel(s), please refer to Notice No. 20121118 from the International Buddhism Sangha Association which forwarded the public announcement titled "Replies to Inquiries" from the United International Buddhism Headquarters, available on the internet at http://www.ibsahq.org/news_view.php?id=161.)

The great holy and virtuous one left quietly into seclusion without leaving a name. The situation in today's world is just the contrary. Some people who are small figures with little accomplishment fill their minds with vanity. They love to boast about themselves and use all means to get attention from the world to show off how great they are and how high their lineages are. For prestige, power, wealth, fame, and so on, they use all kinds of low-class ways to pretend to be an insider, untruly boasting and overstating their status, and using famous names to grab disciples, fight for worshipping sites, form gangs, and snatch offerings. There is no possibility of seeing any pure and tranquil characteristics of Buddhism in them.

These people of little ability do not have any true power of realization from Buddha-dharma but are very good at boasting and posing. This is especially true when they are on the dharma rostrum wearing dharma robes. The posture would be very impressive, with their disciples repeatedly addressing them as venerable ones or great dharma kings. They would hold up a document of recognition and shamelessly claim themselves to be the nirmankayas of so-and-so great Bodhisattvas or reincarnations of great venerable ones or great rinpoches.

These people may even use the name of H.H. Dorje Chang Buddha III to arm themselves. However, they dare not to take the exam proctored by seven monastic masters and ten witnesses. Any easy inspection of their speech and conduct would find them violating the 128 Evil and Erroneous Views. Even if some of them were holy ones in the past, because of deviating from cultivation and the Buddha's teaching, they must have already degenerated into ordinary beings. Yet, they still keep on claiming to be holy ones. That was why, for protecting cultivators' opportunity of acquiring wisdom, the Office of H.H. Dorje Chang Buddha III issued a public announcement to inform cultivators that they should only listen to the recorded dharma lessons expounded by H.H. Dorje Chang Buddha III. Other cultivators with whatever status can only organize their disciples to listen to the dharma lessons and teach some regular dharmas with fixed rituals and are not allowed to give discourses so as to avoid misleading cultivators.

The definition of "holy and virtuous one" refers to one who has the bodhicitta of great compassion established from the foundation of being a holy one with the realization of nirvana at different depths. He or she is unselfish, selfless, and free of attachment to the dharma, and takes up saving and transforming living beings toward accomplishment as his or her own responsibility. Thus, such a one [he or she] possesses the virtue of formless Bodhi. Only a Bodhisattva at such a state of virtue can be regarded as a holy and virtuous one. Only a Mahasattva can be called a "great Bodhisattva" or "great holy and virtuous one." Maha means big or great, indicating great vow, great cultivation, great power of realization, and great effort made to save living beings. Only a Bodhisattva with great state of virtue and great realization or a Mahasattva can be called a great Bodhisattva or a great holy and virtuous one. The status of great holy and virtuous one cannot be claimed by a so-called patriarch of a lineage, dharma king, venerable one, great dharma master, or great rinpoche. Whether a great holy and virtuous one is true or false and what weights and contents there are must be proven with Sun-Moon Wheel(s).

Above the level of Mahasattvas are Bodhisattvas at the levels of universal enlightenment and wonderful enlightenment. Higher than

Bodhisattvas at the levels of universal enlightenment and wonderful enlightenment are Buddhas having realized supreme, non-differentiating, and perfect enlightenment, possessing perfection of the three bodies and four wisdoms, and coexisting with the entire universe.

These nouns and terms are simple to say. A so-called dharma king, venerable one, rinpoche, or great dharma master would generally lift a pen and easily grab one of these names as a cover for himself or herself. Then this type of person would have big self-pride and, for the purpose of self-promotion or pursuing gains and offerings, boast to be a great holy and virtuous Bodhisattva. Actually, this type of person is not even a small holy and virtuous one and simply does not have wisdom in the Five Vidyas and does not have any true realization. Doing so can only lead him or her as well as his or her disciples into the hell realm.

24

Where Can True Assemblies of Buddha-Dharma Be Found?

There are many dharma assemblies in the world. However, who has seen a true dharma assembly? Where are true dharma assemblies? They are right here!

I attended in person many grand dharma assemblies. All were holy ones. At every dharma assembly, Buddhas and Bodhisattvas, or at least dharma protectors and the yidam, would be present. Therefore, holy feats were certain to manifest. Examples are:

Holy Buddha-Bathing Dharma Assembly

Buddha-Bestowed Nectar Dharma Assembly

Dharma Assembly of Fetching Karma from Hell to Eliminate Hindrance

Dharma Assembly of Selecting Karmic Condition, Eliminating Hindrance, and Conferring Initiation

Dharma Assembly of Golden Throne Captured by Dharma King Mohe with Realization

Dharma Assembly of Testing the Ability of Creating a Mandala Underneath a Stone Slab

Torma Offering Dharma Assembly

Dharma Assembly of Celebrating the Dharma Expounded during the Trip to the East Coast

Initiation with Bodhi and Vajra Seeds Dharma Assembly

Examination of Holiness and Virtue Dharma Assembly

Examination of Master's Qualifications with Sun-Moon Wheels Dharma Assembly

Inner Tantric Refuge Ceremony Dharma Assembly

State Practice Mapeng Terma Initiation Dharma Assembly

Refining Da Ba Bu Qiong Pill Dharma Assembly

Refining Ka Zhuo An De Pill Dharma Assembly

Selecting Karmic Condition by Divine Forecasting Dharma Assembly

Selection Made in Dark Confinement from One-Hundred Letters of Petition for Clarification/Verification Dharma Assembly

And Others

Every one of these dharma assemblies demonstrated extremely mighty power and were absolutely not just theories of worldly Buddha-dharma, popular Buddhism, and the study of Buddhism. Rather, holy states that were seen by people with their own eyes manifested as a reality. If there were no presence of Buddhas or Bodhisattvas, then at least the yidam or dharma protectors of the dharma assembly would definitely come. Each dharma assembly exhibited boundlessly mighty power and unique holy scenes as the characteristics of holiness and non-worldliness, and was absolutely not a theory-exercising worldly dharma assembly with the activities of chanting mantras, reciting sutras, and repenting.

Among the dharma assemblies that I attended, the most inconceivable and shocking one was the Dharma Assembly of Celebrating the Dharma Expounded during the Trip to the East Coast. It brought me into the holy state and made me not want to leave it. This was the Dharma Assembly that impressed me the most.

The dharma bowl was on the lawn and was washed with a powerful hose by the attending people. Even we onlookers were splashed with a lot of water. After being washed clean, the dharma bowl was put on a stool in front of us and covered with a transparent glass plate. It could be seen clearly that there was nothing in the dharma bowl. Dozens of people were listening to the Buddha Master expound the dharma from a faraway dharma rostrum, while watching the dharma bowl in front of us. The Buddha Master prayed,

"If my 'Dharma Expounded during the Trip to the East Coast' represents Buddha-dharma with correct knowledge and views, Buddhas would bestow a little nectar, as a manifestation of the dharma of Tathagata. I am not requesting nectar. The purpose is to use Buddha-bestowed nectar to prove whether the dharma I expounded is the dharma of Tathagata or not. For the perfection of the dharma, we are holding this dharma assembly of celebration to demonstrate that Buddha-dharma is true and real and is not hollow theory. This is all we wish."

"We also set up a dharma bowl here. I hope that Buddhas in the ten directions can give some sort of manifestation of the dharma, considering the presence of the true incarnation of Dorje Chang Buddha III. Even just emitting a beam of light, or producing some very fragrant scent would be fine. I will not insist on getting nectar, even very few thin silk-like threads of nectar would be sufficient. In summary, this is not for other purposes. It is for stating that this set of recorded dharma lessons of 'Dharma Expounded during the Trip to the East Coast' is true and correct, containing no errors."

After H.H. Dorje Chang Buddha III had said the prayer, He continued to expound the dharma. In about a little over half an hour, Buddhas did come from the sky and bestowed a large lump of nectar into the dharma bowl that could be seen clearly through the glass plate. Even the traces of tiny dots that were left on the glass plate were very clear. Since we all saw this extremely magnificent holy feat on the spot, how could we not cultivate ourselves, learn Buddhism, and benefit living beings? The bodhicitta of Anuttara-samyak-sambodhi naturally rose from within.

Additionally, the Dharma Assembly of Testing the Ability of Creating a Mandala Through a Stone Slab, the Selecting Karmic Condition by Divine Forecasting Dharma Assembly, the State Practice Mapeng Terma Initiation Dharma Assembly, and the Holy Buddha-Bathing Dharma Assembly also left the deepest impressions on me. I could only state one fact. These were definitely not what the so-called dharma kings, venerable ones, and great dharma masters who were ordinary persons could accomplish.

The same was true for other holy dharma assemblies that simply could not be held by one who was not an extremely great holy and virtuous one or a great holy and virtuous one. That was why many people admired us very much, since we had the opportunities to attend the holy dharma assemblies, could commune with Buddhas and Bodhisattvas in person on the spot, could receive the bestowed kindness in person, and could get supremely magnificent empowerment. Of course, the strength of the empowerment was very mighty. That was without a doubt.

Just as the Buddha Master, H.H. Dorje Chang Buddha III, said, "You cannot just rely on empowerment without cultivating yourself to attain accomplishment." What the Buddha Master meant is that living beings must use their self-cultivation to transform and reschedule causes and effects. The reason is that the consequences of the law of cause and effect cannot be ignored. If one does not do self-cultivation and does not have one's three karmas in correspondence, merely relying on empowerment is useless. Even though empowerment can have the effect of temporarily blocking karmic hindrance, without self-cultivation, one eventually has to pay for consequences and retributions. This is because "the consequences of the law of cause and effect can never err."

25

What Is the Truth about Reversing An Old Age Back to Youth?

Throughout these many years, the Buddha Master really worked very hard and never had any time to have a good rest. Every day, He had to talk a lot and was constantly busy with the endless matters of Buddha-dharma. Additionally, the Buddha Master vowed to bear living beings' karmic retributions, as stated in *The Supreme and Unsurpassable Mahamudra of Liberation*:

"I bear all of the negative karma and offenses of living beings.

I give to you all the good karma and merits I have planted."

This vow of His Holiness the Buddha did come true. As a result, during a period of several days, all black karmas from the outside were transferred to the Buddha Master. The Buddha Master suddenly became very tired, exhausted, and aged. He looked like a seventy or eighty year old person. Upon seeing the Buddha Master's situation, Venerable Long Zhi Tanpe Nyima, a fellow brother who was very good in his cultivation and conduct and who was the reincarnation of Denma Tsemang, one of the twenty-five major disciples of Master Padmasambhava, spoke respectfully to the Buddha Master, "Buddha Master, it can't go on like this! Otherwise living beings' good roots will be severed. Living beings are unable to understand why the Buddha could become so exhausted."

The Buddha Master said, "Even Sakyamuni Buddha became exhausted. If not, why would He enter into nirvana and leave for the Buddha-land? This was exactly how Buddha manifested impermanence." Brother Tsemang looked very sad and was greatly worried. Then the Buddha Master said, "Let me think about this a bit first." Brother Tsemang still felt very worried and sorrowful. The Buddha Master felt that what he said did make some sense and told him, "You go and get the camera to take a picture of me." The Buddha Master then also said, "Don't worry. I am not going to die! Let's address this after the dharma assembly!"

On October 18, 2012, I saw in person the Buddha Master reversing His appearance back to a youthful look. Within ten minutes, the Buddha Master reversed His aged appearance to that of a youth. At that time, the Buddha Master was at the mandala on the lawn praying for peace and auspiciousness. He told several of us to go and fetch the offering objects and the prayer manual. When I returned, I suddenly saw that vicissitudes and age were completely removed from the Buddha Master from the skin to the bone structure. The Buddha Master now had a childlike appearance. I was so astonished by what I saw that I dropped the offering apples to the ground! Good Heavens! The changes were like between two different persons. Furthermore, the other monastics present also said that they saw this surprising change.

What was the truth about this change of reversing old age back to youth? The United International World Buddhism Association Headquarters published this article of "Announcement of Good Fortune to Cultivators" on December 5, 2012.

On December 12, 2012, several hundred people saw H.H. Dorje Chang Buddha III during the Dharma Assembly of Decision by Selection with their own eyes. They all witnessed the fact that the Buddha Master reversed His appearance back to that of a youth.

In a recorded dharma lesson, some people stated that they first saw the Buddha Master's appearance turning from an old-aged one to a baby-faced appearance, resembling the statue of Amitabha Buddha at Hua Zang Si in San Francisco. Several days later, the Buddha Master's appearance again altered into that of a young person. Some people said that the Buddha Master's appearance was now ten times more graceful and majestic than when He was in Chengdu, China. One said that she saw the Buddha Master having turned younger and she told other people that the Buddha Master had suddenly returned to His appearance of over twenty years ago and looked extremely elegant and majestic.

行人的福音

我們藉祈禱迎接 2013 年吉祥殊勝法會的因緣，希望大家共同發願，祈請十方諸佛加持美國國泰民安，五穀豐登，無災無難，世界各國、人類、眾生安樂，祥瑞豐盈，和平恆昌，敬祈第三世多杰羌佛，不捨我等行人，能法駕佛鑾親臨法會加持。趁發此文公布一個振奮人心的好消息，在 2012 年 10 月 18 日很多行人拜見過偉大的第三世多杰羌佛，又在 10 月 25 日見到羌佛，她們說當時都不敢相信遠才隔七天，與幾天前所見到的多杰羌佛完全判若兩人，太神奇驚煞人了！只隔幾天時間，佛陀師父竟然回春年輕，更重要是遠比二十多年前童顏英俊，據禪房的法師們說：「這七天佛陀師父在草坪壇城做新平吉祥祈禱，由於多年來一直辛苦沒有得到休息，免不了疲勞滄桑，一天中午，佛陀師父知道大家的心情難過，說：『你們不要為我難過，生老病死無常，這世界就是無常性啊，所以釋迦佛也走了。』當時佛陀師父讓法師去取供品、祈禱文來，當法師把供品、祈禱文送去，怎麼看到佛陀師父已經變成童顏了！法師一驚之下，供品中的蘋果都掉下地了。」頓珠和幾位法師說佛陀師父返回在成都時的年輕，趕快趕到現場第一眼看到佛陀師父時，全都驚呆了！哪裡是幾天前看到過的蒼老形象！也不是在成都時的那種年輕概念，而是骨格體貌都變了，返回年輕相貌、膚質，精神煥發，用一句不該用的世俗話來說：太帥、太漂亮！當年在成都時和訪問台灣時的形象，根本無法比擬現在第三世多杰羌佛的童顏英俊、威武莊嚴！徹底說明「回春童顏法」就在佛陀的手中。可是光佛嚴屬呵斥我們說我們看花了眼，胡說八道，說：「我是用恆河沙和甘露水洗掉了臉上的皮膚腐垢而已」，這是醫術之法，哪個人都可以把臉洗乾淨，塗油脂面霜還會讓臉光亮呢，你們太誇張了，胡說什麼變成二十幾年前成都的我，你們看像嗎？成都時的我平凡一人，膚識寡見，慚愧的很，有什麼可效仿的，如果我懂這個法要仿嗎？也不會去回春一個成都的我吧！你們看了《解脫大手印》頂聖法錄中有這老還童回春童顏法，就不躲事實朝我身上套，《解脫大手印》中是提到過這些法，但是到今天沒有人修過，怎麼知道效果怎麼樣，我不了解這個法，我還差啊，沒有道功夫。」佛陀師父雖然否定，但是羌佛回春童顏是否認不了的鐵證事實，你們想想看，不要說十幾分鐘的時間就返回童顏，就算是七天，這是用恆河砂沈臉就能返回中年輕嗎？尤其是還超二十年前的英俊、莊嚴、威武，這是人為能力能達到嗎？歷史上還沒有過這樣的先例！這裡深深提示我們一個嚴峻值得思考的問題，在這世界上的一些高高在上自居聖者、狂傲吹噓的著名法王、尊者、法師，他們不但連智慧都沒有開動，因此展示不了五明，而且年齡越大越老越衰竭，至於形相就越來越困難等等，但是相反的，他們卻竟然依賴傳承法位，大言不慚，聖者自居，高升法王台，升坐法王台上，迷惑行人，剝奪供養，說心裡話，除了蓮花生大師，這些人沒有一個有真功夫回春年輕了的，真可憐！反之而第三世多杰羌佛不收供養，五明高峰無缺，三藏圓通登峰造極，一切圓融無礙，而且返蒼俊回春童顏，驚世駭俗，但是祂卻不承認自己有道行，處處說自己差、自己慚愧，這是謙遜、這福慚愧，那些虛假而大言不慚、以凡充聖的滿口活佛們，應照之下，貽笑大方，皮毛而已，他們真是可憐到了極點！對比之下，這兩種不同的言行自然透露出了真聖者和凡夫充墨的本質，眾人深思啊！！！我們相信，只要有一個真心誠意的心，佛陀師父會傳給我們「回春童顏法」的，否則《解脫大手印》中就不會有這個法的名福。

聯合國際世界佛教總部
2012 年 12 月 5 日

Figure 25-1 - The article of "Announcement of Good Fortune to Cultivators," was published by the United International World Buddhism Association Headquarters on December 12, 2012 (See Appendix D.)

People all wanted to learn the dharma of reversing an old age back to youth. Thus, they beseeched the Buddha Master to expound the dharma, which was recorded. The name of this recorded dharma lesson is "This is scary! The disciples did not give in to the Buddha: They insisted that H.H. Dorje Chang Buddha III did restore youth and childlike appearance!" However, H.H. Dorje Chang Buddha III said,

"I do not know the dharma of restoring youth and childlike appearance. I only know a little bit about the methods of medical treatment.

Looking at the comparison from the recorded videos, it would be false to say that I did not become younger at all. However, what you disciples said was much too exaggerated. I simply do not know the dharma of reversing an old age back to childlike youth."

At this time, Kaichu Rinpoche spoke by the side of the Buddha Master, "Buddha Master always spoke and acted as a humble one. However, now He is right in front of us. We can judge with our own eyes. Do we really exaggerate? Can worldly medical treatment change the bone structure or reverse an old age back to youth? Why has there not been even one such example in the world?"

Today, we saw the fact clearly and vividly with our own eyes. We did not exaggerate or speak baselessly. Even though it was denied by the Buddha Master, the iron-clad fact of the Buddha Master's restored youth and childlike appearance was undeniable. Think about it. Can this be achieved by ordinary abilities of any human? There has not been such precedence in history!

This instance made us think about a serious situation that is worthy to deeply ponder. In this world, there are famous dharma kings, venerable ones, and dharma masters who pose as holy ones with high statuses, arrogantly boasting about themselves. They have not developed their wisdom and are not able to demonstrate any accomplishment in the Five Vidyas. Moreover, they become more frail and exhausted as they age. Their appearances also deteriorate at the same time. However, they just rely on their statuses and positions within their lineages to shamelessly boast of themselves and pose as holy ones. They falsely present themselves as dharma kings and sit high on the dharma-king seats to swindle cultivators out of their offerings. To tell the truth, no one, other than Guru Padmasambhava, had any true ability of reversing old age back to youth, including current famous dharma kings, venerable ones, and dharma masters.

Conversely, H.H. Dorje Chang Buddha III does not accept offerings; He has achieved perfect accomplishments that are at the acme of the Five Vidyas and commands perfect proficiency in the Tripitaka. Everything His Holiness does is in perfect harmony with the karmic condition without any impediment. Moreover, His Holiness was able to turn His aged yet still handsome appearance to a youthful and childlike appearance with astonishing, extraordinary effect. However, He does not admit to having the power of realization and always says that He is nothing but a humble cultivator who does not accept offerings.

Actually, this kind of genuine modesty provides a contrast to those dharma kings and rinpoches who falsely claim and shamelessly boast about their importance. The comparison makes them superficial and laughable. They are extremely piteous! Comparing these two kinds of speeches and deeds, it naturally reveals the different characteristics of a true holy one and ordinary people who fake as holy ones. This is really worth pondering.

26

Forecasting the Arrival of a Million Birds
Ahead of Time

There are two things that we do very often. As religious teachers at the temple, we provide assistance to believers for them to respectfully listen to the recorded dharma lessons expounded by H.H. Dorje Chang Buddha III. Even though we dharma masters are not at a high level yet, we are still able to tutor beginning cultivators. The other thing is releasing captured living beings. The compassionate and kind wife of the Buddha Master, whom we addressed as Fomu ("Fomu" literally means Buddha mother, a female Mahasattva whose status is next to only the Buddha) often leads us to release captured living beings. This is a kind conduct to benefit others that can be done by all without any differentiation in terms of one's status.

The Compassionate and Kind Fomu is a Ph.D., a university professor, and a famous artist. She often uses the money from selling paintings to release captured living beings. Often, the fish bought and later released are in several cabins weighing a few or even tens of tons and numbering more than ten thousands. Sometimes even the entire boatload of fish in a large fishing vessel are bought. The fishermen even know us. The activities of fish releasing have been carried out continuously for more than ten years. Fomu's speech and conduct have earned our total admiration, and we have been deeply edified and transformed. Her acts of kindness have impelled us to carry out acts of great compassion to all living beings.

The compassionate and kind Fomu has taught us that all animals coming here are our family members. Even those who have not come here yet are also our family members, the only difference being their karmic conditions having not matured yet. Since beginningless time, they have always been closely related to and inseparable from us. Therefore, we should truly treat them equally and love them.

Strangely enough, because such a holy place of great compassion exists, all kinds of birds and animals have been coming and creating a bustling atmosphere of happiness and excitement. Everywhere in the yard, birds are crowing and chirping, parrots are singing, and animals are playing joyfully. It can be said that such an interesting wilderness environment cannot be found in any garden in private homes in the entire Los Angeles area. Even though this place is separated from the neighbors by just a wall, these birds and animals do not stop at their gardens. This holy and interesting phenomenon is really incredible. The good karmas and merits here invite living beings to come and pay homage happily.

Animals having the karmic conditions to come here all have very good karmic roots. For example, a fluffy Shih Tzu dog at the home base was named "Xiang Rui" (which means auspiciousness) by the Buddha Master. It had originally been a homeless dog and we took it in. Soon after arriving at the home base, it took refuge with the Buddha Master. It was very respectful to the Buddha Master and would prostrate anytime upon seeing the Buddha Master. Additionally, when you held money in your hands to present as offering to the Buddha Master and the Buddha Master declined, Xiang Rui would jump up and bite the money off. Then it would run to the Buddha Master to deliver the money to the Buddha Master's hand. Of course, the Buddha Master still would not accept it and would return the money.

Figure 26-1 - The dog Xiang Rui

More recently, a friend temporarily placed a dog looking exactly like a polar bear here for boarding. Its name was "Miao Miao." On the third day of its arrival, it took refuge with the Buddha Master. It would prostrate anytime upon seeing the Buddha Master.

Figure 26-2 - The dog Miao Miao

All living beings are equal and have the Buddha nature. Just like the dogs Xiang Rui and Miao Miao and the one million birds, they know that they should pay homage and present offerings to the Buddha Master.

In the evening of December 19, 2012, a number of people including Venerable Long Zhi Tanpe Nyima (Denma Tsemang II), Layperson Kuan, Akou Lamo Rinpoche, Yongdeng Gongbu Rinpoche, Luoben Rinpoche, Queji Gele Rinpoche, Xuan Hui Acarya, Sister Dun Zhu, Sister Du Yingci, Wen Li Acarya, Dharma Master Hua Kong, Mei Ling Acarya, Sister Zhi Hong, and others followed the Buddha Master on a trip.

When the Buddha Master's motorcade stopped at the city of Lost Hill, we all took a break at a gas station. Because the gas station was located in the desert, there were only a few small trees nearby. The Buddha Master suddenly told us all,

"This place is called 'Bird City.' Although there are only two or three birds now, a million birds will come after a short while."

Sister Du Yingchi asked, "Is that true?"

The Buddha Master said, "You don't think so?"

Exactly as we were told, in less than ten minutes, when we walked out from the restroom, the sky seemed to be covered up by dark clouds. A large black area formed by a huge crowd of birds moved over. There were at least one million birds in the sky above our heads. They grouped into three or four layers and were all showing dance movements by flying and moving back and forth. The highest layer was as high as the clouds, and the lowest layer was at the height of the roof, which was three to four meters above the ground. Therefore, the sounds of birds flying with flapping wings could be heard very clearly.

Additionally, the dance of the bird flock was directed by a leading bird. Their movements were coordinated and in unison. The sounds lasted for different intervals and were very much in sync. The birds turned and rolled in unified changes of formations. Their elevations also moved up and down in waves.

Figure 26-3- Over a million birds were offering their dance performance in the sky (Birds at the highest and middle levels could be seen with naked eyes at the scene but were not visible in the recorded video. Only the birds at the lowest level were visible in this picture. On the right side of this picture were street lights.).

The birds presented various kinds of dancing skills in the sky above the Buddha Master. The flocks of birds flying high formed groups to present figures of different shapes: circles, closed rings, flat contours and long lines. Sometimes, the birds at the highest layer even dropped suddenly like an opened parachute, and then soared back high again.

People all shouted happily and said the scene looked like that of exploding fireworks. This performance lasted about twenty minutes and never moved away from the sky above the Buddha Master. The Buddha Master felt rather embarrassed and said, "Thank you very much! Thank you very much!"

After finishing their performance, the birds flew to the trees near the Buddha Master's vehicle. Some perched on leafy trees, and some perched on withered trees. Every branch was fully occupied. The formerly withered trees now formed a wondrous scene with black-colored "leaves."

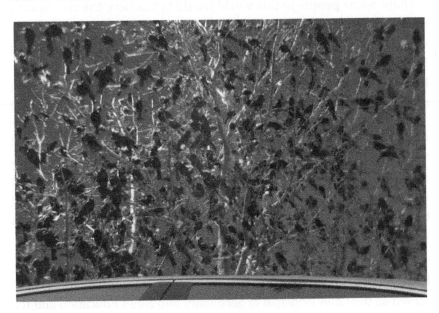

Figure 26-4 - After the flock of birds had offered their performance, many birds raced to the trees next to the Buddha Master's parked car for the opportunity to respectfully view and salute the Buddha Master. The lowest tree branches were almost willowed by the standing birds as low as the door of the car. The car top seen at the bottom of this photo was the car in which the Buddha Master was seated. The dark figures seen in the picture were all birds, not tree leaves.

At this time, the Buddha Master took out food to empower them. Of course, this amount of food was not enough for them. Even a truckload of food, if brought here, would not be enough for all these birds. They seemed to be waiting politely for others to go ahead first and none went to the ground to eat.

The Buddha Master told Brother Kuan to drive the vehicle to the side of a big road and park there. Then the birds at other trees also flew to the tree next to the Buddha Master's vehicle to respectfully watch and salute the Buddha Master. The tree branches were almost broken. The birds standing at the lowest level bent the tree branches to almost the height of the door of the Buddha Master's vehicle. The birds were most crowded in front of the door of the car, and they were not worried about the fact that people were right next to them. The Buddha Master opened the car window to praise them and empower them.

Perhaps some people in this world would not believe the scenes they read and saw here. However, this was a fact that many people experienced. They first heard the forecast made by H.H. Dorje Chang Buddha III and then witnessed the prediction's fruition. This fact could never be created by any man-made effort. Is there any holy one who can forecast ahead of time by ten minutes? No, it is impossible to find one!

At that time, Venerable Denma Tsemang used his cell phone to record the scene. Because the distance was too high and too far, the video recording function was not able to capture the scene at the highest layer. Only the view at a close distance was recorded. Therefore, I had to make inquiries of many of the people who went on that trip and verified this iron-clad fact.

For example, one of the witnesses was Sister Du Yingci. She had once served as the Chief Principal of Secondary and Adult Education and the Director of Community Education at the Alhambra Unified School District in the greater Los Angeles area in the United States. She had also served as a President of the Kiwanis International in the San Gabriel Valley. She is currently the Director of Operations for the International Art Museum of America in San Francisco. She is a person of very high morality.

Also, Venerable Denma Tsemang, who was one of the twenty-five major disciples of Master Padmasambhava, related to me in person the entire event. His was of course speech with regard to the law of cause and effect without a doubt because he is a person who upholds justice in his cultivation and conduct. I can only say that, among the venerable ones and dharma kings we commonly saw, there is almost none who is comparable to him in terms of cultivation and conduct. He is also a holy and virtuous one with master's qualifications with Sun-Moon Wheel(s).

According to what we know, he and Dharma King Gar Tongstan and Kaichu Rinpoche all have their own strengths in cultivation and conduct. They are all holy and virtuous ones with the same classification of realization. They have advanced step by step through cultivation. They first progressed from being a great virtuous one to the level of a holy and virtuous one with One Sumeru Wheel. Then they progressed and achieved the levels of holy and virtuous ones with Two Sumeru Wheels and holy and virtuous ones with Three Sumeru Wheels successively. After that, through intensive real practice in cultivation and conduct, they have surpassed the levels of holy and virtuous ones with Sumeru Wheels and entered into the holy realization of holy and virtuous ones with master's qualifications with Sun-Moon Wheel(s).

The Buddha Master also approved these observations of mine. The Buddha Master said,

"The three of them are all different in their gain and loss in terms of cultivation and conduct. Dharma King Gar Tongstan emphasizes undistracted cultivation of the dharma nature and true suchness. He is very diligent day and night and is not interrupted even by eating and wearing clothing. His goal is in realizing the equanimity of the dharma nature. However, he does not communicate or interact with cultivators. That is why he lacks the deeds of a Bodhisattva's benefiting living beings."

"Kaichu Rinpoche focuses on strictly abiding by the precepts and quietly engaging in self-cultivation. His esoteric practices embody subtleties of uncommon import and he does not publicize the teaching or the dharma. His realization is very reputable, but he has not diminished external affinities with worldly matters yet."

"Venerable Denma Tsemang makes an earnest effort to cultivate and act in accordance with the Buddha's teaching. He uses his correct views to propagate Buddha-dharma. He is low-key in his speech and conduct and never slanders others to elevate himself. He does not show the appearance of a holy and virtuous one with master's qualifications with Sun-Moon Wheel(s). His work is very hard and extremely laborious. He is a meritorious hero who has truly established the merit of a Bodhisattva's cultivation and conduct in propagating Buddha-dharma and benefiting living beings. He is easygoing and is close to people. However, he is somewhat too straightforward in his speech and conduct. That can sometimes hurt his own karmic condition and expend his merit."

"Though the three of them are all different, they are already excellent. Some others of those so-called venerable ones, dharma kings, and great dharma masters cannot be mentioned in the same breath with them. That is why they have achieved the realm of holy and virtuous ones with master's qualifications of Sun-Moon Wheel(s)."

Venerable Denma Tsemang narrated the whole event to me. I was greatly moved. It could only be accomplished by an extremely holy one with the status of a Buddha, and is impossible for any other holy and virtuous ones to have done so.

After I finished recording the event by writing about it, I took the photo of birds perching on the tree in front of the Buddha Master's vehicle taken at that time to respectively show to the Buddha Master. I said, "This holy feat was too magnificent! Too amazing! Buddha Master's forecast was too astonishing! It was unprecedented. Moreover, one million birds came. Not only did the birds perform an elaborate dance, they were not afraid of people and also respectfully came over to get close to Buddha Master."

You wouldn't be able to imagine what the Buddha Master said then. The Buddha Master said,

"How could I have the ability to forecast? That was a coincidence. It just so happened that many birds did come. Birds in America knew that people wouldn't hurt them, and they developed the habit of not fearing people. So this was a very normal phenomenon. What merit do I have! You should not put diamonds on me for decoration. No matter how you try to elevate me, I am still a humble one. What you should do is cultivate well and benefit living beings!"

在佛陀师父预言后约十分钟，百万飞鸟就在空中为HH第三世多杰羌佛献舞，这是真实不虚的，我是现场的见证人之一，特此证明

陈智

看到这篇文章感触很深，因为当时我正是在现场的幸运者之一。佛陀师父跟大家说"这个地方叫鸟城，等会会有上百万只鸟来"佛陀师父跟杜师兄讲话时我就在现场，不一会儿大约十几万只鸟从四面八方向佛陀师父飞来，黑呼呼一大片一大片分层往下飞，几乎遮盖了整个天空，不是身临其境无法想像就在佛陀师父预言后十几分钟内，预言真的实现了，当时的景像我一辈子也忘不掉。

此篇文章是详细又真实的记录，我是现场目击者可以作证。

娟瑞 合十

這篇文章是絕对真實的記載，當时我也在現場！

文… 合十

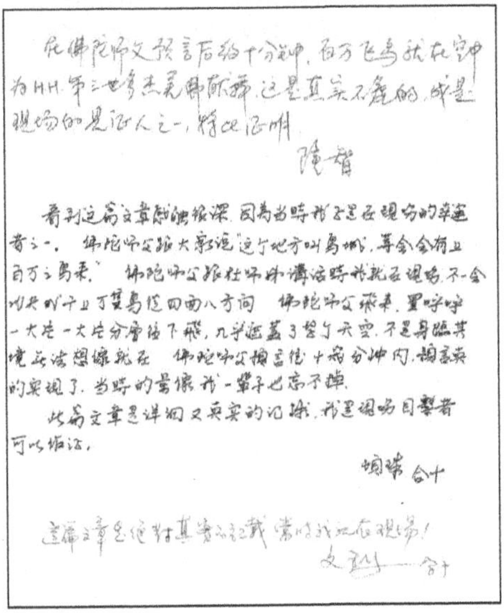

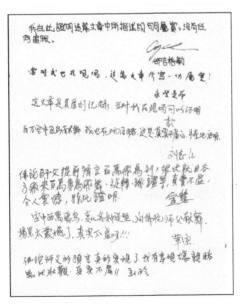

Figure 26-5 - These were hand-written testimonies with signatures by individuals who were present at the scene and witnessed this dance performance by one million birds, submitted as proof of the truthfulness of this event (See Appendix E.)

我在此證明這篇文章中所描述的句句屬實，沒有任何虛假。

鄧吉格勒

當时我也在现场，这篇文章所写一切属实！

永登曼布

这文章是真实的记录，当时我在现场可以证明

敖

百万空中飞鸟献舞，我也在场目睹，这是真实不虚的，特此证明。

刘德红

佛陀師父提前預言百萬飛鳥到，很快就自各方飛來百萬隻鳥飛舞、旋轉、跳躍等，真實不虛，令人震撼，特此證明。

宣慧

空中百萬飛鳥，变化各种造型，向佛陀师父献舞，場景太震撼了，真实不虚呀!!!

華宜

佛陀師父的預言真的實現了，我有幸現場親睹無比壯觀，真實不虛!! 郭玲

Figure 26-6 - These were hand-written testimonies with signatures by individuals who were present at the scene and witnessed this dance performance by one million birds, submitted as proof of the truthfulness of this event (See Appendix E.)

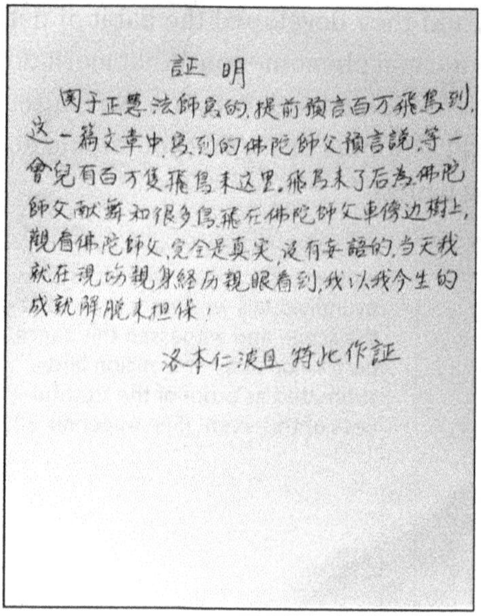

証 明

　因于正愚法师兒的,提前预言百万飛鳥列,
这一篇文章中鸟到的佛陀师父预言說,等一
會兒有百万隻飛鳥未这里,飛鳥未了后为佛陀
师父献舞和很多鸟落在佛陀师父車傍边樹上,
觀看佛陀师父,完全是真实,没有妄語的,当天我
就在现场親身経历親眼看到,我以我今生的
成就解脱未担保,

　　　　　洛本仁波旦 将此作証

Figure 26-7 - These were hand-written testimonies with signatures by individuals who were present at the scene and witnessed this dance performance by one million birds, submitted as proof of the truthfulness of this event (See Appendix E.).

27

I Did Not Know That My Taking Refuge and Cultivation Were False for So Long; the Six Dharma Treasures Can Show What an Idiot with Low Character Is

I cultivated for these many years. However, I just did not make progress. There was only a very short period of a little over one month, when the state of taking refuge and the yidam mandala of Green Tara could be clearly seen to appear. However, whenever I spoke to communicate with Them, the holy state dissipated immediately like smoke. Many times the situation was just like this. As long as I did not speak, the state was very true and real. Once I tried to communicate with Them, the state became fuzzy right away and then vanished into thin air.

I always wondered how the dharma transmitted by the Buddha Master could be so insubstantial? Could it be that the dharma transmitted by the Buddha Master was incomplete?

However, I also believed that my Master was the Buddha, H.H. Dorje Chang Buddha III, because many people had learned great dharmas from Him, such as the Great-Cross Justice Dharma King, Tangtong Gyalpo Rinpoche, Mozhi Rinpoche, Venerable Denma Tsemang, Dharma King Gar Tongstan, Kaichu Rinpoche, Holy and Virtuous One La Zhen, and others.

Then, why didn't I get to learn the highest dharma? I now clearly understood many truths and principles. I corrected many of my mistakes and sins. I also did my best to do my daily dharma practice according to the Dharma of Cultivation and the dharma of the yidam's ritual transmitted to me by the Buddha Master. However, there still weren't firm beneficial effects. Why had I still not learned a great dharma and why didn't I have realization power to manifest? I could not comprehend at all, so understandably, some thoughts arose in my mind

Could it be possible that the Buddha Master was not a Buddha and treated people with differentiation? No wonder that lack of unity existed among fellow sisters at the home base. Also, could it be possible that the dogs had been trained to make those movements?

On the other hand, I also thought about some other facts. Could a million Yellow Jackets and a million birds be trained to come when you wanted them to? How could you train a dead person to revive by your instruction? Furthermore, why didn't the Great-Cross Justice Dharma King, Dharma King Mohe, and Mozhi Rinpoche harbor such doubts? Why didn't Dharma King Gar Tongstan and Kaichu Rinpoche whom we were with all the time have such problems either? Why were their realization powers so superior?

As soon as I became aware of the emergence of these thoughts, I repented right away. This was really terrible. Not having realization power was my own problem and it even became my excuse for having doubt. It seemed that I should caution myself against such bad thoughts that were rooted in ignorance. Thus, I went to the Great-Cross Justice Dharma King to seek advice.

I organized my thoughts in preparation for inquiry. The first time, He looked at me but did not give any answer. The second time He did not say anything either. The third time, I changed the topic for seeking advice.

I said, "Great-Cross Justice Dharma King! According to what I know, you are recognized by the world's highest-level great dharma king as a dharma king who has reincarnated from a very famous upper level great venerable one. Then, why do many people address you as Great-Cross Justice Dharma King?"

The Great-Cross Justice Dharma King said, "Sorry that you notice this embarrassing practice! I did not ask people to call me the Great-Cross Justice Dharma King. Whatever they call me makes no difference."

I again asked respectfully, "Why do they respectfully address you this way?"

The Great-Cross Justice Dharma King said, "Perhaps it was because I got the title of the Great-Cross Justice Wearing Red Robe and Carrying a Sword. Some people used this opportunity to change their way of addressing me. Actually, however I am addressed is not important, be it the Great-Cross Justice or a small cultivator. We shall not be attached to status or title. What we need to do is to really cultivate and learn Buddhism in concrete steps."

I respectfully inquired, "Why can't I make progress in cultivation? Why, Dharma King, did you become proficient in sutras when you were only a few years old? Why is your power of realization from cultivation so high and profound beyond imagination?"

The Great-Cross Justice Dharma King said, "You should not flatter me!"

I said, "Kaichu Rinpoche who is inferior to you has shown in front of us a live test of his tummo practice with a heat-sensing apparatus. His power of tummo is so amazing, but I do not have such an ability!"

The Great-Cross Justice Dharma King said, "Cultivating as you are doing now, you will not get the power of tummo, you will not become accomplished in this lifetime. Moreover, your cultivation will get worse lifetime after lifetime."

I asked, "Why? I also practice the dharma very hard. And I am cultivating myself!"

The Great-Cross Justice Dharma King said, "Since you think this way, let's wait until you have figured this out clearly." After that, He did not talk to me.

A few days later, I had done all my thinking but still did not know why I could not make progress in my cultivation, why I could not pass the dharma of decision by selection, and why I did not learn a great dharma. I again went to the Great-Cross Justice Dharma King. He said, "Did you find the answer? If you did, don't come to ask me again."

I said, "Just because I cannot come up with the answer, I come to beseech you Dharma King to point the way and lead me out of this maze."

The Great-Cross Justice Dharma King said, "First go and prostrate to the visage of the Buddha Master and then come and ask me."

After I did the prostrations and came back, the Great-Cross Justice Dharma King said, "Now you calmly and seriously listen to what I have to say to you. Many people are in the same situation as you are in. They cultivate earnestly and practice the dharma diligently for their entire lives, but do not get beneficial effects and do not attain accomplishment. They cannot even derive power of realization or beneficial effects from any dharma. The reason is that many non-conformances to the dharma block their opportunities to acquire wisdom. The key is non-conformity to the dharma, not abiding by the precepts, and incorrectly abiding by the precepts. They do not recognize holy ones or they regard ordinary beings as holy ones, causing them to commit enormous sins. Separately, among those who are masters, some falsely claim to be holy and virtuous ones even though they are not. Some small holy and virtuous ones falsely claim to be great holy and virtuous ones. There also exist the situations of a holy and virtuous one degenerating into an ordinary person for violating precepts. After that, the person still poses as a holy and virtuous one to deceive his or her disciples. That is a serious offense to the precepts!"

I did not quite understand what He said. I replied, "I recite 'the Fifty Stanzas of Guru Devotion' ('the Fifty Verses Regarding How Disciples Should Treat Their Master') twice every week. I also recite 'the Fourteen Fundamental Precepts of Esoteric Buddhism' once every day and check if I have committed any violation. I pay special attention to the first precept. I respect venerable ones, dharma kings, rinpoches, and great dharma masters very much. They are all masters. There are many masters who come here to pay homage to H.H. Dorje Chang Buddha III. They are venerable ones, dharma kings, rinpoches, or great dharma masters. I always treat them according to 'the Fifty Stanzas of Guru Devotion.' I do follow the teaching."

The Great-Cross Justice Dharma King closed His eyes and did not say anything. I beseeched repeatedly, "Why don't You speak?"

The Great-Cross Justice Dharma King opened His eyes and spoke seriously, "You are extremely foolish and naïve. You are cultivating. However, you are not even aware of the problems you have created. Why do you only recite 'the Fifty Stanzas of Guru Devotion' and follow 'the Fourteen Fundamental Precepts of Esoteric Buddhism' in your conduct, but do not use the 128 Evil and Erroneous Views to check and verify the so-called masters who are venerable ones, dharma kings, rinpoches, and great dharma masters? Without checking and verifying, how do you know who are true masters? If you apply the first precept of 'the Fourteen Fundamental Precepts of Esoteric Buddhism' and 'the Fifty Stanzas of Guru Devotion' in treating unqualified masters, your sin would be terribly big!"

"Your fault is in reciting 'the Fourteen Fundamental Precepts of Esoteric Buddhism' every day and always following 'the Fifty Stanzas of Guru Devotion' to treat masters with fame. Are the masters you have been dealing with, be they venerable ones or dharma kings, truly qualified masters? Do they speak falsely to deceive their disciples? Do they let you work with them to engage in falsification and do things that hurt living beings? Have they ever untruly used the title of an even higher holy and virtuous one to fool their disciples? Have you verified and investigated? You are so stupid to the extent of not verifying and not investigating! If one uses the name of holiness to collect money and engage in conduct causing other people's loss to benefit oneself, even if this person was a holy and virtuous one in the past, he or she must have deteriorated into an evil master due to contamination by profits and gains. Such a person is not a master at all. You even abide by the contents of the precepts in treating evil masters. Are you perpetrating sin or accumulating merit?"

"The supreme holiest Tathagata, H.H. Dorje Chang Buddha III, never let people treat Him according to 'the Fourteen Fundamental Precepts of Esoteric Buddhism' and 'the Fifty Stanzas of Guru Devotion.' Rather, He has taught people to use the 128 Evil and Erroneous Views to check and verify. Today, I clearly tell you that your sin and bad karma are very severe!"

"The best dharma treasures in the dharma realm are the verification using the 128 Evil and Erroneous Views and the mind-essences of *The*

Supreme and Unsurpassable Mahamudra of Liberation. These are su-preme dharma treasures that are incomparable throughout history."

"Among the venerable ones, dharma kings, great rinpoches, and great dharma masters you have met, which one of them could surpass Mozhi Rinpoche? Even Mozhi Rinpoche who has Two Sun-Moon Wheels has told me that His cultivation and realization are too insufficient to qual-ify him for receiving the respect and following as specified in 'the Fifty Stanzas of Guru Devotion' and 'the Fourteen Fundamental Precepts of Esoteric Buddhism.' I think He is quite right. I praised Him as a holy and virtuous one with correct knowledge and views."

"What kinds of people are you Zheng Hui respecting and worship-ping all this time? Do they have certificates of holiness and virtue with Sun-Moon Wheel(s)? If they hold certificates of holiness and virtue with Sumeru Wheel(s), have you carefully checked whether they fall into the 128 Evil and Erroneous Views? If yes, that person can turn into an evil master, because he or she is not a great holy and virtuous one at the level of Two Sun-Moon Wheels or higher. Could you be sure that among them there are no swindlers, no evil spirits or demons, no mountain spirits, no aquatic demons, and no monsters? Could you be sure that there are no incarnations from the categories of various devilish monsters, ghost spirits, and evildoers?"

"They know very clearly that they have to put on cassocks, red robes, or dharma kings' gowns. Then, they hold up the certificates showing their recognized statuses and use 'the Fifty Stanzas of Guru Devotion' and 'the Fourteen Fundamental Precepts of Esoteric Buddhism' to har-ness those extremely foolish people like you into being loyal to them. Correspondingly, you uphold the conduct and mentality of abiding by the precepts to respect and follow them. You are actually promoting evil and spreading poison. You must clearly know this!"

"The Buddha Master H.H. Dorje Chang Buddha III has said already, The Fifty Stanzas of Guru Devotion' and 'the Fourteen Fundamen-tal Precepts of Esoteric Buddhism' cause more sin than merit. This is true especially for the first precept of the 'Fourteen Fundamental

Precepts of Esoteric Buddhism,' which has the effect of promoting evil and destroying goodness. 'The Fifty Stanzas of Guru Devotion' and the 'Fourteen Fundamental Precepts of Esoteric Buddhism' are only to be applied toward great holy and virtuous ones who are incarnations of great Bodhisattvas; they should never be applied to masters who are demons, evil spirits, and swindlers. Otherwise, one not only cannot attain liberation, but also will be certain to descend into one of the three lower realms.' The Buddha Master has very clearly expounded the dharma in His discourse. If we practice 'the Fifty Stanzas of Guru Devotion' and 'the Fourteen Fundamental Precepts of Esoteric Buddhism' with regard to true Buddhas and Bodhisattvas, there will be boundless merit. However, it is difficult to find a true holy and virtuous one or a genuine Buddha or Bodhisattva even among ten thousand venerable ones, dharma kings, rinpoches, and dharma masters in this world."

"Those with big undeserved titles are in fact false masters. They can be seen everywhere, even some who were recognized by eminent dharma kings. Some were holy ones in the past but later became corrupted. Nine thousand nine hundred ninety-nine out of ten thousand are swindlers. With the appearances of venerable ones or dharma kings, they are completely imposters or swindlers. They do not know Buddha-dharma at all."

"If you ever apply 'the Fifty Stanzas of Guru Devotion' and 'the Fourteen Fundamental Precepts of Esoteric Buddhism' toward ones who are incarnations of evil spirits and demons, the sin is unlimited. I can only feel sorry for the questions you have raised. You do not feel that you are naïve and foolish to the extreme. Your conduct is assisting evil and destroying goodness! Who can you blame for your not passing the decision by selection? You have only yourself to blame!"

"Even if you have done well on all these aspects, it still depends on whether you have taken real actions in the bodhicitta of saving living beings. That admission criterion is to see how many people you have led to cultivate solidly and to listen to the recorded dharma lessons. If you do not proselytize living beings into learning Buddhism to establish the merit of saving living beings, the circumstance will be imperfect."

"Additionally, there is an issue that is the most important to cause you not to pass the decision by selection and to be unable to learn great dharma. This is mainly because of your impure karma. Furthermore, this impure karma is different from other types of impure karmas. This impure karma is against the Buddha and great Bodhisattvas. This is a fundamentally impure karma. For instance, you do not honestly and sincerely take a pious refuge in the Buddha Master. That is equivalent to not taking refuge. Without taking refuge, you are simply not a Buddhist at all."

I immediately expressed my disagreement and replied, "I am very pious! I am very honest and sincere!"

The Great-Cross Justice Dharma King said, "That belongs to your reluctant action of forceful adjustment to suppress your mind consciousness and restrain yourself, and is not out of the true awareness and genuine faith from your inner mind and deep self. Such devotion is like a piece of grass growing on a wall and will waver left and right. For example, when you see that the Buddha Master manifests holy states and boundless merit, you are very pious. At that time, the Buddha Master is truly a Buddha in your mind. However, at other times when you see the Buddha Master being the same as a common person or even having some illness, you consciously or unconsciously think different kinds of thoughts, and regard the Buddha Master as a common person."

"Why don't you realize that this is the karmic condition and manifestation of the Buddha Master taking on living beings' suffering? Why do you generate thoughts of impure karma over that? Why don't you think about the Ancient Buddha Vimalakirti being ill and confined to bed when doing so for the sake of living beings? Why don't you think about the fact that the Buddha Master does get very seriously ill but, once not suffering for living beings, His illness immediately goes away? Can this be understood by your mentality of an ordinary person?"

"People in ancient times said, 'Wavering back and forth reveals the mentality of low-class people, just as the flooding and receding of water in a mountain creek.' This is exactly what you are. Even more serious is the problem of how you took refuge. That was the original cause for the non-correspondence of your three karmas. The seed of impure karma in your mind made you falsely take refuge."

I said, "Although I do have this kind of situation, my three karmas are absolutely in correspondence. I am a true Buddhist and I have truly taken refuge."

The Great-Cross Justice Dharma King said, "If your three karmas were in correspondence, how could you have the mentality of wavering left and right, and see the Buddha with ordinary people's view? How could you judge the Buddha depending on whether something is holy or mundane? Why don't you have such mentality toward Sakyamuni Buddha? Why don't you have such mentality toward Kuan Yin Bodhisattva? Your three karmas are not in clean and pure correspondence. Rather, the correspondence is a forced and restricted one. That is why you have such a mentality. This is not the conduct of a truly faithful believer, not the conduct at the upper level."

"You have to know clearly, why the Buddha Master comes to this world in the current lifetime, and what the purposes of other dharma kings and great venerable ones are. Of course people would all say that it is for enlightening oneself and others and for widely saving living beings. Actually, how many of them truly have the realization power to widely save living beings? How many are for all living beings and not for themselves? At least in modern history, the Buddha Master is the only one."

"For example, who can work hard and do things for living beings all the time without accepting any money or wealth presented by living beings? Even when people left the money there without leaving their names, the Buddha Master always let the dharma masters collect the money for use by the temples or donate to non-profit organizations. Are there any people like Him? Are there great dharma kings, great venerable ones, and great dharma masters like this? At least I have never seen one. There is simply no one who has the conduct as that of the Buddha Master! Can you Zheng Hui find one who has the same conduct as that of the Buddha Master? Other than the Buddha Master, who else only propagates the dharma, benefits living beings and does not accept offerings?"

"The Buddha Master not only does not accept offerings, but also uses the money He earns from hard work to support the monastics at the temples and to help disaster relief efforts. Even an uneducated person should think about this fact. Who has such conduct of sacrificing oneself and selflessly benefiting others? Wouldn't this cause people to ponder deeply? If not a Buddha, can one have such supreme conduct of a Buddha?"

"Of course evildoers and bad people would say doing so is a pretense. Then, who dares pretend this way? Do you dare to pretend this way? Since you have said this is a pretense, we would just accept it as a pretense. Now I will talk to you about a few things that cannot be pretended. Can H.H. Dorje Chang Buddha III's Five Vidyas and the thirty major categories of accomplishments in the treasure book be pretended? Can you find one who can pretend these accomplishments and prove it to me? Who is that person? You can find no one! You are not able to pretend either!"

The Great-Cross Justice Dharma King asked me again, "Did you take true refuge?"

I replied without hesitation, "Of course I did! If not, how could I be a monastic bhiksuni now?"

The Great-Cross Justice Dharma King said, "You who wears the robe of bhiksuni cannot represent a Buddhist who has truly taken refuge, and it does not indicate that you have taken true refuge in the Three Jewels. You should clearly know what taking refuge means. Taking means taking on. Refuge means reliance. Moreover, it means taking on this reliance throughout this lifetime while your body is in this world. Any day while your life and body exist in this world, the three karmas of body, speech, and mind of that day should reflect 'having taken refuge.' That means taking on the reliance on the three karmas of body, speech, and mind without the slightest deviation from the Three Jewels and from the Buddha. Have you accomplished that?"

I said, "Of course I have!"

The Great-Cross Justice Dharma King said, "If you did, you would not have the thoughts as well as the speech and conduct that are just the opposite. You not only have not taken true refuge, but also are a betrayer and a bad person making evil slanders against the Buddha! There are very many such people in Buddhism. You are one of them. That is why many Buddhists who have cultivated for their entire lifetime and even have had some states of realization eventually still cannot attain accomplishment and liberation. The reason is that they unintentionally took false refuge and did not know this fact themselves. You are a notable example of these people."

Upon hearing what He said, I was not convinced and my guts were exploding with anger. I said, "You can't talk about me baselessly! Your judgment and conclusion disregard the facts. I am a Buddhist disciple who has taken true refuge, and I am learning Buddhism and cultivating honestly. I believe in the Buddha Master. That is why I have followed the Buddha Master at this home base of His for more than ten years. If not having taken true refuge, I would not be at this place of the Buddha Master. Would I continue to be a monastic? Dharma King, You represent the Great-Cross Justice and are a great holy and virtuous one with extremely high status. I know You are great. I respect You. However, You cannot apply Your accomplishment as pressure on people. I am now cultivating, learning Buddhism, and practicing the dharma without interruption for even one day. I have never slandered the Buddha. You must not misunderstand me, Dharma King!"

The Great-Cross Justice Dharma King said, "Ignorance and affliction can cause people to degenerate completely. You are so angry now, so you have already been pulled by the attachment to self and have deviated from cultivation. I will still say that you are a Buddhist taking false refuge. You are deceiving yourself."

"Now, you answer me honestly. You see the lack of unity and struggle among fellow brothers and sisters and keep that in your mind. Then you blame the Buddha Master and think that is the Buddha Master's fault. Just because of this, you have already departed from the refuge you took and are no longer a Buddhist. You are a worldly person wearing a monastic robe and no longer have one-hundred-percent sincerity toward the Buddha Master."

"An even more ignorant thought of yours is that you think that the Buddha Master should replace these monastics involved in conflicts at the home base with upper-level holy and virtuous people. You are too foolish and even have thoughts in your mind that would violate the law of cause and effect. You do not understand the relationship between causes and effects and the karmic conditions between them. Sakyamuni Buddha should have kicked out Devadatta and other disciples who did not behave well and replaced them with Bodhisattvas at the tenth stage or higher. In that case, how could you ever have the opportunity of learning great Buddha-dharma? You would be among those who should be replaced by H.H. Dorje Chang Buddha III. You are a stupid person. Quickly generate the recognition and knowledge of truth from your inside!"

"The causality, results, and karmas since beginningless time existing among fellow brothers and sisters, the intercrossing between good and bad, as well as the conflicting inductions and retributions are relationships involving causality and cultivation. What do these have to do with the Buddha Master, H.H. Dorje Chang Buddha III? Why don't you blame Sakyamuni Buddha? Why don't you blame Kuan Yin Bodhisattva? Why don't you think that these are caused by Kuan Yin Bodhisattva, since they are practicing the mantras of Kuan Yin Bodhisattva and the mantras have not empowered them to cultivate well?"

"You must clearly wake up to one point. The Buddha Master can only teach and transform them according to the available karmic conditions. The non-conformity of their cultivation and behavior to the Buddha Master's teaching and transformation has nothing to do with the Buddha Master. There are many people of this kind in Buddhism. Otherwise why would there be public announcements reminding people over and over again? That means they have been treating the announcements as mere wind blowing by the ears or as birds flying by upon hearing and reading them. The Buddha Master has already used all possible means to teach the disciples."

"The situation is similar to Sakyamuni Buddha's teaching and transforming of the five hundred bhiksus and some small Bodhisattvas. Many of them simply treated what the Buddha said as wind blowing by the ears and did not listen to the teaching. They continued to do what they were used to. This was due to the problems in their good roots and karmic forces, which confined them. That is why there was the lesson of visiting Dorje Chang Buddha II, Venerable Vimalakirti, when He was ill. Could their conduct be Sakyamuni Buddha's problem? Your thinking already means you are a person blocked by karmic hindrance."

"Now I'll remind you of one more problem. The fellow brothers and sisters you deal with do not get along well with one another. Is this true? This is not what they should do and is not the conduct of cultivators, right?"

I replied, "Of course that is not the conduct of a cultivator and goes absolutely against cultivation. However, I have been very careful in this regard. I do not mix with them to cause conflicts."

The Great-Cross Justice Dharma King said, "Actually you are even more terrible than they. They are just having conflicts among fellow brothers and sisters, but they do not slander the Buddha as you have. Blaming the Buddha for other people's impure karma from their speech and conduct is a very bad way of slandering the Buddha! Do you dedicate your three karmas of body, speech, and mind to relying on the Buddha Master every day? I will answer this for you. No. You take fellow brothers' and sisters' non-conformity to the dharma and not acting according to the teaching as reasons to doubt whether the Buddha Master is a Buddha or not. Your big, notorious sin is created right at that moment. This is a worse sin than the conflicts existing among fellow brothers and sisters."

"How stupid and naïve are you really? It is preposterous. When the Buddha Master asked you about certain matters, you even lied to deceive the Buddha Master. As a person who lied to deceive H.H. Dorje Chang Buddha III, which Buddha, Bodhisattva, or yidam dare accept you who had the record of deceiving the Buddha? Which yidam would be willing to take you in the decision by selection as a qualified disciple for the dharma? They absolutely will not do wrong with regard to the law of cause and effect. Then how could you have beneficial effects from the dharma. How would you be able to learn great dharma? Consequently, how could you attain accomplishment and liberation?"

"You do not even realize that you are even more detestable than your fellow brothers and sisters. You are like a pile of dog poo but you think of others as being stinky. Why haven't you discovered that you are in the same category as some brothers and sisters? This is like a crow seeing a pig as black but not seeing itself as even blacker than the pig."

"Additionally, the self-centered view and selfish behaviors that you inherently have are also worthy of your introspection and contemplation. Let us start from some little things. When you are not on duty, you are not willing to help others to do things. Even when people ask you to just open the door, you do not want to help. Then where are the four limitless states of mind in you? Just because of this attitude, you will not learn the great dharma. This is because any great dharma is controlled by the yidam who makes the decision from selection. Could people like that be in the world of Buddhas and Bodhisattvas?"

"Your vision is so narrow. You only see that you have not learned the great dharma. Why don't you see that some famous venerable ones and dharma kings also have not learned the great dharma? The reason is that they have not taken true refuge just like you haven't. I'll tell you clearly. The world of Buddhas and Bodhisattvas does not accept people who take false refuge and engage in false cultivation because people in the world of Buddhas and Bodhisattvas are all holy ones."

"Today, I only talk about you in these aspects. There are problems in other aspects of your cultivation and conduct as well, but these are enough reasons already. How could you possibly say that you do not understand why you have not learned a great dharma yet? You now understand, right?"

"You should clearly know that no person who doubts the Buddha can be found in the world of Buddhas and Bodhisattvas, not even one. This is similar to the fact that there is no pig or dog in the population of humans since the mentality, shape, and structure of pigs or dogs are simply not that of a human. On the other hand, a human's mentality, structure, speech, and conduct are not the mentality, structure, speech, and conduct of Buddhas and Bodhisattvas."

"As another example, say the sand in the Ganges River is pure sand, and the mud and sand in the worldly rivers is sand mixed with mud. To turn the sand mixed with mud into pure sand, the mud in the sand must be washed away. Then the sand will become pure and be in the same category as pure sand. "

"To enter the world of Buddhas and Bodhisattvas, one has to become one in the realm of Buddhas and Bodhisattvas. Then one must truly take refuge and truly cultivate oneself. In particular, when facing Buddhas and Bodhisattvas, one must eliminate all thoughts, deeds, and languages that belong to evil karmas. One should cultivate one's character and substance to match that of Buddhas and Bodhisattvas. Only then can one have the realization power and accomplishments of Buddhas and Bodhisattvas."

I felt that the Great-Cross Justice Dharma King's discourse made great sense. My cultivation and conduct were truly driven by such mentality to cause me to fall into the situation of taking false refuge. I even thought that I was smart and had the ability to analyze. Actually I was not pious at all. I was very piteous!

Although I knew that the Buddha Master is the true incarnation of an ancient Buddha, sometimes I still treated the Buddha Master with worldly views. Even though it was only a very brief flash in my mind and I adjusted and repented right away, the adjustment was forcefully done in mind after all.

For example, although I attended many holy dharma assemblies, impure karmas were still produced by my shortcomings in the form of tiny thoughts. All would reduce the level of purity of my three karmas toward Buddha-dharma. I could not find what my problems were and even blamed the Buddha Master for not being merciful to me and not teaching me great dharma. Why did the Buddha Master teach other people but not me, showing differential treatment?

In another instance, when many dharma kings, regent dharma kings, and rinpoches had recognized the Buddha Master as H.H. Dorje Chang Buddha III, I happily added my praises with an excitement that was difficult to describe in words. I was very respectful toward the Buddha Master, Who then appeared to me like a Buddha in every aspect. However, when the extremely few dharma king(s) or rinpoche(s), who had lost morality and had the nature of ordinary people, denied that they had written their recognition documents, I immediately generated unkind thoughts with impure karma toward the Buddha Master, and even contemplated who was telling the truth after all.

Actually I was already very terrible. The Buddha Master was an extremely great holy and virtuous one with the supreme wisdom of prajna. How could He intend to forge a false recognition by anyone? The Buddha Master made it very clear that we were in the age of the internet. Any falsification involving celebrities would be exposed within two days after the news was published on the internet. Then you could be sued in court. Doing so, doubtlessly, would be like looking for trouble, looking for bad luck, and looking for disaster for yourself. Even if the party involved was not famous, pirating other people's names to elevate one's own status would be quickly found out once the contents were published on the internet. Doing so would land one in jail as well.

The Buddha Master often taught us that we should be truthful in doing anything and must not falsely fabricate. In these many years, we saw the Buddha Master's sublime morality that was extremely clear and pure. I could say that no one else could be compared. It was true that no heavyweight person in Buddhism was any comparison. I was speaking from my heart. Then how could the thoughts carrying impure karma toward the Buddha Master emerge in my mind? That meant I truly did not recognize the Buddha Master in my inner and deep mind.

What the Great-Cross Justice Dharma King told me brought up many feelings in me. This was truly my fatal flaw. I beseeched the Great-Cross Justice Dharma King to teach me how I could remove the inferior worldly views in me, and how I could truly grow the correspondence of the three karmas naturally, to become one with the clear and pure correspondence of the three karmas.

The Great-Cross Justice Dharma King said, "To achieve the clear and pure correspondence of the three karmas and become one who has truly taken refuge, you must solve the problem fundamentally. Your recognition and knowledge about the Buddha Master should not be superstitious and, rather, should be based on rationality and reality. That means the absolutely true recognition and knowledge that is not just based on the recognitions, congratulations, and praises of those many dharma kings and rinpoches. The Buddha Master is truly a Buddha, but being recognized by these documents of recognition does not necessarily determine that He is a true Buddha. Even if these recognitions do not exist, you cannot say that He is not a Buddha. A Buddha has the enlightenment capacity of a Buddha. We must recognize and know a true Buddha based on the Buddha's actual enlightenment capacity."

"As an analogy, let's assume that the Buddha is pure gold, that dharma kings, venerable ones, and great rinpoches are brass, and that ordinary people are rusty iron. The nature and elements of these three metals are completely different. If you apply the same color to cover these three pieces of metals, no difference can be seen. However, you must be clearly aware that, although these three things have been colored the same and cannot be distinguished from one another by their external appearances, gold is gold and is not brass. Brass absolutely is not gold. It is not necessary to appraise the gold before it is gold, because gold is gold by itself and brass is brass. You cannot say that a piece of gold that is not appraised would become brass or a piece of appraised brass is gold."

"The realities of gold and brass are not determined by appraisals. The differences between them are that they have their own weight, nature, and elements. The fact of whether one is a Buddha or not is determined by the truth. A Buddha is a Buddha even without undergoing the process of being recognized. Conversely, one who is not a Buddha is not a Buddha even if recognized as such since a Buddha's holy realization and state of enlightenment are completely different from the content, structure, and realization of dharma kings and venerable ones. Therefore, the Buddha Master absolutely does not need the recognition or non-recognition of any dharma king or rinpoche. This is similar to the situation of gold, brass, and rusty iron. Regardless of being appraised by an appraiser or not, pieces of these three materials still have their own individual weight, contents, and nature. Gold is gold, and brass is brass."

"Sakyamuni Buddha did not have even one recognition document. However, He is a true Buddha. A Buddha is not elected by any documents of recognition and, rather, is determined by His inherently perfect enlightenment capacity."

"Just looking at Our Buddha Master, H.H. Dorje Chang Buddha III, from the angle of causality, His many enlightenment capacities and accomplishments are unprecedented. What I am trying to say is that retribution from causality and the manifestation of causality are scientific, following us just like a shadow following the body and never having the slightest deviation."

"For example, the accomplishment of a Bodhisattva at the second stage cannot be achieved by a Bodhisattva at the first stage. On the other hand, the accomplishment of a great Bodhisattva is not sufficient enough to be compared with that of a Bodhisattva at the level of universal enlightenment or wonderful enlightenment. The accomplishment of a Buddha is absolutely not what a great Bodhisattva can do. All will be exhibited in worldly phenomena and manifested in the dharma realm in the form of causality. Whatever knowledge, accomplishments, and achievements all come from cultivation and practice since the beginningless time and are manifestations of the induction and retribution from causality."

"If one is a Buddha, then the accomplishments and achievements manifested by the Buddha in this world are absolutely not what the achievements manifested by a great Bodhisattva can reach. Simply speaking, the Buddha's wisdom is absolutely much higher than that of a great Bodhisattva. The Buddha's abilities are absolutely much greater than a great Bodhisattva's abilities. The Buddha's enlightenment capacity is absolutely superior to the holy realization of a great Bodhisattva. Therefore, the Buddha shows the strongest performance in all aspects in the world."

"You can reflect upon H.H. Dorje Chang Buddha III's accomplishments in the Five Vidyas. Who can win by comparison from ancient time until now? Has there been a holy and virtuous one who surpasses His Holiness the Buddha? Also, if you look at the dharmas as well as sutras and commentaries that the Buddha Master expounds, which patriarch master or holy and virtuous one throughout history to the present time has achieved the unimpeded perfection that the Buddha Master has demonstrated? Regardless of any sutra, any commentary, or any dharma, there is not one that the Buddha Master cannot explain with proficiency."

"I'll ask you another question. Throughout history, whose discourse on the ultimate truth of prajna that you read is as clear and thorough as the discourse expounded by the Buddha Master? There isn't even one. From ancient time till now, not even one extremely holy and virtuous patriarch master comparable to the Buddha Master can be found. In history, not even one Buddhist figure that surpassed the Buddha Master ever appeared. The fact can be shown just in terms of the achievements in causality. If H.H. Dorje Chang Buddha III were not a Buddha, could people inferior to Him be a Buddha?"

"Now let us talk about the holy states manifested by His enlightenment capacity. Take for example the various initiations that manifested unlimited mighty power and holy states, if not a Buddha, who can reach that level? Also, the disciples taught by Him have had such high accomplishments; many of them have achieved holy capacities that transcend the mundane."

"Of course all of these could be denied and negated by people. Taking the dharma of tummo concentration for example, there were stupid ones who declared that heat could be generated by putting an electro-magnetic stove behind one's back and a piece of iron in front of one's belly. This was really an unscientific statement to deceive people. First, heat cannot be transmitted across the thickness of a human body by an electromagnetic stove. Secondly, even if you press your palms on the electromagnetic stove and then put a piece of iron on the palm, no heat can be transmitted to the back of the palm. The reason is that the human body will block the heat wave from the electromagnetic stove."

"These people, who represent the gangs and syndicates of evil spirits and demons, lack true abilities and can only recourse to attacking and slandering others to cover up their inability. When they have time, they just like to make up things to delude people. It is piteous that hell is expecting their arrival. People can verify this fact by doing an experiment with an electromagnetic stove for themselves.

I said, "Those people were talking nonsense! There was a time when nothing was put on Kaichu Rinpoche's belly and an infrared heat sensor aimed directly at his belly. The measured temperature was 197.4°F. When Mozhi Rinpoche was practicing the dharma, a porcelain plate was put on his belly, not an iron plate. Many dharma kings and rinpoches were scorched. Those rinpoches who were scorched all took oaths against severe consequences to guarantee that this was a true fact. I was an eye witness at the site on that day. If this were not a true fact, would every one of them take an oath against severe consequences? This dharma assembly was video-recorded. The evidences were iron clad and witnessed by all who were present. People all saw it. There were too many people who made up lies about these events even though the facts were clearly present! Those who told these lies will be caused to descend into the uninterrupted hell!"

The Great-Cross Justice Dharma King continued, "They will descend into the uninterrupted hell. However, we should not scold them. They are all living beings. We should chant the Buddha's name for them, to pray for their wellbeing. When thinking about pity for others, we should also shine light on and inspect ourselves. Perhaps we are even more stupid and more terrible than others."

I said, "The effect of tummo concentration can be proven. However, some people had other questions like: When Kaichu Rinpoche was receiving the initiation of 'Xian Liang Great Perfection,' he entered the world of rainbow body within one hour. This could only be stated verbally and could not be seen by others. How can this be proven?"

The Great-Cross Justice Dharma King said, "I cannot speak for this. You can go and ask Kaichu Rinpoche!"

At that time, the Great-Cross Justice Dharma King called out loudly to ask Kaichu Rinpoche to come over. He said, "Kaichu Rinpoche! Please come! We have a question for you! Evil spirits and swindlers questioned your 'Xian Liang Great Perfection.' They said you were lying. This will affect living beings' cultivation."

Kaichu Rinpoche said, "Buddha-dharma is for self-cultivation and does not need to be argued about with demonic and evil people. Today, the venerable and honored Great-Cross Justice Dharma King wants me to testify for 'Xian Liang Great Perfection.' Considering the fact that living beings are deluded by them, I will testify with my entire being from the beginningless time to eternity. I hereby take an oath against severe consequences."

"When the Buddha Master was holding the initiation of state practice of 'Xian Liang Great Perfection,' in no more than one hour, I entered into the five-colored bright world of rainbow body in Buddha-land. Several years have passed since that moment. In daytime or at night, I can enter into the Buddha-land of rainbow body right away at any time I wish. This is the accomplishment that I have already realized."

"If I lied, not only I would descend into the uninterrupted hell, but also my family including my son, daughter, and grandson would all meet with evil retributions and suffer forever without happiness and joy and would only be in misery until eternity. If what I said here today are all true facts, they not only will not meet evil retributions but also will enjoy perfect good fortune and be happy forever."

"Buddhist disciple Kaichu takes this solemn oath in front of all Buddhas and Bodhisattvas, dharma protectors in the sky, and all gods and deities. May induction and retribution come soon as I have pledged. Now my oath is complete."

"What I just did should have satisfied these evil spirits and swindlers! Do they dare to take oaths on their own speech and conduct? They dare not! No one dares take an oath for what is false. This is like the situation of Sakya Trizin. He lied and then dared not go to the temple to take an oath with the monastics, since taking an oath against severe consequences on what is false will cause one to meet serious retribution in the end."

The Great-Cross Justice Dharma King said, "We are not going to discuss these powers of realization. Anyone can be attacked and slandered by people who make up stories. Let's put all these aside. I just want to mention a few things for you to verify and prove. Then you can recognize the fact that our Buddha Master is a true Buddha. Upon recognizing the proofs, you will know from your inner heart that H.H. Dorje Chang Buddha III, is a true Buddha."

"The first verification of proof: The sky was completely clear at the holy Buddha-bathing dharma assembly. However, the day before, the Buddha Master said, 'There will be big winds rolling in tomorrow. Therefore, you should plant the curtain poles firmly.' At the beginning of practicing the dharma on that day, the weather was completely cloudless and the hot Sun was high in the sky. There was not even any wind. After the start of beseeching all heavens, a fierce wind suddenly came in less than a minute. The curtain poles were almost broken. If the wind was not called by the Buddha, would ordinary people be able to invoke the wind? You should think carefully about this fact."

"When practicing the dharma of invoking dharma protectors in all heavens, heavenly deities suddenly arrived in the sky. Astonishing thunders struck with explosive sounds. This was a time when the sky was clear everywhere and the hot Sun was shining. How could the explosions of thunder arise and roaring thunder roll? If not invoked by a Buddha, who else could have the ability to do so? You should think carefully about this fact also."

"Moreover, dharma protectors were invited to manifest the Vajra form in the Buddha-bathing pond. If not invoked by a Buddha, who else could invoke Mahakala Vajra to demonstrate miraculous transformations in the Buddha-bathing pond? The scene was witnessed by people with their own eyes."

"The Buddha-bathing pond weighed more than 4,000 pounds and could not be lifted by fourteen people. However, the Buddha Master designated two disciples to lift it up. If they were not disciples taught by the Buddha, how could an elderly person and a young person lift such a weight? Just this Buddha-bathing pond can provide the proof. What else can be questioned? These facts are worthwhile considering more carefully. Aren't these only accomplishable by a Buddha? How can these possibly be achieved by human efforts?"

"The second proof: Only the Buddha Master is the extremely holy one who truly has the purpose of benefiting all living beings. Just look at today's world, which patriarch master have you seen take action to clean up his or her organization from inside? In contrast, the Buddha Master never thinks about Himself and only thinks about benefiting, helping, and liberating living beings. To prevent living beings from being cheated and harmed, His Holiness the Buddha keeps cleaning up figures at the levels of elder masters within the inner circle including dharma kings, venerable ones, great rinpoches, and great dharma masters who are reincarnations of patriarch masters by teaching and transforming them rigorously and informing cultivators how to appraise and recognize them. People are alerted not to be fooled by using the 128 Evil and Erroneous Views to evaluate masters. In the public announcements and statements from the Office of H.H. Dorje Chang Buddha III, there have been a lot of content in this regard. Who dares to clean up one's inner circle this way? Only His Holiness the Buddha dares to clean up His inner circle for the benefit of living beings without worrying about His own dharma kings, rinpoches, and dharma masters collapsing and without making the effort of strengthening His power base. Whereas, all other big figures would protect their inner circles by praising and promoting one another. In order to protect the inner circle and present a colorful, pleasant image, they never criticize the conduct of impure karma by people at the level of masters. They do not care about the fact that living beings are being poisoned and deluded. Why don't you think about this fact? Other than the Buddha, who else is unselfishly doing such things?"

"The third proof: One day, in the afternoon, the wind was just starting to blow. The Buddha Master said, 'Stop talking! Hail will be coming right away.' About ten seconds after the Buddha Master's speech, hail did fall. The size was about that of a pellet. It stopped after a few minutes. The surrounding area was covered by a whole layer of hail. What superior human scientific means are capable of making such a prediction?"

I said, "I was present and witnessed this event!"

"Don't interrupt me!" The Great-Cross Justice Dharma King said. Then, He continued, "Moreover, the hail covered the whole ground. At that time, the Buddha Master used a stick to draw a circle on the ground. When all hail pellets melted, the ones inside the circle that the Buddha Master had drawn still did not. What did all these phenomena mean? If not by a Buddha, can a Bodhisattva do this?"

"The fourth proof: People washed the dharma bowl for holding nectars clean and then were watching on the spot to guard the nectar bowl. Meanwhile, H.H. Dorje Chang Buddha III invoked Buddhas to come from the vast sky to bestow nectar. Didn't this prove He is a Buddha? Could a Bodhisattva invoke Buddhas? This event of the Buddha bestowing nectar was seen by many with eyes wide open. Other than a Buddha, who could invoke Buddhas to bestow nectar?"

"The fifth proof: When a group of people including Ven. Elder Dharma Master Wu Ming, Ven. Elder Monk Yi Zhao, and others were receiving the initiation of sprinkling nectar from the Buddha Master, the Buddha Master unexpectedly said, 'In a short while, a million Yellow Jackets will come in the sky. However, they will not bite to hurt you.

You can take it easy.' When the dharma was practiced, a million Yellow Jackets did come and were right above people's heads. They did not bite or hurt even one person. Could this be done by an ordinary person? Would an ordinary person dare to let people stay under the Yellow Jackets?"

"The Yellow Jacket is the most venomous or deadly kind of bee in the world. Moreover, they particularly like to bite people. In a situation of Yellow Jackets flying in a crowd of people and a million Yellow Jackets being present above people's heads, any person could have been killed by a million Yellow Jackets. They are called Yellow Jackets and are notorious for stinging and biting people. Only two or three Yellow Jackets could cause a person to die, not to mention such an enormous presence of Yellow Jackets covering the entire sky! Just this fact was not achievable by a human effort, and could only be accomplished by a Buddha! Even a most stupid idiot would clearly understand that this could only be done by a very great Buddha or Bodhisattva."

"The sixth proof: I only mention the fact that 'What Is Cultivation' and the two great mind essences of The Supreme and Unsurpassable Mahamudra of Liberation, 'Contemplating the Magnificence of Perfect Prerequisite Oceanic Mind Essence' and 'the Most Magnificent Bodhi Dakini Oceanic Mind Essence,' clearly revealed the Buddha's nature. Additionally, the 128 Evil and Erroneous Views were provided to people as criteria for distinguishing what is right or wrong. If He were not a Buddha, could you downgrade Him to a great Bodhisattva?"

"From ancient times till now, who else can present this precious, concise, and yet perfect system of expounding the precepts and the dharma? There has never been one. Why don't you give some good thought to these facts? Why don't you make a comparison between the Buddha Master and those famous great dharma kings, great dharma masters, great rinpoches, and great venerable ones in today's world? Can you think of or find anyone who has one-third of the Buddha Master's holy capacity and accomplishments? Even if you think for days and nights, you will not come up with any Buddhist figure for comparison. The reason is that there isn't any great virtuous one in Buddhism who can be identified as comparable with the Buddha Master. There exists not even one! Isn't this a true fact?"

"Then, how do you measure and consider this utmost supreme Buddha? You have already been contaminated from inside. You hold onto impure karma that blocks your vision, desensitizes your heart, and causes you to expose your ignorance and black karma. How can your three karmas be pure and correct? Do you know that whenever the Buddha Master expounds the dharma, our mind and conduct are always involved? If mind and conduct are not correct, there will be no beneficial effects from learning any dharma. This is because every dharma has its own yidam. The yidam will not accept a person whose mind and conduct are not correct, because the yidam will bear the responsibility of causality. The yidam is responsible for applying His power to empower the person. Having empowered a bad person will add to His sin and negative karma."

"Therefore, among billions of people, not even one whose mind and conduct are not correct would successfully receive an initiation of state practice. This is mainly due to the fact that, in a holy initiation or an even higher initiation of state practice, the yidam and dharma protectors will be present in person to accept the disciple. If the disciple's mind and conduct are not correct, the yidam will not accept the disciple because He dares not accept. Therefore, the accomplishments from all dharmas must be established on mind and conduct and be carried out in upholding the precepts."

"If your mind, behavior, and upholding of the precepts are not up to a sufficient degree, even if you were taught the dharma through special circumstances, you still will not receive the benefits anyway. Additionally, any initiation of a great dharma must be done through the process of decision by selection. If one's cultivation and upholding of the precepts are not up to the standards, the yidam of the dharma will not approve it."

"For example, a dharma assembly was held to authorize some fellow brothers to conduct initiations of exoteric dharmas. Some brothers received quite a few dharmas. One of the brothers received some initiations of exoteric dharmas and learned some mantras and some dharmas. However, when he requested practicing 'the Great Perfection' and 'the Phowa Dharma,' because his cultivation and conduct at that time did not reach the required merit for practicing the dharmas he requested, the Buddha Master told him that his affinity with the dharma was not mature yet. However, he kept requesting over and over. The Buddha Master relented and conducted the selection for him."

"When the Buddha Master reached out to take the letters of petition for 'the Great Perfection' and 'the Phowa Dharma,' within just one or two seconds, a very strong tornado started all of a sudden. The whirlwind went into the dharma bowl containing dozens of dharma books and letters of petition and dredged up and removed both 'the Great Perfection' and 'the Phowa Dharma' from the bottom. People saw the two letters of petition get buried in the underbrush. All other dharma books and letters of petition were not moved out of the bowl. This whole process was video-recorded."

"However, the Buddha Master still let this rinpoche brother take back these two letters of petition from the underbrush and held the selection of learning the dharma for this brother. As soon as the selection got started, a round of wind came again. The result from the selection also indicated 'affinity with the dharma not mature.' Although the brother learned some dharma that day, he did not receive the two dharmas he requested. Also, the sudden winds were very strong, making even big trees waver left and right."

I said, "I was present on that day and saw that with my own eyes."

The Great-Cross Justice Dharma King said, "If you are not up to the standard of corresponding to the dharma, the yidam of the dharma will not approve you and will not accept you. That is why you have not gotten to learn great dharma. You have to rationally and clearly recognize the Buddha Master's true enlightenment capacity of a Buddha. Then you can prevent the thoughts of impure karma from arising. Only then can you truly take refuge and cultivate with your three karmas in true correspondence."

"Today, you do not even admit that you took false refuge. Why don't you think about the six true verifications of proof that I mentioned? Our Buddha Master has accomplished all of these. Just think about how great, utmost high, and supreme our Buddha Master is. Once you do that, even if now He is a handicapped person or a beggar, or has the appearance of an idiot, He is still in real essence the utmost high and great Buddha."

"Once you become clear in this aspect and always remember these key points, you will truly recognize that your master is a true Buddha. Whatever He does will no longer appear like ordinary to you."

"How can ordinary people totally understand the Buddha's selfless perfect enlightenment capacity? If you had not hidden like a thief under the offering table at Hua Zang Si, you would still regard the Buddha Master as a disciple of Tangtong Gyalpo Rinpoche today! You would not know that even Master Padmasambhava had recommended Tangtong Gyalpo Rinpoche to quest for great dharma from the Buddha Master. You should deeply ponder about this!"

"Arhats have accomplishments at the Arhat's levels of fruit. Bodhisattvas have the states of realization defined by Bodhisattva's stages. A Buddha has the enlightenment capacity of a Buddha. We shall recognize and know a true Buddha from the Buddha's actual enlightenment capacity. As a matter of fact, H.H. Dorje Chang Buddha III has perfectly achieved the true accomplishment and status in both worldly dharmas and transcendental dharmas. There has been no second patriarch master, dharma king, venerable one, great rinpoche, great dharma master, or great layperson that is comparable. In terms of transcendental dharmas, all His accomplishments demonstrate the enlightenment capacity of a Buddha. There is no dharma king, rinpoche, or great dharma master who could be on a par."

"Speaking from the worldly dharmas, dharma kings and rinpoches in the world wrote their recognitions, corroborating recognitions, and congratulations. Although the Buddha Master thought that these recognitions were meaningless to Him and could not represent the nature of reality, these dharma kings, venerable ones, and rinpoches did seriously and earnestly write these documents. Resolution No. 614 of the Senate of the United States Congress also used the title of H.H. Dorje Chang Buddha III. You can also see from the report published by a newspaper in Washington, DC that H.H. Dorje Chang Buddha III not only has the accomplishment of a Buddha and not only has been recognized as a Buddha in Buddhist circles, but also was addressed as H.H. Dorje Chang Buddha III in the Senate's Resolution. The government gave Him the statuary title of H.H. Dorje Chang Buddha III. This is also not achieved by any dharma king, rinpoche, venerable one, dharma master in history. In other words, with the exception of Sakyamuni Buddha, this is unprecedented by any person ever before."

"Actually, there are too many examples to cite. I would like to mention the following facts in particular to show that these ironclad accomplishments of the enlightenment capacity of the Buddha, cannot be achieved by Bodhisattvas. Let me ask you:"

"If not a Buddha, who can summon Mahakala Vajra to arrive at the scene to let people all see?"

"If not a Buddha, who can invoke Buddhas to bestow nectar from the sky into the bowl and let all people at the site see?"

"If not a Buddha, who can forecast the arrival of one million birds and then let people all see the fact a while later?"

"If not a Buddha, who can let a person tour the World of Ultimate Bliss first and then return here to prepare for ascending there?"

"If not a Buddha, who can make a knife wound heal with flesh grown back in three hours and let people see the fact?"

"If not a Buddha, who dares forecast the arrival of one million Yellow Jackets and let people see the scene?"

"If not a Buddha, who can let a non-sentient thing transform as told and let people see the scene on the spot?"

"If not a Buddha, who can make a person who had been received by Amitabha Buddha to stay and be revived, as seen by all people at the site?"

"If not a Buddha, who can reverse an aged appearance to that of a youth after a little over ten minutes as witnessed by people with their own eyes?"

"If not a Buddha, who can solve all problems and answer all questions?"

"If not a Buddha, who can be unmatched in the Five Vidyas and unprecedentedly and singlehandedly achieve accomplishments in the thirty major categories?"

"If not a Buddha, who can forecast the coming hail which started right after and also draw a circle to keep hail pellets inside the circle from melting?"

"If not a Buddha, who can create artworks that cannot be duplicated and even place mist from the sky into a sculpture, which is now on exhibit to the public at the International Art Museum of America."

"If not a Buddha, who can, during a trip to Taiwan, write predictions of all events that day in a tour of more than 500 miles that the group experienced without any discrepancy?"

"If not a Buddha, could His disciples who received initiations of state practice be all holy ones with unmatched abilities?"

"If not a Buddha, could His disciples of eminent monks who passed away have almost all realized the state of non-decomposing flesh body and even emitting rainbow lights?"

"If not a Buddha, how could the white clouds instantly drop to the top of a tree and manifest the Sambhogakaya form of Dorje Chang Buddha?"

"If not a Buddha, who can apply unlimited great compassion to bear living beings' suffering and bestow good fortune and happiness to others?"

"You answer me, who can accomplish these holy capacities and states of enlightenment?"

I said, "Ordinary people or Arhats cannot do these. Bodhisattvas can't either. Absolutely only a Buddha can do these." Then, I also said, "The holy states manifested by the Buddha Master were so many. I saw so many of them, a lot more than these."

Figure 27-1–News report about the Senate of the United States Congress unanimously passing without dissent its Resolution No. 614 on December 12, 2012 that celebrates H.H. Dorje Chang Buddha III's being awarded the Top Honor Prize of the World Peace Prize, published in the Washington Chinese News on January 12, 2013

The Great-Cross Justice Dharma King said, "You don't need to say these flattering words. It is still useless even if you say a lot more because you treat them as clouds seen by the eyes and wind blowing by the ears and will totally forget them all. You just need to hold onto these examples of "Who can do so if not a Buddha" facts that I have mentioned. Hold onto them tightly and think back whenever you need to use them as the fine medicine to cure your illness of dark hindrance. They are also the fine medicine for curing anyone's hindrance of doubt and dark karma."

"Once you have such awareness and become totally clear, then everything will be clear. It is not a question of repenting in front of the Buddha statue and verbally saying you will correct yourself. This is a question that you must clearly understand in your inner self. You have to truly experience, recognize, and introspect this way. Once you achieve this, your mind will truly be calmed down. Whenever demonic hindrances arise, you will think about these facts, and think about my questions to you and my reminder to you, which is also the reminder to all cultivators. Doing so will be more effective and more powerful than any powerful mantra. Only then, will you not be constrained by your demonic hindrance. Your knowledge and views will become correct."

At this moment during the Great-Cross Justice Dharma King's discourse, I suddenly recalled a past memory, which was the magnificent state I saw at the time of attending the dharma-protecting night-guarding duty in the early morning shortly after I had started at the home base. In the sky right above the offering table, an extremely solemn and majestic Buddha emitting five-colored golden light rays appeared. Now I know that I saw the Buddha Master's true Sambhogakaya form, Dorje Chang Buddha, at that time. I did not realize for so many years that the true Buddha had already appeared for me long ago!

After listening to the Great-Cross Justice Dharma King's discourse, I felt extremely ashamed. Using these key points for verification and analysis, I became aware that I simply was not a Buddhist with the three karmas clear, pure, and in correspondence. I was just an idiot. No wonder I did not have beneficial effects. I finally discovered the horrible hidden peril in me. At the same time, my karmic hindrance began to be vanquished. Thinking about the six verifications of proof reminded to me by the Great-Cross Justice Dharma King, plus the seventh, the scene that I saw while hiding under the offering table at Hua Zang Si, and this series of facts of "if not a Buddha, who can?" I woke up. The question really is: if not a Buddha, who can do these with human efforts?

I finally stood up from this awakening. My body and mind suddenly felt extremely light and delighted. For seven whole days, I stayed in constant joy with a purified self. Suddenly, one morning, the Buddha Master said, "Zheng Hui, your good roots matured! I am going to conduct an initiation of state practice for you, to transmit a profound great dharma to you!"

Heavens! It turns out that the difference between whether one can learn Buddha-dharma or not is just the separation from it by hindrance. It is a question of whether the refuge one has taken is true or false, and whether the correspondence of one's three karmas is true or false. After that, the Buddha Master held an initiation of state practice just for me.

28

True Buddha-Dharma Cannot Be Acquired and Learned with False and Untrue Conduct

No matter how high you are or what great fame and status you may have, even if you have the title of a great dharma king, a great venerable one, a great rinpoche, or a great dharma master, it is still very difficult for you to learn true Buddha-dharma. First, the great dharma of Tathagata is not easy to find. The true great dharma of Tathagata is simply and certainly not what a great dharma king, a great venerable one, a great rinpoche, or a great dharma master has. The question is where Buddha-dharma is and who has the true dharma.

It is necessary to find a great holy and virtuous one who truly possesses the great dharma of Tathagata. That is very difficult. It is hard to find even one out of 100,000 rinpoches and dharma masters. Therefore, it is even more difficult than retrieving a needle lost in the ocean.

According to what I have seen in real life, it is not true that every famous venerable one, dharma king, rinpoche, or dharma master possesses true Buddha-dharma. Actually, they still need to search for the great dharma of Tathagata. Basically, the dharma kings, venerable ones, great rinpoches, and great dharma masters who are known to have Buddha-dharma and lineages of great dharma of Tathagata only have a Buddha-dharma that is ineffective. Holders of true Buddha-dharma cannot be identified just based on holding a lineage. At the home base of H.H. Dorje Chang Buddha III, I have seen very many dharma kings, venerable ones, and famous lineage holders. I do not see that they possess true Buddha-dharma. People have all kinds of experiences on the path of learning the dharma. These include sorrow, bitterness, torment of time, and possibly happiness. You should be prepared to taste them all. In the end, you still have to caution that Buddha-dharma is not there.

Even if you have found a holder of Buddha-dharma, would you be able to pass the test given without notice? The most important fact is that any genuine Buddha-dharma is sure to be directly controlled by the yidam. Because the yidam cannot be deceived, you would not be able to learn the true great dharma of Tathagata by untrue acts. Both the great holy one who transmits the dharma and the yidam would be clearly aware of your falsification. The yidam absolutely will not accept anyone who commits falsification. Therefore, one would not be able to learn true Buddha-dharma by fraudulent acts. Simply speaking, all problems are created by one's self.

I spent twelve years learning the dharma but truly woke up to this fact only at the very end. To learn true Buddha-dharma, there mustn't be any false conduct. The outcome is controlled by one's own effort. One's fate can only be adjusted by one's self. Transmission of Buddha-dharma must be approved by the yidam.

Transmission of false Buddha-dharma and common Buddha-dharma does not require the decision by selection. However, in the case of transmitting true Buddha-dharma and, in particular, the Buddha-dharma of state practice or the Buddha-dharma that enables the disciple to attain accomplishment and see the holy state on the spot, the process of decision by selection is a must. All must go through this test.

The dharmas of decision by selection are classified into six types, including three types of exoteric/esoteric dharmas (common dharmas) and three types of holy dharmas (upper-level great dharmas).

The first three types are:

"Divination of Esoteric Buddhism"
"Drawing a Lot and Turning a Pill Across the Curtain""
"Casting a Flower into the Mandala"

These are common dharmas that belong to the category of exoteric dharmas but are often used by practitioners of esoteric Buddhism.

The following are the three types of holy dharmas:

"Vajra Selection"

"Selection Made in Dark Confinement from One-Hundred Dharmas to Choose the Door toward Enlightenment"

"Selection by Divine Forecasting"

The first three categories are not very accurate in selecting one's affinity to the dharma and rely completely on the Buddhist disciple's devotion and faith. The latter three categories are selections controlled by truly great holy and virtuous ones and extremely great holy and virtuous ones. It is very difficult to find one of these selections, especially the "Selection Made in Dark Confinement". As to the "Selection by Divine Forecasting", it is even more difficult to find than climbing to the sky. That requires the holy realization only possessed by an extremely great holy and virtuous one.

Additionally, the dharma of "Inquiry by a Flying Lot" is also used for selection. Actually this is not a regular dharma of decision by selection. The key of determining whether a selection of "Inquiry by a Flying Lot" is accurate or not depends on whether this dharma was conducted by a great holy and virtuous one or not. If done by a great holy and virtuous one, it will be accurate. If done by a small holy and virtuous one, the result will absolutely not be accurate. This is because a small holy and virtuous one could only invoke a small deity to issue the deity's flying-lot decree, rather than inviting a great deity who knows the causality.

Whether done by a great holy and virtuous one or a small holy and virtuous one, we must see whether the flying lot is just jumping at the same place or flying entirely into the sky. Jumping at the same place but not flying entirely into the sky means the result is absolutely not accurate, unless the dharma is conducted by a great holy and virtuous one at the level of Two Sun-Moon Wheels or higher, or a great holy and virtuous one who is capable of conducting "Vajra Selection." Then the result will be accurate. Therefore, "Inquiry by a Flying Lot" is not a regular dharma for selection or inquiry. Its accuracy depends on the level of the person who practices it for the disciple.

The dharmas of decision by selection that I am going to talk about today refer to selections in these categories of holy dharmas. To learn any great dharma of Tathagata, one must pass a test from these three categories of holy dharmas. There can be no exceptions. This barrier must be crossed.

There are also some dharmas that are rumored to be selections, such as "Inquiry by a Flying Lot," "Selection with Mani Stone," "Lot Drawing from Golden Vase," "Card Drawing Across the Curtain," and others. These are less accurate. Many of the people who underwent such selections later devolved.

I have experienced decisions by selection many times. I beseeched the dharma from H.H. Dorje Chang Buddha III many times. The Buddha Master almost always declined. Even when it was not a definite declination, I would be told, "Your affinity with the dharma is not mature yet. You are not able to learn this dharma."

Of course I was not convinced and the Buddha Master saw that. Sometimes seeing that I felt really sad and was unconvinced, the Buddha Master would immediately conduct the decision by selection for me and say, "You watch this! I am going to pray openly. The outcome will have nothing to do with me!" In the end, the yidam appeared and did not approve the dharma I requested. The answer was completely the same as that given by the Buddha Master. Therefore, if you want to learn true Buddha-dharma, you must first have the Buddha Master's approval. Only then would the yidam agree.

On real occasions, I saw many dharma kings, venerable ones, great rinpoches, and great dharma masters from all over the world. The Buddha Master told them, "You are not qualified to learn this so-and-so great dharma." Sure enough, the process of decision by selection showed that the yidam did not admit this person. Why was the outcome such? I specifically sought teaching from the Great-Cross Justice Dharma King about this.

The Great-Cross Justice Dharma King said, "You had such an idea because you saw that they didn't pass. However, you did not see that they were falsely cultivating with ordinary people's thinking. Sakyamuni

Buddha patiently taught cultivators to have the ten good virtues, the four limitless states of mind, and bodhicitta. If you measure them, do you see that they have all of those?"

"H.H. Dorje Chang Buddha III has told them over and over that they should remove self-centered views and attachment to self and unselfishly benefit living beings. They should not speak behind people's backs about rights and wrongs to belittle others and promote themselves. That is not the behavior of true cultivators. They should shine light on themselves to introspect and find their own shortcomings and should learn the conduct of Buddhas and Bodhisattvas. Did these kinds of people accomplish these?"

"They ignored the teachings of Sakyamuni Buddha and H.H. Dorje Chang Buddha III and continued to do what they wanted, with the flame of selfishness raging. Those who were masters but not holy and virtuous ones even slanderously commented on holy and virtuous masters, who passed the exam held with three masters and seven witnesses, behind their backs. Those who were holy and virtuous masters with the credential issued by three masters and seven witnesses should have set examples for others with their demeanor of holiness and virtue. On the contrary, they did not serve as role models to teach morality. Rather, they shamelessly exposed their lack of virtue to living beings and spread gossip about those who passed the exam of seven monastic masters and ten witnesses to insult more senior holy ones."

"These people did not think about their own realization. Without taking the exam proctored by seven monastic masters and ten witnesses, they were not in a position to comment on or gossip behind holy and virtuous ones who passed the exam proctored by seven monastic masters and ten witnesses. They did not have the mentality of feeling ashamed and becoming polite and respectful; rather, they shamelessly commented on the holy and virtuous ones who passed the exam proctored by seven monastic masters and ten witnesses. Doing so was turning the truth upside down, was opposite to basic morality, and belonged to the category of deeds committed by people with sin and dark karma."

"With such mentality of ordinary beings, can they be genuine dharma kings, venerable ones, great rinpoches, and great dharma masters? Can they represent the mind, conduct, and speech of an Arhat or a Bodhisattva? If they can and since they are so good at self-promotion, why don't they dare to take the exam proctored by seven monastic masters and ten witnesses to show the proof? Actually, some of them are not even as good as ordinary people who cultivate well without titles! If people at such levels can pass the decision by selection, the world of Buddhas and Bodhisattvas would be thrown into chaos. With such thinking as mentioned above, you are already within the domain of being unable to pass."

I only began to notice a fact when I became completely clear and aware. The Buddha Master knows everything about you and me. He knows what you and I are and whether we can learn a certain dharma or not. The yidam absolutely will not accept an unqualified disciple for the dharma of state practice. Let's take someone who is a master or a Buddhist disciple with good cultivation for example. Say, this person has lied to deceive people. Or this master has spoken falsely to deceive disciples for his own benefit, or this master has worked with his trusted accomplice(s) to create a scheme to profit him or herself and bring damage and loss to the disciple(s). The yidam will never let a person who has such speech and evil conduct pass the selection. The Buddha Master knows about this clearly. The yidam also is aware of everything. Therefore, this person will not be able to learn Buddha-dharma.

Additionally, you should be especially clear that affiliating with three or more of the 128 Evil and Erroneous Views will cause the yidam to reject you. Therefore, any false speech or conduct is just playing games, as in the world of ordinary people. The impediment of sin when seen by the Buddha and the yidam, will cause you the consequence of not getting the opportunity to learn true Buddha-dharma. That is why a holy and virtuous one determined by the exam proctored by seven monastic masters and ten witnesses will definitely be one who has true realization and will not be a false holy and virtuous one.

On the other hand, masters who do not have certificates of holiness and virtue really should cultivate earnestly. Status based on praise and boasting is a castle in the air after all, and will definitely collapse. The fact is that whatever is false will not be true, and whatever is true can't be false. Any person who has any false element in cultivation will not pass the decision by selection. The yidam will not approve it. In this aspect, I have very deep impressions from the setbacks I experienced!

Actually, the decision by selection is a very simple formality. However, its connotation embodies boundless wonders and is a sky-shaking event that must not be underestimated. At the scene, the extremely great holy and virtuous one would first conduct "the Dharma of Divine Forecasting" and publicly announce what dharma you will learn or what dharma you cannot learn. The forecast determines your affinity with the dharma. At this time, the verification immediately follows to see if the extremely great holy and virtuous one's prediction is true.

First, the dharmas to be learned are written on tens of pieces of paper that are of the same size, texture, and color. They are individually rolled and squeezed into nubs and thrown into a golden vase. After shaking, you will draw one nub out. When opened, its contents will be what has been forecasted by the extremely great holy and virtuous one with one-hundred-percent certainty. Then this piece of paper will again be rolled and squeezed into a nub and put into the golden vase. This process will be repeated continuously for two more times. The same piece will be selected for a total of three times. So the result is unquestionable and in complete agreement with the forecast by the extremely great holy and virtuous one. This is the official verification regarding the Dharma of Divine Forecasting.

Suppose this extremely great holy and virtuous one does not have the enlightenment capacity of Divine Forecasting. That would mean not possessing master's qualifications at the highest level of holy realization. If so, no one could be sure that you would draw the same piece for three consecutive times. The key is that, if you ever draw out a piece that is not the one in the forecast, the extremely great holy and virtuous one will be seen by people as a false extremely great holy and virtuous one. Therefore, whether the extremely great holy and virtuous one is true or false, and whether the dharma of decision by selection is true or false can be seen at a simple glance.

An extremely great holy and virtuous one is unselfish. If your affinity with the dharma has matured, the extremely great holy and virtuous one will tell you that the time for practicing a certain dharma has come. Once verified, the correspondence will be one-hundred-percent.

Through my continuous effort of beseeching, I experienced a number of decisions by selection. Every time, the result was accurate without any discrepancy. However, none had the great dharma that I wished to learn. The yidam of the great dharma did not approve me. I almost completely lost hope. However, I still had the mentality of rather giving up my life than the dharma. While I was at a loss as to what to do, I brought some questions to seek teaching from the Great-Cross Justice Dharma King. His discourse and counter questions made me feel extremely ashamed and caused me to wake up completely. I made up my mind and once again went to the Buddha Master to quest for the dharma.

The Buddha Master said, "Very good! Your awareness is thorough. However, you still need to strengthen yourself in two aspects. You should strengthen your cultivation and implementation of the two great mind essences of *The Supreme and Unsurpassable Mahamudra of Liberation,* and strengthen your comprehension and deepen your insight into *Expounding the Absolute Truth through the Heart Sutra* by reading them a few more times."

Then, I did so according to the Buddha Master's teaching. At this time, my longing of the past twelve years finally bloomed and bore fruit.

In 2013, I underwent the rigorous decision by selection conducted by my Buddha Master, H.H. Dorje Chang Buddha III. The yidam inspected my cultivation and my upholding of the precepts. Everything was finally settled. The Buddha Master conducted the selection. I was accepted by the yidam to enjoy the initiation of state practice of the dharma of "Xian Liang Great Perfection."

At three o'clock in the afternoon on that day, the Buddha Master held the initiation of state practice and transmitted the dharma of

"Xian Liang Great Perfection" in *The Supreme and Unsurpassable Mahamudra of Liberation* to me.

This dharma of "Xian Liang Great Perfection" surpassed the dharma of the "Mind Essence of Great Perfection," surpassed the dharma of the "Shortcut to the Mind Essence of Great Perfection," and surpassed the dharma of the "Shortcut to the Six Dharmas of the Profound Practice of Great Perfection." In summary, the Dharma of "Xian Liang Great Perfection" is a distinguished great dharma among great dharmas and surpassed all dharmas of Great Perfection. For example, the dharma of Great Perfection in esoteric Buddhism requires practicing for at least twelve years before getting the effect. If one's practice is not good enough, there wouldn't even be any correspondence. On the other hand, "Xian Liang Great Perfection" will lead to realizing the state at the time of initiation. That is why it is called "Xian Liang," meaning the actual capacity is displayed and the state is instantly manifested on the spot.

When the initiation started, because of my deep and heavy karmic hindrance, I only saw some normal shadows of light and could not enter the profound holy state. The Buddha Master, H.H. Dorje Chang Buddha III, saw this situation and knew that the path was blocked by my karmic force. Thus, the Buddha Master made an even stronger prayer request. However, I still did not enter into the state. At that time, I deeply questioned in my heart how I could be qualified to learn such a high dharma! Based on my speech and conduct of all these years, I was just a common person carrying black karma. From now on, I would no longer think that the problems were with the Buddha-dharma. Rather, events exactly proved that my cultivation and practice in daily life had truly been very bad.At this critical moment, the Buddha Master did not give up the initiation for me and told me, "Now I am going to do one last initiation of utmost-precious nectar to strengthen the force of empowerment."

When nectar was poured to the top of my head, my body felt a kind of indescribable magnificent feeling. It was too wonderful to describe in words. Several minutes passed. Suddenly, the sky cracked open. The curtain of this earth-shaking experience was pulled open. A green-colored state manifested before me. I no longer had the feeling of the existence of mind and body and was immersed in the state. The Buddha Master once had told me that his was the state manifested by Green Tara, for lighting up my path to the Buddha-land. Now, being involved in the leading green, I was quickly led into the Buddha-land. I finally entered the world of holy states. I succeeded!

My excitement was beyond description. I could only tell you that "it was amazingly magnificent." I am afraid of losing my realization power due to revealing the holy state. That is why I could not tell you everything about the holy state.

I saw all kinds of wonderful and extremely beautiful scenes of the Buddha-land that were changing and transforming in all possible auspicious ways. However, it was very pitiful that I was not able to recognize the names and characteristics there. In the state, I also saw four or five rows of characters written in navy blue color that disappeared quickly. I did not recognize the writing either. Then I saw a line of dark-green characters. I was able to recognize the words "twenty one" only. Before I could continue recognizing them, the characters had disappeared.

Let me state one more time that I could not reveal the more magnificent states to people in this world. At that time, I was chanting the secret mantra and forming the mudra in my hands. My body was very light and floating without feeling the weight. My entire body and mind were in the world of rainbow light. I was so blessed! This was the first time I saw the unprecedented holy state. I had succeeded!

After the Buddha Master had finished conducting the initiation and transmitting the dharma, the Buddha Master taught me the secret mantra and how to visualize and told me to close my eyes. I did and still saw the state. Then the Buddha Master let me open my eyes and I still saw the state. Thus, with my eyes either open or closed, I stayed in the state of Buddha-dharma. I truly tasted the endless flavors of the dharma and the supremely majestic and magnificent power from the initiation of state practice of "Xian Liang Great Perfection."

Before, I had thought that perhaps the Foreword titled "the Supremely Precious Voice of Good Fortune" written by several holy and virtuous ones was too grandiose and exaggerated in describing *Expounding the Absolute Truth through the Heart Sutra*. Today, the state of "Xian Liang Great Perfection" made me truly realize how ignorant and piteous I had been before. No work by ancient virtuous ones is comparable to *Expounding the Absolute Truth through the Heart Sutra* in terms of its greatness and profound wonders. "The Supremely Precious Voice of Good Fortune" depicted very accurately that, in its principle, in the opportunity it offers, and in its mantra, *Expounding the Absolute Truth through the Heart Sutra* is an utmost supreme dharma treasure for entering cultivation, becoming enlightened, and attaining accomplishment.

On the day when I wrote to this point, I was so moved that I broke down crying. Tears were all over my face. I can only say that the Buddha's Sect is Buddhism. True Buddha-dharma of Buddhism — the Buddha-dharma of state practice initiations in *The Supreme and Unsurpassable Mahamudra of Liberation* of the Buddha's Sect is the highest Buddha-dharma. It is very magnificent and very great, and truly cannot be compared with anything else.

What virtue and ability did I have that I could receive this distinguished great dharma among the great dharmas? The Buddha's kindness is so vast that I cannot describe it in words. All I can do is to be grateful from within to my utmost supreme great Buddha Master who manifests supreme and perfect enlightenment, to all Buddhas in the ten directions in the dharma realm, and to the yidam and dharma protectors of the dharma of "Xian Liang Great Perfection." I can never repay this great compassion and great virtue even if I exhaust my mind and body!

This ashamed bhiksuni who spent twelve years at the home base of H.H. Dorje Chang Buddha III now finally dares to state firmly that I have learned truly supreme Buddha-dharma. However, I am still very ashamed because the Buddha Master told me, "You should unrelentingly continue to be washed clean in this state of Buddha-dharma and elevate your realization to the level of flawlessness. Only then can you truly become a great holy one and be able to enlighten yourself as well as others." I bear in mind this teaching and will definitely uphold my conduct in accordance with this teaching.

As a monastic person, I must bear my responsibility to the law of cause and effect. I hereby take this earnest and serious oath:

"My Buddha Master held an initiation of state practice for me on a summer day in 2013, to transmit the dharma of 'Xian Liang Great Perfection' to me. It was true that, within two hours, I was led into the world of Buddha-land to realize the magnificent holy state. The circumstance and state that I mentioned above are all true facts. If there is anything untrue, I am willing to receive the retribution of suffering and descend into the uninterrupted hell and never get out. On the contrary, if what I said is all true, I dedicate all my merit to all living beings in the dharma realm, to let them leave suffering and obtain happiness, acquire perfect good fortune and wisdom, and attain enlightenment early to become liberated and accomplished."

I can only take this oath against severe consequences to testify that this book of *Revealing the Truth* that you read today is a true record of facts. Now, I must state the karmic conditions that led to this book's coming into being.

As early as 2011, I wrote a draft of a book titled *I Truly Met the Buddha*. I presented the manuscript of the entire book to the Buddha Master for review. After seeing the book's title and reading several chapters, the Buddha Master felt very disgusted and said, "What Buddha! What Buddha I am does not need your false flattery and inflated exaggeration. What you wrote is not factual. It is an exaggeration without a doubt. This is like gold plating my face and can be called flattering me with nonsense. Seeing such an act in the world of Buddhism, I feel ashamed of you. It is okay that you and others write books. Writing about me is also fine. However, as a Buddhist, what is written must be true and factual. Even a little bit of falsification should not be mixed in. Doing so violates the precept against lying!"

The Buddha Master threw the manuscript to the ground and said, "You don't write books anymore. False propaganda is an insult to me, and is disrespectful to all Buddhas in the ten directions!"

I took the manuscript back and felt very bad. The Buddha Master reprimanded me severely. My writing did have exaggerations. I only wrote good things and circumvented what was not good. This really wasn't the conduct that a Buddhist should have. After that, I did not know how to work on this book. I was depressed for quite a long time.

One day, the Buddha Master asked me, "Why are you showing a worried face all the time?"

I said, "I want to write a book. Earlier, I only wrote good things and did not write what was not good. Some facts were thrown out. I repent. I now want to write a book based on true stories. Is it okay that I write about my becoming a monastic and some little facts about life here?"

The Buddha Master said, "If you can do that, that means you are a Buddhist."

I said, "Is it okay that I also write some of the things about Buddha Master's life? Would Buddha Master delete those, or stop me from publishing it?"

The Buddha Master said, "I want you to write what is true. As long as it is true and as long as it is not prohibited by the precepts to be said, you can write facts about me. I absolutely will not delete it and will not stop you from publishing the book."

I said, "Buddha Master, please remember this. Then this is our agreement! I will write truthfully this book of true stories. However, may I please ask Buddha Master, which aspect would violate the precepts?"

The Buddha Master said, "As an example, you were taught a dharma. This dharma is very precious. You must not write the way of practicing this dharma in the book to teach others. Writing in the book to teach others means disrespecting the dharma and violates the precepts. Other examples include some great holy and virtuous ones coming here to learn the dharma as well as what dharma they learned. Writing these facts in the book also violates the precepts."

From then on, I started to write and complete this book of true stories. After completing the initial draft, I once again presented the manuscript to the Buddha Master. After the Buddha Master had finished reading it, I asked the Buddha Master if there were contents that needed to be deleted.

The Buddha Master said, "It seems that you over praised me."

I said, "If Buddha Master does not think that is true, of course it can be deleted."

The Buddha Master put up a reluctant smile that had never been seen before. I said, "Then it's a deal!"

The Buddha Master said, "Then it could only be left like that! I will not change your writing. However, do not write things about me anymore in the future. I will not have an agreement with you again!"

Thus, this book, *Revealing the Truth*, with the facts recorded herein was born.

Appendix A - The Account of a Holy Incident by Layperson Kuan

What I am about to say is about the Yun sculpture "A Pillar Holding Up Heaven" created by H.H. Master Wan Ko Yee, my Buddha Dharma King Master. One year and nine months ago, this holy work of art was completed and its shape finalized. A year and nine months had passed, and several of us decided to place the artwork "A Pillar Holding Up Heaven" into a display cabinet. First, the bottom edge of the artwork had to be closely traced on a baseboard. This was done to make sure that the sculpture would be centered. I personally traced a black line very carefully around the artwork. At that point, we all figured out that the size of the display cabinet that had previously been calculated and built was too small and the upper portion of the artwork would go beyond the baseboard. Because the body of the artwork was too large, it was impossible to fit in the display cabinet. H.H. Master Wan Ko Yee strictly criticized us, "Why didn't you measure it right in the beginning? Will this display cabinet, worth thousands of dollars, now be discarded?" The Master faced "A Pillar Holding Up Heaven" and casually said to Himself, "It would be nice if you could become smaller!" After the Master finished saying that, six of us lifted "A Pillar Holding Up Heaven" and placed it down on the floor. Because it was such a precious piece and worth so much, we all guarded the spot.

Approximately five hours passed. We then lifted it to the baseboard preparing to take a picture. Just as "A Pillar Holding Up Heaven" was moved up to the baseboard where I had previously traced the black line, a fellow disciple suddenly yelled, "Hey, it has become the magic stick of Sun Wu Kong (the Monkey King)!" Everyone looked. To our surprise, "A Pillar Holding Up Heaven" had actually shrunk. With only H.H. Buddha Dharma King's words "Let it be smaller"..., it actually shrank and now fit perfectly into the display cabinet. At this moment,

I traced a red line around the bottom edge of the artwork once again on the same baseboard that showed the previously traced black line. When comparing the two lines, the widest part of the artwork had actually shrunk and the line was now more than two inches smaller than the previous line. The entire upper portion of the artwork shrank and fit perfectly into the area of the display cabinet. This inanimate piece of artwork that had already finalized its shape was truly magnificent and unbelievably amazing.

I am a Buddhist disciple. I would not fabricate false testimony that would violate the law of cause and effect. These two lines were traced by me that day based on the bottom edge of the actual artwork that day. Moreover, the artwork indeed shrank because of the Master's words. If any of the above is falsely fabricated, I shall be punished, enter the three evil paths and become an animal. If this account of said facts is authentic, I will greatly gain good fortune and wisdom and dedicate the merit to the well being of everyone.

Now, I have some honest words that come from my heart that I would like to give everyone. Everyone should think about just what level this great and authentic Buddha-dharma actually is on for such power to be demonstrated. Shouldn't we take this opportunity to take refuge and learn the authentic Buddha-dharma?

Buddhist Disciple,

Qi, Pengzhi, who documented this account.

August 18, 2004

Appendix B –Written Testimony by Layperson Yang Huei-Chin

Before confronting the bloody demonic ghost, I prepared a big piece of crisply fried pork chop for him. After putting it into a bowl and turning myself to another direction, the pork chop disappeared immediately. I couldn't believe that the ghost completely ate the meat along with the bone.

Within the gloomily dark woods, the gloomy atmosphere was extremely strong. Before the vicious ghost launched his assault, the sounds of opening a coffin and fierce beasts running around and other formidable sounds and scenes appeared in the forest.

We all practiced our dharma and used the Vajra rice to confront him. Without notice, I was sprayed by the wet poisonous vapor he gushed out. The situation was very nerve-racking. The foul smell was very strong and irritating to the nose. At this extremely urgent moment, the Buddha Master's holy presence appeared, enabling us all to break away from the demon's control.

Because of concern that unknown harm might be incurred from the wet poisonous vapor, I tried to wash the parts of my body that were sprayed with water from the swimming pool that was adjacent to the forest. However, for several days, I still could not wash away the leftover fetid smell.

Every sentence of what I stated above is true about the situation at that time, without anything false.

Person taking this oath: Huei-Chin Yang

Appendix C – Complete Listing of the One Hundred Letters of Petition Used in the Dharma of Decision by Selection

No. 1: For a decision of selecting the door toward enlightenment from one hundred dharmas, I am very ashamed to write the letters of petition. I thank the dharma protectors for doing me this favor, to expose my secrets for the purpose of benefiting living beings.

No. 2: The letters of petition I submit today set a sky-high goal. Please do not think that I am ridiculous. Deciding my identity from the selection facilitates saving living beings. Benefiting living beings is the correct path.

No. 3: Zhengda's identity is most important. I am not afraid of your laughing at me. For saving living beings I must prove my identity. That is why I wish to be identified as high.

No. 4: H.H. Dorje Chang Buddha III is the holiest. I am a trusted aide of the Tara. A cultivator building temples has great merit. You will be brought to see the Buddha and become a holy one.

No. 5: I'd like to beseech H.H. Dorje Chang Buddha III to transmit me the secret dharma of state practice. I will be free to choose from the dharmas of four major Vajras. There are three letters of petition with close causes. Please bless me to pick this one.

No. 6: Dorje Chang Buddha and Sakyamuni Buddha have high achievements in the Five Vidyas. The sutras of all Buddhas are the best. With the presence of dharma-protecting Dakini, I will be able to learn the most complete yoga dharma.

No. 7: Though I, Awang Deji am piteous, and everyone dislikes my arrogance, I cannot lack my identity, however. Otherwise it is difficult to save living beings with an ambiguous identity.

No. 8: I am at the upper level among those who are close to the Tara. I am at the same level as those who received the dharma of Vajra Body Substitution Meditation. My crown has been opened by the dharma of Mud-Pill (soft spot on the crown, the fontanelle) Lamdre. I am a little holy monastic disciple of H.H. Dorje Chang Buddha III.

No. 9: I, Zhengda, have a most compassionate heart. I am a reincarnated one cultivating humbly. I am already an eminent monk surpassing the esoteric sects. I am free of sin even with the act of transcribing and copying the recorded dharma lessons.

No. 10: I was enlightened at the dharma assembly in Hong Kong. People all want to follow H.H. Dorje Chang Buddha III. Being a holy and virtuous one with two star wheels my realization is shallow. I want to engage in real cultivation to pursue master's qualifications at the middle level of holy realization.

No. 11: Awang Deji is a false holy person. She is selfish and exploits people. She looks down on people and is an arrogant person. She is really a big bad person.

No. 12: There exists the great dharma of reversing an old age back to childlike youth. The dharma is held by the extremely great holy H.H. Dorje Chang Buddha III. Youthful appearance was restored in seven days. I beseech to be transmitted with this same great dharma.

No. 13: Transcribing and copying the recorded dharma lessons was a foolish violation. Making errors in sentences to cause the loss of true meanings deemed me a person of guilt. I must repent seriously and correct thoroughly. Otherwise the outcome would be my being detained in the mundane world.

No. 14: Seven monastic masters and ten witnesses observed on the spot. This Buddhist nun became a kind god. As a nun master with the ability of letting my spiritual consciousness leave the crown, I am a great patriarch of esoteric Buddhism.

No. 15: Transcribing and copying of the recorded dharma lessons violated the decree. My wish is solely for benefiting living beings. How could that cause black karma to be attached to me? It is certain that the merit of doing so is broad and deep.

No. 16: Cultivators do not follow an ugly master. They look for masters with a majestic and virtuous appearance. Please let me expel my hindrance and become beautiful, with the dharma of reversing an old age back to childlike youth transmitted by the Buddha.

No. 17: What kind of person is Awang Deji, whose entering the order of monastics makes all Buddhas happy? Earlier at the time of holy Venerable Vimalakirti, she was already a trusted disciple.

No. 18: Awang Deji is a great holy one. I am a holy virtuous one with Mud-Pill crown-opening. Following me to learn Buddha-dharma, one will be on a smooth path. One will surely become a holy one very fast.

No. 19: This is a gossip-making, false holy one, who deceives living beings and Dakinis. Anyone who follows and receives teaching from her is certain to degenerate. Her disciples are truly piteous.

No. 20: I was afraid of causality before learning Buddhism. I am selfish and deliberately indulged myself. I lost my consciousness long ago. My three karmas are not in correspondence with the Buddha.

No. 21: Kuan Yin fulfilled my wish and I became a monastic. Grand vow has been made in my mind to save living beings. All people, regardless of being kind or evil, can become holy ones by following me.

No. 22: Sakyamuni Buddha and H.H. Dorje Chang Buddha III have the highest dharma. I did transcribe the teaching of the dharma from the recorded dharma lessons. I am doing all I can to benefit living beings. The mantra of the great dharma will be transmitted to me today.

No. 23: The highest holy one H.H. Dorje Chang Buddha III is the venerable one among Buddhas. I am not guilty for printing dharma books. I did it for benefiting living beings, not myself. That is why my crown was opened by the Mud-Pill dharma.

No. 24: An initiation of Bodhi-Vajra Seed will enable me to ride the cloud to reach the Heaven of Peerless Devas (akanittha deva in Sanskrit, the highest heaven in the form sphere), and become a superior person with the accomplishment of master's qualifications at the middle level of holy realization. I will broadly propagate the holiest dharma of H.H. Dorje Chang Buddha III.

No. 25: Awang Deji is a humble one, who made a grand vow of cultivation in her mind. How could an ordinary worldly person have accomplishment? She must be transmitted the dharma of tummo with third-stage realization.

No. 26: If transmitted with the great dharma of Corpse-Laying Tummo Concentration, I can attain great accomplishment to save living beings. My wish of entering the monastic order is not for other matters. Being able to save living beings makes me smile broadly.

No. 27: The dharma of Corpse-Laying Tummo Concentration will certainly be transmitted to me. I will learn the dharma of Vajra Body Substitution Meditation. Before-Sound Meditation and One-Taste Meditation (samarasa in Sanskrit) will all be taught to me. I should acquire master's qualifications at the middle level of holy realization.

No. 28: Zhengda wants to learn the dharma of Before-Sound Meditation. Deji should not sleep much at night. Life and death are a big matter and impermanence is fast and quick. Please transmit to me the highest dharma of One-Taste Meditation.

No. 29: Please transmit to me the dharma of initiation with holy Bodhi Water. I want to acquire master's qualifications at the middle level of holy realization. I, the disciple, will definitely help living beings. I will benefit living beings and liberate them.

No. 30: I came by cloud from a holy palace, to broadly propagate the eighty thousand dharmas of Buddhism. I am a bhiksuni with my crown opened at the Mud-Pill spot. Bodhisattvas in front of the Buddha also praise me.

No. 31: H.H. Dorje Chang Buddha III is venerable among Buddhas. His

Five Vidyas is a summit that no holy one ever achieved before. I am not guilty for transcribing recorded dharma lessons, because that is for benefiting all living beings.

No. 32: I would rather give up my life than give up the dharma. Please transmit to me the dharma of Xian Liang Great Perfection. I am not qualified to learn the dharma of reviving a dead person. Please teach me the dharma of reversing one's appearance back to a childlike look.

No. 33: I do not commit a crime by printing the recorded dharma lessons. The purpose is to save living beings and propagate the true dharma. My three karmas are always doing matters of Buddha-dharma. I will draw this one if I can learn great dharma.

No. 34: Tara and I were in the same family. I lived in heaven for a long time. Sometimes my appearance resembles that of Kuan Yin Bodhisattva. I have a mind of great compassion all the time.

No. 35: I, Zhengda, am just a little nun, and have received and committed myself to the complete set of Grand Precepts awarded in three dharma assemblies. Presumably my origin must be extraordinary, because I have the holy realization of crown opening.

No. 36: Who is this monastic Zhengda? She is just a common and ordinary person. She is only able to say nice words to deceive living beings and is a fake nun.

No. 37: Living beings do not understand the language from listening. They will only know from reading the written text. Transcribing to duplicate the recorded dharma lessons is for benefiting living beings. It is not for making myself a hero.

No. 38: Not complying with the Buddha's instruction and having committed the act of transcribing the recorded dharma lessons, Zhengda feels sorry for violating the precepts. Making errors in the writing is a despicable sin. There is no way to escape even after thorough repenting.

No. 39: I have already had the ability of letting my spiritual consciousness exit my crown. I also made a genuine determination as indicated by cutting off my hair and getting the three scars from receiving the complete set of Grand Precepts awarded in three dharma assemblies. I must learn the dharma of reversing one's aged appearance back to a childlike appearance.

No. 40: H.H. Dorje Chang Buddha III is my highest Buddha Master. Tara has designated me as upper level. Tara has transmitted to me dharma from the division of supreme yoga, and appointed me to supervise many people.

No. 41: I have completely received the complete set of Grand Precepts awarded in three dharma assemblies. The examination of letting spiritual consciousness exit the body by the realization of Mud-Pill Lamdre has been passed by me and Long Hui. The seven monastic masters and ten witnesses expressed their admiration.

No. 42: Please transmit to me the dharma of reversing one's appearance back to a childlike appearance. I will become beautiful after a night's sleep. My appearance will resemble the handsome, good looking, and majestic appearance of H.H. Dorje Chang Buddha III.

No. 43: My mind is always greedily thinking about other people's wealth. I do all I can to get their money. I deceive people who want to learn dharma from me. I teach false dharma as the genuine dharma.

No. 44: H. H. Dorje Chang Buddha III's status is the highest. I am ranked in the upper level among His disciples. I attained the realization of an Earth deva long ago, as testified by the seven monastic masters and ten witnesses.

No. 45: I am a most trusted aide of Tara. Tara conducted initiation of great dharma for me. I can recall that experience in my current lifetime. I play an authoritative role in Tibetan esoteric Buddhism.

No. 46: Guests of Tara coming from outside were all checked and examined by me. My status is in the upper level of first class in Tibetan esoteric Buddhism.

No. 47: Guests of Tara were holy ones. There existed great differences among holy ones. They all prostrated on the ground when paying respect to Tara. I saw many such occasions when I was by Tara's side.

No. 48: I first thank the extremely great holy H.H. Dorje Chang Buddha III. Then I thank the great holy master conducting the selection. If I can draw this one, the karmic condition indicates I shall be transmitted with the dharma of Vajra Body Substitution Meditation.

No. 49: The great holy master practices the dharma of decision by selection. Please appear and let me see your appearance. I am grateful that you practice the dharma to make a forecast for me. Please transmit to me the initiation called for by the decision of selection.

No. 50: The Bhiksuni Zhengda has a most poisonous heart. She harms people and commits arson. Wearing a set of monastic robes, she is a false rinpoche from the beginning.

No. 51: How could I dare to generate arrogance from cultivation? However, one must have an identity to engage in the conduct of saving living beings. Without a correct name one cannot make statements be heard well. That is why the letters of petition greedily embody high expectations.

No. 52: The highest Buddha-dharma in the holiest division will be transmitted to me by H.H. Dorje Chang Buddha III this year. Let me receive holy inner tantric initiation. Then my status will change from Sumeru Wheels to Sun-Moon Wheel(s).

No. 53: Zhengda does engage in true cultivation. That is why I accomplished the dharma of Mud-Pill Lamdre. I wish to accomplish a great state of realization, to let me be personally in charge of a holy dharma gate.

No. 54: It is not necessary to listen to the recorded dharma lessons. As long as one is compassionate with a kind heart and does deeds to assist the poor and relieve suffering, the merit is no less than that of people who listen to the dharma.

No. 55: I beseech H.H. Dorje Chang Buddha III to be certain to transmit to me the dharma of reversing one's appearance back to a childlike appearance. Then when anyone engaging in evil practice meets me, I will be able to keep this person to stay on the path toward enlightenment.

No. 56: Awang Deji is not human and is just a worldly person who dislikes poor people and is fond of rich ones. When people come to visit from far away, she would still be unruly with them and humiliate them.

No. 57: I passed the exam proctored by seven monastic masters and ten witnesses. My spiritual consciousness can exit the body and see Bodhisattvas. I am a reincarnated superior person. The Tara often praises me before the Buddha.

No. 58: As a disciple, I am very ashamed. I do not have the ability to create a mandala in the presence of a separation by a stone slab. Though I am not remotely close to master's qualifications at the highest level of holy realization, I should be able to pass the exam for master's qualifications at the middle level of holy realization.

No. 59: Please transmit to me the highest Vajra dharma, so I will be able to make Vajra pills dance. I want to conduct initiations for cultivators, and change my status to the level of one Sun-Moon Wheel.

No. 60: The dharma of Selection Made in Dark Confinement to Choose the Door toward Enlightenment from One Hundred Dharmas is difficult. I will devote myself to quest for the state practice dharma of Fire Offering. I do not want to learn the worldly version of this dharma from Tibetan esoteric Buddhism. I want to learn the holy dharma with the flame ignited by a dharma protector.

No. 61: I know how to be in charge of holy initiations, and will comply with the precepts and will not confer the initiation without reason. I beseech the Buddha to apply great compassion to transmit the dharma to me, so I can have effective supernatural power during the three periods of the day.

No. 62: I am not greedy for gold, silver, or other treasures. I only want to save living beings with the ability of riding the cloud to fly in the sky. Please let me learn the dharma of conducting holy initiations. Then the dharmas I transmit will be higher than inner tantric dharmas.

No. 63: Awang Deji is very ordinary. Her cultivation is common and she fears difficulties. She is not a reincarnation of a great holy one, and is just a little monastic person.

No. 64: Awang Deji truly entered the order of monastics. She dedicates her merit to her family members and relatives in the mundane world. May they all quickly perfect their good fortune and wisdom in the current lifetime, and all will realize the perfect status of a Buddha!

No. 65: The dharma of reversing an old age back to childlike youth is not untrue. H.H. Dorje Chang Buddha III is an example. The youth was restored in just seven days to have a young appearance. Please transmit this dharma to me so I can show evidence.

No. 66: There is a stipulation that does not allow transcription of the recorded dharma lessons. However, the problem is that people from Guangdong cannot understand the Sichuan accent. For others to read and know the contents in order to benefit their cultivation, transcribing and printing the recorded dharma lessons is a just conduct.

No. 67: I am not in a position to ask for the dharma of Divine Forecasting. Then please let me be in charge of the initiation of decision by selection. My status will be elevated to Two Sun-Moon Wheels, so I will be able to teach and transform dharma kings of esoteric Buddhism.

No. 68: I beseech the honored greatly compassionate H.H. Dorje Chang Buddha III to transmit to me the supreme holy dharma. I will enable all sentient beings to break away from demons' constraints and be liberated from all consequences of heretical practices.

No. 69: The dharmas of Lamdre have many levels. The Dharma of Mud-Pill Lamdre is the highest. Having passed the exam proctored by seven monastic masters and ten witnesses, my status is at the summit of esoteric Buddhism.

No. 70: I know I am a person of holy reincarnation. I beseech the Buddha to transmit to me the dharma at the highest level. If I do not get the highest dharma, how would I answer when the Tara reprimands me?

No. 71: Having already accomplished the dharma of highest Lamdre, Zhengda can let the spiritual consciousness exit during all three periods of the day. Now I should change to the dharma of Vajra Body Substitution Meditation, plus the dharma of Xian Liang Great Perfection.

No. 72: Awang Deji is a true cultivator. I beseech the Buddha to transmit to me a great Vajra dharma. The dharma should be a top dharma ranked Number One or Number Two, to let me achieve the third-stage accomplishment of tummo.

No. 73: Zhengda is originally a little nun, and is far from the realization of a great holy one. She wants to use the excuse of building a temple to cheat other people out of money. If this is true this one will be drawn.

No. 74: The Buddha will transmit to me the dharma with the benefits He manifested. In seven days, an aged appearance will be restored to a childlike appearance. I can serve as an example to teach and transform false rinpoches. Other people will also emphasize genuine transmission when questing for the dharma.

No. 75: All I want is to learn well and benefit living beings. I absolutely will not be an enemy to someone. Please transmit to me a great dharma that is more superior than the Mud-Pill dharma, so I can carry out the endeavor in the sky or underground.

No. 76: I beseech the holiest Buddha H.H. Dorje Chang Buddha III to transmit to me the dharma of Lion Vajra, with the highest dharma protector Rehula. The entire dharma will be transmitted by an initiation of state practice.

No. 77: I became a nun to engage in true cultivation. I am not a person who deliberately takes on evil views. Please do not blame me for occasional mistakes. That is due to my not listening to the dharma earnestly.

No. 78: Living beings are in poverty because of their ignorance. The phenomenon reflects current retribution from the non-ignorable manifestation of causality. Listening to and cultivating true Buddha-dharma belong to true cultivation. Following me one can acquire endless material enjoyment.

No. 79: I am far from the dharma of Buddha-Bestowed Nectar; I am not qualified to learn the dharma of Creating a Mandala in the Presence of a Separation by a Stone Slab; and I am not able to practice the dharma of Divine Forecasting. I can master the dharma of conducting initiation of decision by selection.

No. 80: I remember that the Tara was my master and transmitted to me seventeen great dharmas. Now Tara dispatches me to be a disciple of H.H. Dorje Chang Buddha III. I will definitely be taught the great dharma of Corpse-Laying Tummo Concentration.

No. 81: I, Awang Deji with the monastic name of Shi Zhengda, sincerely beseech the countless dharma protectors to safeguard me to establish a big temple in Taiwan to broadly propagate Buddha-dharma.

No. 82: I am ashamed in the ability of knowing what I am. I wish to beseech the initiation of Ma-Peng Terma Dharma. With the ability of knowing what happens outside the tent including everything in the world, I will become a great holy Bodhisattva to save living beings.

No. 83: Awang Deji is a lady involved in matters of rights and wrongs. Superficially she is a Buddhist nun, but in reality an asura. This fact is undeniable if this one is drawn out.

No. 84: Awang Deji was born from hell. Her good root is rather poor from the beginning. To learn the highest Buddha-dharma, she must transmigrate into another lifetime.

No. 85: Awang Deji cultivates falsely. While she appears to be propagating Buddha-dharma by broadcasting recorded dharma lessons, in reality she is using this opportunity to collect offerings. She then uses the money to enjoy life including traveling to China.

No. 86: I want to learn the dharma of Before-Sound Meditation. This is because I am dispatched by the Tara. Otherwise my crown would not have been opened at the spot of Mud-Pill. I beseech the greatly compassionate H.H. Dorje Chang Buddha III to let my wish be fulfilled.

No. 87: I beseech the Buddha to transmit the dharma of Vajra Body Substitution Meditation. The initiation will be conducted within three days. I, the disciple, do not make such a request baselessly. I have already accomplished the dharma of Mud-Pill Lamdre.

No. 88: I learned the unmatched highest dharma. My success in propagating Buddha-dharma is incomparable to anyone else. The dharma is one hundred times better than the dharma of Lamdre. That is why my spiritual consciousness could exit the crown at the Mud-Pill spot.

No. 89: Awang Deji who is me, Zhengda, has the dharma of Mud-Pill Lamdre to let my spiritual consciousness exit. Now I beseech the greatly compassionate H.H. Dorje Chang Buddha III to transmit to me the dharma of conducting holy initiations.

No. 90: I am a common one among living beings in samsara. I request for the dharma of the highest vehicle. I am sincerely learning Buddhism and truly cultivating myself. I believe that I will get a certificate of master's qualifications at the middle level of holy realization.

No. 91: The purpose of entering the order of monastics is nothing other than liberation. Seeing that the mundane worldly life is just a process of sin and karma. I have already learned great dharma. The dharma, the Buddha transmits to me, is certain to have me liberated.

No. 92: I, Awang Deji with the monastic name of Shi Zhengda, have just paid for my retributions in the hell realm. Being afraid of the great suffering in the hell realm, I will cultivate diligently to reap the correct accomplishment.

No. 93: I beseech my master, the Holy Tara, to teach me the dharma of Empowering Meritorious Resources. Disciples who follow and learn from me can all be empowered perfectly. Each and every one of them can manifest rewards of good fortune and accomplishment in the Five Vidyas.

No. 94: If I do not cultivate sincerely, and have a purpose of only benefiting myself not others, that is the nature of false cultivation by a demon in human-form. Then I should draw this one and suffer retributions.

No. 95: Awang Deji has heavy worldly manners. Her field of vision is often blocked by ignorance. In order to cheat for the Buddha's dharma, she kneels down below the seat of H.H. Dorje Chang Buddha III.

No. 96: I received my precepts through three dharma assemblies held at Hua Zang Si. All Buddhas and dharma protectors happily gave their praises. As early as Sakyamuni Buddha's time, I was already a cultivator.

No. 97: Awang Deji falsely entered the order of monastics, sitting on a lotus seat to deceive her disciples. I am an ordinary person making false statements. I have neither accomplishment nor virtue and am very inferior.

No. 98: Awang Deji falsely entered the order of monastics. She tries to deceive the Buddha for the dharma and scams people. If this text is drawn out, the fact is determined by Buddha-dharma. Numerous disciples following her will have difficulty becoming liberated.

No. 99: I am originally a false cultivator. Under the cover of propagating Buddha-dharma and saving living beings, the reality is that I am scamming for money and deceiving living beings. Having this one drawn out would be the evidence.

No. 100: Awang Deji has great dharma, which is higher than the nine levels of esoteric Buddhism. I am an eminent nun and a great holy mother who benefits living beings to rid them of the nature of ordinary beings.

Appendix D - Announcement of Good Fortune to Cultivators

With the karmic condition of praying for holding auspicious and magnificent dharma assemblies in 2013, we hope that people can all make vows together to beseech and invite all Buddhas in the ten directions to bless the United States with prosperity of the country, safety of its people, abundant harvest of all kinds of crops, and being free of disasters and hardship. We wish all countries in the world, mankind, and living beings happiness and tranquility, with auspicious phenomena blooming everywhere and peace staying forever. We respectfully beseech that H.H. Dorje Chang Buddha III does not leave us and comes to and bestows the Buddha's holy presence at the coming dharma assemblies.

At this time, we would like to bring you all a piece of very exciting good news. On October 18, 2012, many cultivators had the opportunity to pay homage to H.H. Dorje Chang Buddha III in person. On October 25, 2012, they saw His Holiness the Buddha again. They said that they were totally astonished and could not believe their own eyes. Within just seven days, H.H. Dorje Chang Buddha III had changed and was like a completely different person. That was extremely miraculous and surprising! In just a few days, the Buddha Master turned back the clock of aging and became much younger. More importantly, He looked much younger and far more handsome than even His childlike complexion of more than twenty years ago.

Dharma masters guarding the meditation room said, "During the last seven days, the Buddha Master was at the mandala on the grass-covered lawn praying for peace and auspiciousness. Due to His working hard for many years without a good rest, marks left by the vicissitudes of life were unavoidable. At noon time on that day, knowing people's sorrow in mind, the Buddha Master said, 'You should not feel sorry for me. Life, aging, and illness belong to impermanence. Impermanence is the nature of the world. That is why Sakyamuni Buddha also left.' At that time, the Buddha Master let the dharma masters depart to fetch the offering objects and the prayer manual. When the dharma masters came back with the offering objects and the prayer manual, they suddenly saw that the Buddha Master's face had changed to a rosy child-like complexion! Being greatly astonished, they dropped the apples to be offered to the ground."

Upon hearing that the Buddha Master has returned to His youthul appearance as He was while in Chengdu (the provincial capital city of Sichuan Province, China), Dunzhu and several dharma masters hurriedly came to the scene. At their first sight of the Buddha Master, they were all struck dumb with surprise! How could this image be the aged handsome one seen just a few days ago! Nor is this appearance the same as the youthful-looking appearance while in Chengdu. Instead, the whole skeleton and figure of the face changed. The complexion turned back to a youthful appearance that is highly spirited and full of vigor. Describing with an inappropriate worldly sentence, He is just too handsome and good-looking to describe! The images we knew from the times of living in Chengdu and visiting Taiwan simply could not be compared to H.H. Dorje Chang Buddha III's current handsome and childlike appearance that is also majestic and dignified! This fact absolutely indicates that the "Dharma of Restoring Youth and Young Appearance" is in the hands of the Buddha.

However, H.H. Dorje Chang Buddha III seriously scolded us and said that our eyes got blurred and what we said was nonsense. The Buddha Master said, "This is because I washed my face with the sand of the Ganges River and nectar water. That is just a method of curing. Any person can wash his face clean. Even applying ointment or facial cream can make the face look shiny. You have exaggerated too much and baselessly said that I look like I did when I was in Chengdu more than twenty years ago. Do you see a resemblance? I was just an ordinary person while in Chengdu and had only shallow knowledge and limited opinions. I was very ashamed of that. There was nothing worthy of imitation. Even if I knew this dharma and wanted to do some imitating, I wouldn't want to imitate and restore the 'me' that existed when I was in Chengdu. You read from the list of holiest dharmas in *The Supreme and Unsurpassable Mahamudra of Liberation* that there are dharmas of reversing an old age back to youth and restoring vitality and childlike appearance. Then you try to link the dharma to me without considering the fact. It is true that these types of dharmas were mentioned in *The Supreme and Unsurpassable Mahamudra of Liberation*. However, no one has practiced these dharmas yet. How could people know how good the dharma's effect is? I do not know this dharma. I am still inadequate. I do not have this ability."

The Buddha Master made the denial. However, the fact that H.H. Dorje Chang Buddha III restored His youth and returned to a childlike appearance is undeniable and is evident without a doubt. You all can think about this. Let's not mention returning to a childlike appearance in just a short while of 10 to 20 minutes. Even if we assume that it had taken seven days, can one return to his youth by only washing his face with the sand of the Ganges River? In particular, the appearance now has by far surpassed the appearance of more than twenty years ago in handsomeness, solemnness, and majesty. Can such a change be brought about by any human ability? There has never been such an example in history!

This instance caused us to think about a serious question that is worthy of deep pondering. In this world, there are some famous dharma kings, venerable ones, and dharma masters who pose as holy ones with high status and arrogantly boast about themselves. They have not opened up their wisdom and are not able to demonstrate any accomplishment in the Five Vidyas. Moreover, they become feebler and more exhausted as they age. Their appearances are also deteriorating at the same time. However, they just rely on their statuses and positions within their lineages to shamelessly boast of themselves and pose as holy ones. They falsely present themselves as dharma kings and sit high on the dharma-king seats to cheat cultivators for their offerings. To tell the truth, Guru Padmasambhava was the only exception in history that achieved such an accomplishment. Not even one of these people has any true ability of returning to youth and a young appearance. They are really piteous!

Conversely, H.H. Dorje Chang Buddha III, who does not accept offerings, has made perfect accomplishments that are at the acme of the Five Vidyas and commands perfect proficiency in the Tripitaka. Everything His Holiness does is in perfect harmony with the karmic condition without any impediment. Moreover, His Holiness is able to turn His appearance from an aged handsomeness to a youthful and childlike complexion with astonishingly extraordinary effect. However, He does not admit to having the power of realization and always states that He is a humble person.

Actually, this kind of modesty and humility really provided a good contrast to those false, shameless, and boastful dharma kings and rinpoches. The comparison made them superficial and laughable. They are extremely piteous! Comparing these two kinds of speeches and deeds naturally reveals the different characteristics of a true holy one and ordinary people who fake as holy ones. This is really worthy of people's pondering!!!

We believe that, as long as we have an honest and sincere mind, the Buddha Master will teach us the "Dharma of Restoring Youth and Young Appearance." Otherwise, the name of this dharma would not exist in *The Supreme and Unsurpassable Mahamudra of Liberation*.

United International World Buddhism Association Headquarters
(Seal)

December 5, 2012

Appendix E – Hand-Written Testimonies from Individuals Who Witnessed the Dancing Performance by One Million Birds

About ten minutes after the Buddha Master's forecast, one million birds presented their dance performance in the sky to H.H. Dorje Chang Buddha III. I was one of the witnesses at the site. I hereby give my testimony.

Long Zhi

I was greatly touched by reading this article because I was one of the lucky ones present at the site. The Buddha Master told us all, "This place is called 'Bird City.' A million birds will come in a short while."

I was there when the Buddha Master spoke to Sister Yingci Du. In a short while, thousands and tens of thousands of birds flew toward the Buddha Master from all directions. They formed big pieces of blackish figures and were flying downward in layers. They almost covered the entire sky. If not personally present at the scene, it would be unimaginable that the Buddha Master's forecast came true after about ten minutes. I will not be able to forget the scene at the time for the rest of my life.

This article provided a detailed and true record. I am an eye witness at the scene and can testify for it.

Dun Zhu, holding my palms together

This article is an absolutely true record. I was at the scene at that time!

Wen Li, holding my palms together

I hereby testify that the descriptions in this article were completely true, without anything false.

Queji Gele

I was at the site at that time. Everything written in this article is true.

Yongdeng Gongbu

This article is a true record. I was at the site at that time and can testify for it.

Kuan

A million flying birds presented their dance performance in the sky. I witnessed the scene at the site. This is true and not false. I hereby give my testimony.

Liu, Zhi Hong

The Buddha Master forecasted the arrival of one million birds ahead of time. Shortly after, a million birds flew from all directions to perform dancing, rotating, jumping and leaping, and other movements. It was true and not false and gave people an amazing impression. I hereby give my testimony.

Xuan Hui

One million birds in the sky changed into various formations to present their dance performance to the Buddha Master. The scene was totally incredible. It was true and not false!!!

Hua Kong

The Buddha Master's forecast did come true. I was fortunate to be present at the site to witness this extremely magnificent view. It was true and not false!!

Mei Ling

Testimony

I hereby testify that what was written in Dharma Master Zheng Hui's article of *Forecasting the Arrival of One Million Birds Ahead of Time*: the Buddha Master forecasted that a million birds would arrive in a short while; after their arrival, the birds presented their dance performance to the Buddha Master; and many birds flew to the trees next to the Buddha Master's vehicle to watch the Buddha Master.

All these are completely true. There is no false statement. On that day, I was at the site. I personally experienced and personally saw this event. I guarantee it with my accomplishment and liberation in my current lifetime.

Luoben Rinpoche, testifying here